Dominant Discourses in Higher Education

Also Available from Bloomsbury

Assessment for Social Justice: Perspectives and Practices within Higher Education, Jan McArthur
Course Syllabi in Faculties of Education: Bodies of Knowledge and their Discontents, International and Comparative Perspectives, edited by André Elias Mazawi and Michelle Stack
Decolonizing University Teaching and Learning: An Entry Model for Grappling with Complexities, D. Tran
Experiments in Decolonizing the University: Towards an Ecology of Study, Hans Schildermans
Language and Decoloniality in Higher Education: Reclaiming Voices from the South, edited by Zannie Bock and Christopher Stroud
Locating Social Justice in Higher Education Research, edited by Jan McArthur and Paul Ashwin
Social Theory and the Politics of Higher Education: Critical Perspectives on Institutional Research, edited by Mark Murphy, Ciaran Burke, Cristina Costa and Rille Raaper
Syntheses of Higher Education Research: What We Know, Malcolm Tight
Why Universities Should Seek Happiness and Contentment, Paul Gibbs

Dominant Discourses in Higher Education

Critical Perspectives, Cartographies and Practice

Ian M. Kinchin and Karen Gravett

BLOOMSBURY ACADEMIC
LONDON • NEW YORK • OXFORD • NEW DELHI • SYDNEY

BLOOMSBURY ACADEMIC
Bloomsbury Publishing Plc
50 Bedford Square, London, WC1B 3DP, UK
1385 Broadway, New York, NY 10018, USA
29 Earlsfort Terrace, Dublin 2, Ireland

BLOOMSBURY, BLOOMSBURY ACADEMIC and the Diana logo are
trademarks of Bloomsbury Publishing Plc

First published in Great Britain, 2022
This paperback edition published 2023

Copyright © Ian M. Kinchin, Karen Gravett and Bloomsbury, 2022

Ian M. Kinchin, Karen Gravett and Bloomsbury have asserted their right under the
Copyright, Designs and Patents Act, 1988, to be identified as Authors of this work.

Cover image © AlexGcs/Getty Images

All rights reserved. No part of this publication may be reproduced or transmitted in
any form or by any means, electronic or mechanical, including photocopying,
recording, or any information storage or retrieval system, without prior
permission in writing from the publishers.

Bloomsbury Publishing Plc does not have any control over, or responsibility for, any
third-party websites referred to or in this book. All internet addresses given in this
book were correct at the time of going to press. The author and publisher regret any
inconvenience caused if addresses have changed or sites have ceased to exist, but
can accept no responsibility for any such changes.

A catalogue record for this book is available from the British Library.

Library of Congress Cataloging-in-Publication Data
Names: Kinchin, Ian M., author. | Gravett, Karen, author.
Title: Dominant discourses in higher education: critical perspectives,
cartographies and practice / Ian Kinchin and Karen Gravett.
Description: London, UK; New York, NY: Bloomsbury Academic, 2022. |
Includes bibliographical references and index.
Identifiers: LCCN 2021035375 (print) | LCCN 2021035376 (ebook) |
ISBN 9781350180291 (hardback) | ISBN 9781350180284 (pdf) | ISBN 9781350180307 (ebook)
Subjects: LCSH: Education, Higher–Research. | Education,
Higher–Philosophy. | College teachers–Training of.
Classification: LCC LB2326.3.K52 2022 (print) |
LCC LB2326.3 (ebook) | DDC 378.007–dc23/eng/20211012
LC record available at https://lccn.loc.gov/2021035375
LC ebook record available at https://lccn.loc.gov/2021035376

ISBN: HB: 978-1-3501-8029-1
PB: 978-1-3502-2977-8
ePDF: 978-1-3501-8028-4
eBook: 978-1-3501-8030-7

Typeset by Newgen KnowledgeWorks Pvt. Ltd., Chennai, India

To find out more about our authors and books visit
www.bloomsbury.com and sign up for our newsletters.

Contents

List of Illustrations — vi
Foreword, *Catherine Manathunga* — vii

Part 1 Considering the Landscape

1 Thinking beyond Neoliberal Discourses — 3
2 Thinking and Doing with Theory: A Polyvalent Perspective — 17

Part 2 Putting Theory to Work

3 Positioning the Student — 33
4 The University Environment — 49
5 Ecologies of Teaching and Ecosystems of Learning — 63
6 Expertise in Context — 81

Part 3 Emerging Polyvalent Lines of Flight

7 Contested Concepts in Higher Education — 99
8 Concept Mapping — 115
9 After Method — 133
10 Towards a Relational Pedagogy — 151

References — 169
Index — 195

Illustrations

Figures

5.1	The chain of practice that comprises the basic act of teaching as content delivery (as perceived by many academics) alongside the elements of pedagogy	66
5.2	The adaptive cycle of ecosystem maintenance set within a variety of mutually supportive philosophical positions	75
6.1	The dominant knowledge structures that are seen to inhabit the quadrants of the semantic plane	84
8.1	The language of rhizomatics presented using the grammar of the concept map	117
8.2	The stabilizing selection pressures that contribute to the maintenance of linearity within the university as exemplified by chains of understanding	122
8.3	Developing links between the key concepts of adaptive capacity, vulnerability, resilience and transformability within the constraints and enablers of the ecological university as a stimulus for further learning	128
10.1	Three lines in the care-pedagogy-salutogenesis assemblage suggesting a tendency towards a triple point	163

Tables

6.1	The contradictions between 'being' and 'becoming' can be seen in tensions between competing discourses	91
10.1	Comparing simple and complex problems	154

Foreword

University teaching and, indeed, all other aspects of university work and life have been increasingly colonized over the past few decades by neoliberal, corporate logics that foreground competition, commodification, consumerism and corporatization. This has hollowed out the mission of universities and ensured that impoverished and instrumental notions about university teaching and students' learning predominate. While research on higher education and educational development within universities has burgeoned during the same time period, there remains a limited commitment in the field to deep, critical engagement with theory that might help scholars, university teachers and students understand and unpack the political work behind these neoliberal shifts.

When Dorothy Bottrell and I coedited the two-volume series *Resisting Neoliberalism in Higher Education: Seeing Through the Cracks* (vol. 1) and *Prising Open the Cracks* (vol. 2) in 2019, we were seeking to offer the higher education sector radical hope that there could be a way beyond neoliberalism and managerialism in universities. Our contributors from around the globe offered strategies not only for resistance to the metric-driven obsessions of the contemporary university but also for counter-narratives that might [re]establish the university's central role in building cultural democracy, social and cognitive justice and an ethics of care.

Ian Kinchin and Karen Gravett's book takes this process a step further by offering a carefully crafted postqualitative and posthumanist critique of dominant discourses constructing university teaching in the twenty-first century. They systematically subject the dualisms and linearity underpinning these neoliberal logics to penetrating scrutiny in this book. In particular, they deconstruct dominant discourses about student engagement, student agency, student voice, student belonging, dialogue and partnership revealing the problematic homogenizations and assumptions underpinning what have come to be regarded as common-sense approaches to 'best practices' in higher education. In a similar way, they also interrogate discourses about widening participation and inclusion, resilience, time and transition in higher education that have the effect of reinforcing rather than dismantling existing social and cultural hierarchies and inequities.

The authors of this book take up the challenge Dorothy and I issued to the higher education field (Bottrell and Manathunga, 2019; Manathunga and Bottrell, 2019) to develop polyvalent lines of enquiry in order to disrupt the narratives and ideologies of higher education. They draw upon a refreshing array of poststructural, postqualitative and posthumanist theories to interrupt hegemonic assumptions about university teaching and the higher education environment. In particular, they draw upon Deleuzian and Guattarian (1987) approaches to deterritorialization, rhizomes and becoming-subjects to open up the cracks in dominant discourses about university teaching and higher education so that new lines of flight become possible.

These lines of flight the authors apply to university teaching include Barad's (2007) ideas about entanglement and intra-action; Braidotti's (2018) work on nomadism, cartographies and affirmative ethics; St. Pierre and Pillow's (2000, p. 1) critique of 'regimes of truth that have failed us' (particularly Enlightenment, humanist binaries); Barnett's (2017) ideas about the ecological university; Biesta's (2013) critique of learnification; and Haraway's (2016) concept of response-ability.

This book is also highly innovative in its methodological use of dialogues between the authors and between the authors and other participants about key readings in higher education. As a result, the theoretical postqualitative work done earlier in the book is then extended in its later chapters to postqualitative dialogic experiments in thinking out loud together. This enacts the intra-action approach to the entanglement of people, objects, environments and others materialities that the authors recommend as a way to encourage collective, collaborative and non-competitive ways of learning and working in higher education.

Ian Kinchin and Karen Gravett explicitly draw upon their interdisciplinary academic and career backgrounds in biology and secondary science teaching and English literature and academic librarianship prior to their work in educational research. This makes for nuanced understandings of ecosystems which thrive on diversity and fascinating dialogues about the richness of poststructural and posthumanist approaches to knowledge that are more familiar to researchers from English literature and the humanities.

I commend this book to you and feel confident that it will open up generative new spaces for entanglement, dissensus and critique of dominant discourses in higher education. This book offers an enticing smorgasbord of theoretical morsels that unravel the tyranny of common sense in university teaching in the twenty-first century. And this field is hungry for theory – enjoy!

Catherine Manathunga
University of the Sunshine Coast, Australia

References

Barad, K. (2007), *Meeting the Universe Halfway*. Durham, NC: Duke University Press.
Barnett, R. (2017), *The Ecological University: A Feasible Utopia*. London: Routledge.
Biesta, G. J. J. (2013), *The Beautiful Risk of Education*. London: Routledge.
Bottrell, D., and Manathunga, C. (eds) (2019), *Resisting Neoliberalism in Higher Education: Seeing Through the Cracks*. Vol. 1. London: Palgrave Macmillan.
Braidotti, R. (2018), Foreword. In V. Bozalek, R. Braidotti, T. Shefer and M. Zembylas (eds). *Socially Just Pedagogies: Posthumanist, Feminist and Materialist Perspectives in Higher Education*. London: Bloomsbury, xiii–xxvii.
Deleuze, G., and Guattari, F. (1987), *A Thousand Plateaus: Capitalism and Schizophrenia*. London: Continuum.
Haraway, D. (2016), *Staying with the trouble: Making Kin in the Chthulucene*. Durham, NC: Duke University Press.
Manathunga, C., and Bottrell, D. (eds) (2019), *Resisting Neoliberalism in Higher Education: Prising Open the Cracks*. Vol. 2. London: Palgrave Macmillan.
St. Pierre, E. A., and Pillow, W. S. (2000), *Working the Ruins: Feminist Poststructural Theory and Methods in Education*. London: Routledge.

Part 1
Considering the Landscape

1

Thinking beyond Neoliberal Discourses

The Authors

This book has emerged from dialogues between the authors over time. We are two academics with very different disciplinary backgrounds and different routes into educational research. One of us has a first degree in biological sciences and had a first career in secondary science teaching. The other has a first degree in English literature and had a first career as an academic librarian and then as a student learning developer. As such, our experiences as students were markedly different, and our experiences as teachers also evolved within very different contexts. However, these different origins have led us both into the domain of higher education teaching and research. In writing these chapters we have drawn upon diverse bodies of literature that reflect our unique professional histories and particular academic interests. We have tried not to compromise too often, or to settle on a mid-way path between our differences, as that would be to aim for the middle ground – the safe option. Safety is an option that satisfies no one. Rather, it results in a bland acceptance of what is and misses the opportunity to offer a radical imagining of what might be. Instead, we have learned from each other and respected our academic differences, and in so doing we have created spaces for new avenues of dialogue, and new questions, as predicted by Andreotti et al. (2016: 85):

> It is precisely by making the limits and juxtapositions (borders) of discursive assemblages visible that social cartographies can open up the possibility of the emergence of new and different discursive assemblages.

We are interested, then, in exploring what might emerge when discourses are made visible. What might happen when the borders of discourses are exposed, akin to the 'radical copresence' needed to generate an 'ecology of knowledges' (as explored by Santos [2014]), or the 'consilience' described by Wilson (1998), where the 'Great Branches of Learning' join forces. It has been suggested that the added complications, uncertainties and apprehensions created by working at the borders in this way may offer a 'fruitful disorientation' (Lenz Taguchi and St. Pierre 2017: 644). This disorientation is one that we have actively welcomed and engaged with in dialogue – between ourselves and with our peers. This has sometimes generated our own 'epistemological shudders' where long-held assumptions are destabilized (Charteris 2014). The result is a text that explores university teaching from a new perspective that is personal to us, but which we hope will resonate with many.

The text offers openings that do not fit with the traditional textbook on teaching, and we readily accept that this may be in tension with the dominant view of current practice, which often 'assumes that knowledge can, and indeed should, be presented efficiently: in concise, simplified, methodized forms' (Doll 2006: 86). We feel that this divergence from the typical is a necessary step for higher education to evolve and for university teaching, in particular, to move away from being regarded as a routine operation that can be measured as a technical competence, towards a scholarly activity that has long been claimed in the literature, but often derided in practice. In recognizing the value of difference and the entanglements of our own academic voices with those in the literature, we concur with Smagorinsky, Augustine and Gallas (2006: 100), who concluded that

> sharing authorship requires the sharing of much more than ownership. It also requires a shared perspective on the part of university-based teachers and researchers on how classroom-based teachers and researchers experience their work. Sharing authorship is rhizomatic rather than arborescent – it involves, as we conceive it, the reterritorialization of cultural practices as part of a new and mutual process of becoming.

For the authors, this 'mutual process of becoming' is now a way for us to perceive our roles as teachers and educational researchers. This aligns with the idea of 'research-as-pedagogy' (Kinchin, Kingsbury and Buhmann 2018), and 'researcher-led academic development' (Kinchin et al. 2018) in which the research-versus-teaching dualism is broken. This book is underpinned by our own non-linear professional transitions (*sensu* Gravett 2021b), and as articulated by Stewart (2015: 1180): our 'contemplation of past pedagogical and curriculum activities has not been linear or sequential … Although the final document may appear linear, its writing and production were anything but'.

Dominant Discourses in Higher Education

In this book we share our belief that teaching and learning should be a thoughtful endeavour. We explore how discourses and narratives underpin the way we understand our environment and shape our thoughts and practices. In 1969, Foucault's writings on discourse surfaced the role of the individual, or subject, as embedded within language, contending that the subject must be 'analysed as a complex and variable function of discourse' (1969: 138). Foucault's work (1969; 1970) encourages us to see discourses as powerful, and to ask certain questions: how does discourse function and what does it do? How does it regulate? As St. Pierre (2000: 485) comments: 'once a discourse becomes "normal" and "natural," it is difficult to think and act outside it.' Indebted to Foucault and St. Pierre, an understanding of how subjectivities are interwoven and shaped by discourses informs this text.

More recently, Charteris et al. (2016) explain how subjectivities are produced and often constrained within powerful higher education discourses. Charteris and colleagues (2016) explore how academic spaces and environments have become 'saturated' with particular dominant 'knowledge economy' discourses, and how academics' relations have become discursively constructed within this frame. Similarly, in 2019, Meyerhoff explored the individual's relationship to higher education's normative narratives, or 'romantic stories'. As Meyerhoff suggests, one example of these stories is that 'for students, the prescribed happiness is seen through their romantic relation to education: they are framed as heroes in a romance narrative of climbing the educational ladder, overcoming obstacles on the way toward a happy life after graduation' (2019: 11). Instead, Meyerhoff (2019: 201) contends that we must 'unsettle our subscriptions to these narratives and expand our horizons to alternative modes of study and world-making'.

In our own consideration of the role of discourses, we have employed the poststructural and posthuman inflected ideas of a breadth of scholars, for example, Deleuze and Guattari, Braidotti, Barad, Foucault, St. Pierre (and many others), in order to offer a similar unsettling. This is not to displace other narratives, but to offer a challenge, and to refresh the perspectives that currently dominate higher education discourses and to escape from the simplistic bifurcations identified in recent work by Macfarlane (2015). We contend that these dominant discourses have become taken-for-granted and have produced various terms and phrases that are often used as shorthand answers to close down debate and plaster over critique – creating a sedative discourse (*sensu*

Guattari 2014). These narratives include commonly accepted and significant terms such as student-centred; widening participation; teaching excellence; student voice; student engagement; resilience; employability and so on. Many of these terms have been borne from good intentions, but meaning may have been lost through overuse and divergence into contested meanings. This is not to say that everything in higher education is wrong! There are many excellent initiatives in the sector, but we contend that all aspects of university practice should be subject to regular scholarly critique, so that we may be in a position to more clearly see and unsettle dominant discourses that romanticize, limit or obscure, and so that any decision to 'stick or twist' is made on reasoned judgements and not because 'that's the way it is'.

Throughout the book, we consider and analyse dominant discourses that are currently shaping teaching and learning in higher education. Some of these act as stabilizing lines of force while others might be conceived as destabilizing lines of flight that disrupt the status quo. We explore this with a number of questions in our minds concerning the value these discourses have added to the lives of those who are engaged as teachers or students at university. For example, the idea that we should adopt a student-centred approach to our teaching seems to be based on good and common sense. However, when we then start to move into the arena of student-staff partnership work (Gravett, Yakovchuk and Kinchin 2020), we start to uncover a tension as it seems unfair to have a partnership that privileges one of the partners. Moreover, adopting a more rhizomatic conception of learning (Gravett 2021b) highlights problems associated with viewing any conception of learning as being 'centred' on one specific location. The student partnership work also uncovers another unhelpful dichotomy in the university. Whereas the world of teaching often stresses values such as inclusivity, collegiality and cooperation for the good of the institution, the world of research is more explicitly concerned with competition between individuals who require personal recognition and accumulated prestige for their work. Although it can also be argued that teaching is becoming increasingly individualistic as a result of neoliberal forces, for example, as evidenced via the adoption of teaching awards across the sector, or metrics such as module evaluation questionnaires that scrutinize individuals' 'performances' in the classroom. Nonetheless, undertaking research with undergraduates places many academics at an uncomfortable junction that challenges their identities as teachers or researchers – a situation requiring considerable mettle (*sensu* Walker 2014).

Dualisms and Linearity

Underpinning our thinking throughout the book are two subtle phenomena that we recognize as inhibitory. The first is the idea of dualisms (or binaries) that acts as a shorthand way of referring to complex descriptions and that constrains thinking. A critique of binary oppositions is a key premise of many posthuman and poststructural theorists, for example, Derrida (1972), who evocatively describes such concepts as 'violent hierarchies', indicating the harmful impact of language and its interrelationship to structures and mechanisms of power. These are ideas we explore more fully in Chapter 2. The other notion we wish to unravel is the concept of linearity. We recognize the effects of linearity within teaching at all levels that impedes and constricts the richness of experience that universities offer to their students. In combination, these restrictive phenomena (often self-imposed) prevent institutions from matching experience with aspiration.

Macfarlane (2015) has identified a number of common dualisms that are likely to resonate with the readers of this book: descriptors such as 'deep and surface learning'; 'research and teaching' and 'student-centred versus teacher-centred teaching'. These dualisms summarize complex notions about the nature of teaching, of learning and of academic practice more generally, as if activities can be neatly compartmentalized in mutually exclusive boxes. These dualisms imply an either/or scenario in each case and fail to acknowledge any blurring of these boundaries. In addition, they have a hierarchical impact because a value judgement is placed on these activities: 'deep learning good, surface learning bad' or 'student-centred good, teacher-centred bad', reminding us of Derrida's surfacing of the violence of hierarchical ideas.

In addition, Macfarlane has identified some more subtle dualisms in higher education that nonetheless may have a deep impact on the psychology of those affected. One example is the distinction between 'academic' and 'non-academic' staff. This dualism is often overwritten with a reinforcing dualism of 'research-active' and 'not research-active'. Rather than seen as 'good or bad', these are more related to the idea of prestige (Blackmore 2015), and how discourses contribute to prestige being unequally distributed across the university: 'teaching = low prestige' versus 'researching = high prestige' (Young 2006). Often underpinning these assumptions of prestige is the categorization of UK universities within the research literature. Macfarlane (2015: 114) has identified how researchers rely on distinctions such as 'old' and 'new' universities to justify their sampling methods and to suggest some kind of inclusive research policy. Someone completely unfamiliar with the UK higher education sector may be forgiven for assuming that if a university was founded in 1096, anyone teaching there must be an integral part of that history, making them a distinct category of teacher. While working in such an institution may colour one's perspective on university life, the binary assumption described above overlooks the mobile nature of academic staff in the twenty-first century, and the range of active connections and collaborations between universities. Macfarlane (2015: 116) concludes that, 'bifurcation dangerously over-simplifies the world of higher education research'.

Once sensitized to its existence, the second phenomenon, linearity, can be observed to be operating within many aspects of university life – from assumptions about student transitions into and through higher education (Gravett, Kinchin and Winstone 2020a) to the ways in which content is presented in lectures (Kinchin, Chadha and Kokotailo 2008). Linearity is also a guiding principle in traditional research methods

> where 'research' is treated as linear stages and series of procedures. In such a model, courses are treated as teaching students how to master methods, rather than how to think about inquiry as a process that is not thinkable without first a consideration of the epistemological and ontological, or rather ontoepistemological positionings (Barad 2007) that make possible a way of thought and questioning. (Mazzei and Jackson 2012: 733)

The problem of linearity is explored by Baker and Irwin (2019: 2) who consider that when dominant discourses that frame development are linear and reductive, then situated experiences are rarely recognized. To move away from such stylized reductionism, Capra (2005) and Capra and Luisi (2014) have explored the value of non-linear systems (or ecological) thinking and have identified several highly significant shifts in perception that are needed to accompany its adoption. These are summarized as shifts from:

- the parts to the whole
- objects to relationships
- objective knowledge to contextual knowledge
- quantity to quality
- measuring to mapping
- structures to process
- contents to patterns
- certainty to uncertainty.

These subtle changes in terminology belie the seismic shifts in thinking and educational practices that they are intended to initiate. These points also offer a challenge to many of the dominant discourses of contemporary higher education, for example, by contesting the fragmentation of university degrees into bitesize modules; by suggesting that *mapping* may offer a different way forward from the current preoccupation with *measuring*, and by questioning the apparent quest for certainty in all things to do with education. Together, the shifts in perception that are listed above offer a radically different trajectory for the renaissance of the post-Covid university that would obviate the maintenance of the status quo.

We return to the idea of mapping (that appears in the list above) at various points in this book and consider it a potential point of overlap between structuralist (Kinchin 2016) and poststructuralist (Deleuze and Guattari 1987) perspectives. When referring to this we focus on the active process of mapping rather than the observation of inert tracings (Deleuze and Guattari 1987). We also employ the use of 'cartography', finding this a meaningful term with potentially dynamic implications:

> The principle of cartography implies that we can compare narrative selfhood with a dynamic map of narrations (and not with a tracing of reality), a map that is always open and always changing. The narrations someone tells about herself or himself are never complete; they form an ongoing process of co-construction and co-reconstruction. As a researcher, one can thus never have a view on the complete map of one's participant, seeing that this map is co-constructed, multiple, and constantly changing. We can only explore several temporal regions and paths knowing that we are taking part in the exploration. (Sermijn, Devlieger and Loots 2008: 632)

As Sermijn, Devlieger and Loots suggest, the notion of cartography encourages us to think about the possibility of a dynamic map of narrations, stories or questions, a map that is always open and always changing. When fundamental questions about the practices of higher education are raised, they are often countered by well-rehearsed responses that rely on pre-packaged ideas that appear rational and well considered. However, the habitual use of pre-packaged responses can remove the requirement for thought, creating the oxymoronic 'thoughtless university'. This may mean that sacred terms such as 'student-centred' or 'teaching excellence' are unlikely to elicit a response where a colleague would argue against the desirability of focusing on our students or trying to teach as well as we are able. But they provide an ambiguous shorthand where colleagues may feel embarrassed to ask what is understood beneath the headline term, as they feel they should probably already know. Schulte (2018) argues that this kind of shorthand allows users not to have to think about the idea being conveyed, and to fall into a habit of using a term in response to certain triggers. With thoughtless overuse, terms that are assumed to be helping to organize thoughts are actually constraining thinking, and rather than help to communicate ideas clearly, they become reductive. The transaction of these labels in this way is likely to lead to a loss of meaning. For example, the term, 'spiral curriculum' is a learned label that typically offers the capital and flexibility that is needed to wiggle free from detailed discussion of curriculum structure (Schulte 2018: 196), until an educational researcher starts to interrogate the understanding behind the doing (*sensu* Roberts and Johnson 2015).

The twin concepts of linearity and dualism provide a point of overlap between the traditionally structuralist view of knowledge creation (Kinchin 2016) and the more fluid representations offered by poststructuralist theorists, for example, by Deleuze and Guattari (1987). As such they provide a helpful point of access to our evolving narrative that should be equally familiar to readers from various disciplinary and epistemological backgrounds. Linearity and its concomitant reductionism lead to a loss of adaptive capacity – a precursor to the condition of pedagogy frailty (Kinchin and Winstone 2017). The loss of associated knowledge leads to a condition observed by Roberts and Johnson (2015) where there is a 'loss of understanding behind the doing', or perhaps, a loss of scholarship.

The Power and Pleasure of Theory

In this book we actively embrace the disorientation that discordant perspectives can create. A belief in the messiness of knowledge, teaching and research underpins the text, and so too does a belief in the power and potential of theory to unsettle and to transform. As St. Pierre (2021: 5) explains:

> Theorists offer us concepts and ideas that can change the world. Why would we not read them and use them? I think of the piles of books at my house that I haven't read yet. I know well that I can read any page in those books and find an idea or concept that will be a shock to my thought (Deleuze 1985/1989). I know some word or phrase on the page will send me spinning down a rabbit hole and tear apart whatever comfort I've made for myself. But I've learned over the years that the terrifying discomfort of being unmoored and lost is what I most desire. I've learned I long for ... what Patti Lather (1996) called working in 'rigorous

confusion' (p. 539). What's important here is that theory should be unsettling, disruptive, confusing, and perhaps that's why we resist it.

In many ways this book celebrates the 'terrifying discomfort of being unmoored' described here by St. Pierre. Engaging with theory can be unsettling ('a shock to the thought'), but also pleasurable, experienced as a desirable dislocation similar to 'spinning down a rabbit hole'. Rather than uncertainty and confusion representing a negative diversion for the teacher or researcher, we consider such confusion to be itself 'rigorous' (Lather 1996: 539). We consider it to be an essential part of learning. Throughout the book, we put theory to work to examine, illuminate and disrupt, and we use theory to explore new ways of thinking and to create new openings in higher education praxis.

We do this by engaging with a breadth of ideas across the chapters, often inspired by thinkers who have emerged from fields sometimes known as poststructuralism or posthumanism. Poststructuralism and posthumanism sit amongst a broad web of variant fields including sociomaterial studies, feminist new materialism and postqualitative inquiry. These overlapping and messy theoretical spaces offer openings to fundamentally rethink how we conceptualize key ideas surrounding language, learning, subjectivity, ontology, epistemology and ethics. Crucially, they offer spaces in which we can consider how as educators we might produce more inclusive knowledge and research practices. Our interest in poststucturalism, posthumanism and other variant fields has evolved over time, and we explain our polyvalent perspective more fully in Chapter 2 where we explore more deeply the value of theory and its relationship with practice. Overall, we concur with St. Pierre and Pillow (2000) that the emergence of poststructuralist ideas in the latter half of the twentieth century has contributed to the troubling of key concepts enabling us to ask new questions 'that produce different knowledge and produce knowledge differently, thereby producing different ways of living in the world' (St. Pierre and Pillow 2000: 1). How might producing different knowledge and producing knowledge differently lead to different ways of learning and working? In what new ways might we think about our teaching, research and relationships in higher education and beyond? These are questions that intrigue us.

We have also exapted some concepts throughout the book. Conceptual exaptation (similar to Bal's view of travelling concepts – Bal 2002) refers to the repurposing of a concept from another disciplinary area. This is a process in which ideas or attributes are co-opted for use in a manner that was not envisioned at the outset (Gould 1991). The concept of exaptation has been successfully translated (exapted) into social systems from its origins in evolutionary biology (Larson et al. 2013). It has been suggested that exapting disciplinary knowledge to forge active links with pedagogic narratives may offer a general route into the professional development of university teachers (Kinchin 2016). The profusion of 'ecological models' in educational research (Keiny 2003; Priestley, Biesta and Robinson, 2015; Leijen, Pedaste and Lepp, 2020) provide instances where this has already taken place. In addition, we have used poststructural and posthuman frames to reshape ideas from the natural sciences (such as biological ecosystems) in ways that may inform the development of education – moving away from linear, instrumental, reductionist measures of complex phenomena towards rich analyses that emphasize dynamism and difference rather than stability and homogeneity. We consider the importance of dialogue to unwrap the diversity that is hidden in the shared labels we use for the exchange of complex ideas (Chapter 7). We have also reconsidered concept mapping (in Chapter 8), a tool for the visualization of knowledge that has a rich heritage in the arborescent structure of science education (where it has been used as a lens to look back at the agreed and the already-mapped). In this book we change the focus from *where-we-have-been* to *where-we-might-go:* from being to becoming.

A Neoliberal Context

Many authors have offered detailed accounts of the problems created by the market-driven, neoliberal culture that currently pervades the dominant discourses of higher education (Giroux 2014; Bottrell and Manathunga 2019; Manathunga and Bottrell 2019). While we do not have space to review that extensive literature within the pages of this volume, we cannot explore higher education without an understanding of how neoliberalism has come to permeate discourses and subjectivities, and so reference to what we perceive as the insidious, creeping pathology of neoliberalism will surface throughout our discussions in the book. Moreover, it is increasingly being acknowledged that recent challenges including the Covid-19 pandemic have exposed just how comprehensively strategies of managerialism and marketization pervade our work and how vulnerable such neoliberal discourses and cultures make institutions and individuals (Blackmore 2020). At this point, we will also refer to comments offered by Fortunato (2017: 184–5). Here Fortunato considers the homogenizing influence of neoliberalism, and his words also provide an overview to flag some of the associated issues that will appear later in this book:

Is it any wonder, then, why the idea of the standardization of something as formative as a young person's education might be culturally viewed with contempt or suspicion in a society whose great heroes deviated from the norm at great cost to themselves in order to build something better? ... Educational standards give the illusion of great freedom and flexibility in designing innovative approaches to meet goals, preparing students for the world's challenges. Rather than creating space for different ways of knowing and different kinds of intelligence, excessive reliance on standardization creates a social stigma by producing fertile ground for exclusion of those who may pursue different goals or learn in different ways. ... Like the monoculturing of plants leading to widespread susceptibility of certain pathogens, will our monoculturing of educational values create long-term fragility to rare but extreme events, or rare but extraordinary opportunities to pursue beneficial social innovations and change?

Fortunato's comments introduce us to conflicts that appear in the inconsistent policy patchwork that has evolved around university teaching – in this case the issue of *inclusion* that appears high up on the agenda of so many committees (as explored in Chapter 4) and the dangers of having a fixed perspective regarding who needs help to be included and by what mechanisms. It also introduces some ecological terminology (e.g. monoculturing) that provides us with a fertile lexicon for development (see Chapter 5) at the borders of our social cartographies, (as mentioned above). Here, for example, monoculturing is seen as a mechanism within the sociology of absences, where it overwrites the diversity that can otherwise be seen within a social ecology (Santos 2014).

It is clear that market-driven managerial cultures have had a profound effect on higher education in recent decades and have encouraged the reconfiguration of institutional and academic norms. It has resulted in the convergent evolution of universities, where distinctive institutional characteristics have been overwritten with gloss and spin to produce 'the hollowed-out university' (Cribb and Gewirtz 2013), in which the quest for exceptionalism has given way to performance ideologies of standardized excellence. Changes in academic norms (including increased pressure to secure research grants, self-justificatory expressions of interestedness and tangential claims to authorship) are considered by Macfarlane (2021: 465) to be evidence of the acceptance of 'practices that might have been regarded as ethically dubious by earlier generations of academics'.

However, rather than encouraging despondency or nostalgia, we set out here to support more optimistic ways of thinking, learning and working in higher education by offering a space to focus on positive reimaginings. This may be seen as an attempt to address a situation described by Wilkinson,

Silverio and Wilkinson (2021: 257) as, 'the deficit of scholarship on the lived experiences of being a contemporary academic', and to move beyond 'the depressing paralysis' of the current system towards 'one that is grounded in a more helpful, democratic, socially just set of sensibilities, values and practices' (Smyth 2020: 716). It also responds to the call to arms offered by Taylor and Bayley (2019: 7) who champion a mode of joyful life-affirming 'doing otherwise' in higher education, that can help us to 'think beyond and outside dominant representations of higher education as a contemporary time-space damaged beyond repair by neoliberalism, and of HE as [already] irredeemably deformed'. Likewise, it responds to Koro-Ljungberg and Löytönen (2017: 301) who write as follows:

> In the fringes, beyond the current major discourses of neoliberal universities, academic capitalism, new public management, key performance indicators, hard times and more within the (global) universities, something else is being created: the free/liberated university. Instead of aiming at the external virtue and goods (such as the economic profit, the research rankings, and innovation stories), the value is in pursuing the internal virtues (such as critical thinking, educated understanding, academic communities, and professional practices).

Conclusion

Our purpose in writing this book is not to try to overturn everything that has come before or to be unnecessarily negative about the current state of higher education. However, it is clear to us that considerable academic energy is expended on developing coping strategies for life in the system we have created. It is also clear that a folklore has been created around educational research and educational practice that appears to constrict the creativity of those engaged in its pursuit. Therefore, in exploring a range of connected ideas and offering some challenge to accepted wisdom, we take the words of Gale (2007: 473):

> to encourage an approach to teacher education practices within higher education that begins to trouble the current acceptance of policy driven grand narratives that attempt to discipline theory and practice.

We have chosen to use ideas from the research literature 'not like bricks that weigh down thought but like toolboxes full of levers and gizmos that open things up' (St. Pierre 1997: 407). Throughout the book, we challenge the grand narratives that dominate the higher education research literature. Some of these narratives appear to have taken on an unquestionable, even sacred, aura, where challenge is almost taken as a sign of disrespect to earlier scholarship. Again, that is not our intention, but it is evident that the context of higher education is unstable to such a degree that a periodic re-evaluation of taken-for-granted assumptions is required. In addition, we suggest that the original intentions of some research studies have been subverted through practice and become obscured. For example, the concept of 'centredness' (most commonly used in the context of student-centredness) has been reconsidered by MacRury (2007: 131) to represent part of the pathology of the university that is both 'structurally and dynamically non-dialogic' and as such 'is anti-creative: a new model of thoughtlessness'. Such extreme criticisms cannot be ignored and should be explored. In our explorations of these ideas, and indeed of our own evolving thinking, we position ourselves as rhizomatic researchers and aspire to the guiding principles summarized by Guerin (2013):

Rhizomatic researchers

- start where they are (nomadic)
- listen to the voices and things connected to them (assemblages)
- embed themselves in the lives of their research
- develop sensitivities to elements/people that are not part of the status quo
- search for research aspects that are sometimes ignored
- desire a life of becoming rather than copying what is seen.

These are principles that have inspired us and that are woven through the text of the following chapters. This book then provides an opening into a space where we can play with a breadth of new ideas, theories and approaches. We hope that this opening offers a new kind of thinking about higher education and its discourses and practices. We hope that you enjoy this space to think differently with us and are both pleased and unsettled by the chapters that follow.

2

Thinking and Doing with Theory: A Polyvalent Perspective

Introduction

In this book we put theory to work. We begin our deconstruction of the dominant discourses that pervade and shape the higher education landscape from a space which upholds the use of theory as a tool to interrupt, to illuminate and to open. Theory, we believe, enables us to create possibilities for seeing and doing things differently, once taken-for-granted certainties are ruptured. In this chapter, we explore some of the key theories that we have found useful. We consider how theory can be used in higher education and beyond, and celebrate the power, potential and pleasure of theory to disorientate and to unsettle. Crucially, we seek to complicate the relationship between two ostensibly opposite concepts: theory and practice, exposing them as fluid, troublesome and interwoven. We do this by revisiting hegemonic, 'arborescent' discourses and reading them again through a breadth of poststructuralist, and posthuman inflected perspectives. Furthermore, we consider how, when taken together, a multiplicity of theoretical approaches can serve us to enact 'polyvalent lines of enquiry' (Manathunga and Bottrell 2019: 293), offering a patchy, plurality of perspectives in which 'new-old (theories, narratives, practices) jostle in entangled matterings' (Taylor 2018b: 372), that invite and encourage us to disrupt the narratives and ideologies of higher education.

What Can Theory Do?

Theory offers the power to interrupt taken-for-granted ways of thinking and working. In his work on the theoretical concept of deconstruction, a concept employed to understand the relationship between meanings and language, Derrida explores how deconstruction can be used to destabilize and create openings (1967). For Derrida, the value of deconstruction is in its capacity to open, to fracture, as well as to offer the possibility of a departure from conventional ways of reading or thinking about language. Similarly, in her article titled 'The Offence of Theory', Maclure (2010) explores theory's capacity to both unsettle and offend. Like Derrida, Maclure contends that the 'offence' of theory lies in its power to disrupt fields of habit and practice. This is also an idea visible in the work of Deleuze (1989: 175). Deleuze writes that theory is needed to show the 'intolerable'. For Deleuze, the 'intolerable' lies masked beneath the habits and practices of 'daily banality'. For Maclure (2010: 278, emphasis in original) 'theory stops us from forgetting, then, that the world is *not* laid out in plain view before our eyes … It stops us from thinking that things speak for themselves – "the data", "practice", the pure voice of the previously silenced'.

However, theory can both please and offend. In this extract, St. Pierre (2021a: 7) describes the desire to become lost in theory:

> Theorists offer us concepts and ideas that can change the world ... I know some word or phrase on the page will send me spinning down a rabbit hole and tear apart whatever comfort I've made for myself. But I've learned over the years that the terrifying discomfort of being unmoored and lost is what I most desire.
>
> What's important here is that theory should be unsettling, disruptive, confusing, and perhaps that's why we resist it. As bell hooks (1989) asked, 'Do we have to go that deep?' (p. 1).

Theory, then, can be deeply disruptive, destabilizing and productive. It can complicate *and* generate. At times this can feel both desirable and discomforting; here St. Pierre quotes bell hooks (1989) in explaining our resistance to feeling 'unmoored' by new words and ideas. Through attempting such a departure from the simple and the plain view, we may be able to question those taken-for granted assumptions that permeate educational discourse as well as to think about what possibilities such a displacement might offer.

Theory as Practice

However, we also wish to move beyond critique, towards offering an affirmative and generative reimagining for higher education. The relationship between theory and practice is complex and can be problematic. Maclure (2010: 280) explains that policy makers and practitioners are often 'put off by theory's tendency to complicate, its vaunted uncertainty, and its fraught entanglement with the "practice" that it is supposed either to explain or to serve'. Complexity and uncertainty may be valued by researchers but far less so by managers and institutional leaders, and researchers will have to work hard to ensure that complex ideas can be clearly communicated. Likewise, St. Pierre (2016: 111) notes that the education sector is afflicted by an urge to 'leap to application', demanding the practical collection of data as a prelude to playing with and creating knowledge, and this is an issue that we discuss further in Chapter 9. Of course, we need to acknowledge the significant voices of those policy makers, managers and practitioners who are alienated by theory's 'tendency to complicate', as well as with those who argue that theory is divorced from practice or not meaningful for educators. Nonetheless, we uphold that such complexity is essential. Not all questions have simple answers. Theory does not simply serve, follow or explain practice.

Our response, then, to this challenge is to continue the critique of the binary conception that has for too long divided theory from practice, within an artificial and unhelpful juxtaposition. Instead, we seek to offer a positive and 'remobilizing critique' (Stronach and Maclure 1997: 93). This critique has been articulated considerably already by a number of key thinkers from within the fields of education, philosophy and critical theory. A disruption of binary oppositions is a key premise of many posthuman and poststructural theorists, for example, Derrida (1972), who evocatively describes such concepts as 'violent hierarchies'. Similarly, in his work *The Pedagogy of the Oppressed*, Freire explores the notion of praxis (now an influential concept for many later theorists) which he defines as reflection and action. Freire (1970) explains that, in his view, discovery cannot be purely intellectual but must involve action. And yet it should also not be limited to activism but must include reflection. Only then will it be a praxis. For Freire, the interconnection of reflection and dialogue can be powerful and transformative.

Binary distinctions are also reimagined in the work of Deleuze and Foucault (1977) who explore how theory and practice can be understood as interwoven. Here, Deleuze and Foucault employ a memorable metaphor: 'a system of relays' (206). They explain their belief that 'we're in the process of experiencing a new relationship between theory and practice ... practice is a set of relays from one theoretical point to another, and theory is a relay from one practice to another ... representation no longer exists there is only action-theoretical action and practical action' (205–7). These ideas have also been developed by Taylor (2018b: 376). Employing the term theory-practice, Taylor explains that, importantly, 'once theory/practice binaries flip, then routes to other flips are more easily created', reminding us of the cumulative impact discursive changes can enact. Likewise, in *What Is Philosophy*, Deleuze and Guattari (1994: 111), contend that

> to think is to experiment, but experimentation is always that which is in the process of coming about – the new, remarkable, and interesting that replace the appearance of truth and are more demanding than it is. What is in the process of coming about is no more what ends than what begins.

To think is to experiment. Theory, then, does not preclude practice. Instead, theory *is* practice: 'Experimentation is always that which is in the process of coming about' and practices enact thought, and these are ideas that we examine further in Chapter 9. Theory, then, can also be understood as material. Indeed, the materiality of language is explored by Althusser (1971) who contends that 'an ideology always exists in an apparatus, and its practice or practices. This existence is material' (166). Similarly, citing Deleuze (1989), Maclure (2010: 281) describes theory as 'a practice of concepts'. Deleuze (1989: 268) writes that 'it is at the level of interference of many practices that things happen, beings, images, concepts, all the kinds of events'. Viewed from this angle, Maclure suggests, 'Theory in educational research has not interfered enough' (2010: 281). What other material interferences might we be able to create, what flips might we be able to make happen?

Theory in Educational Research

We certainly believe that educational research has not interfered enough. Rather, theory's position in educational research has had a problematic history and remains contentious today. Historically, a key feature of higher education research has often been a disengagement or limited engagement with theoretical concepts. In 2004, Tight described higher education as an 'a-theoretical community of practice', and, in 2014, as an 'introspective field of study' (93). Indeed, in 2014, Tight still surmised that 'theories being developed and applied may often be fairly low level in terms of their sophistication' (107). Even today, then, higher education researchers may often be reluctant to explicitly engage with theory for a multiple of reasons. Labels such as pedagogic research and the Scholarship of Learning and Teaching (SoTL) are also sometimes (mis)used to limit the scope and understanding of educational research as a theoretical field. These distinct practices usually signify educational research that may be purposefully local in scope and under theorized. We do not wish to denigrate these practices in any way. On the contrary, local initiatives, grounded in practice, are often extremely useful reflective and developmental activities and can include an important focus on 'quality and enhancement of learning, excellence and recognition' (Canning and Masika 2020: 1). We both engage in local, pedagogic, research ourselves as well as support colleagues to carry out studies designed to enhance learning within a specific area. Nonetheless, we do suggest that these kinds of studies may purposefully not be designed to meet the criteria of 'being public, peer reviewed and critiqued' (Canning and Masika 2020: 1) and that these practices form a distinct area of pedagogic research with different aims and objectives from rigorous research into higher education as a global academic field. This can cause some confusion about the goals and position of educational research. As a result, SoTL has for some come to represent 'a thorn in the flesh of educational research' (Canning and Masika 2020: 1), although we prefer to acknowledge its validity and utility as a branch with its own focus within a broader field. Rather, we concur with Geertsema's (2016) view that attention to SoTL as a more local form of knowledge creation can enable these kinds of pedagogic research to play a strongly developmental role within institutions, and that distinguishing SoTL as something separate from more globally orientated educational research can help with this.

However, educational research is also complicated by the multidisciplinary nature of the higher education field. Many educational researchers (including ourselves) trained in disciplines other than higher education. Educational research takes place within education departments, academic development units, as well as across an array of other practice fields and subject-based disciplinary contexts. As a result, we can understand it as a broad and diverse 'field of study, researched from a number of disciplinary perspectives' (Tight 2014: 95), as opposed to a coherent discipline (although some colleagues still argue for its recognition as a discipline, e.g. Wyse et al. 2020, and others argue it can be usefully understood as both discipline and field). In the introduction to this book, we reflect upon our own very different disciplinary backgrounds and perspectives and conclude that this has been a strength, enabling us to have rich, enjoyable and interesting conversations about different questions. Nonetheless, a diversity of methodological, epistemological and ontological positions can be much more problematic in a less dialogic situation, for example, in the area of anonymous peer review, where education researchers often report that their methods, research questions or theoretical approach may have been misunderstood by reviewers with different expertise.

Moreover, within this diverse field of higher education, educational researchers who do wish to engage with theory have also traditionally been divided into two discrete camps. As explored by Manathunga in her history of the field of educational development (2011), these camps have predominantly attended to either a small scope of psychological, or (less often) sociological, literatures. As a result, Manathunga (358) contends that while 'related fields of adult education, educational sociology, sociolinguistics and educational psychology have moved on to incorporate critical, feminist and postmodernist theoretical and methodological perspectives, these remain highly marginal in educational development literature'. For Manathunga, many researchers 'do not explicitly engage with theory and when they implicitly engage with theory, it is a very narrow selection of theories that count' (356).

Of course, ten years have now passed since Manathunga's portrayal of the landscape of educational research. However, these preoccupations are still visible within the literature that is still today often dominated by a cognitive psychological framing, described powerfully by Manathunga as 'a focus on individual students and on their brains as separate from their raced, classed, gendered bodies and the social, historical, political and cultural contexts within which they learn' (2011: 355). Sociological perspectives may now be more widespread, but other critical theories including posthumanism, new materialism, feminism and poststructuralism are still considered marginal within higher education – although fortunately exciting work is now being done to redress this (Taylor and Bayley 2019; Bozalek et al. 2018b). We believe that a dearth of theoretical underpinning is problematic, as is a failure to engage in the richness of theoretical literatures, with the risk that notions of pedagogy become 'bleached of their complexity and richness ... and reduced to narrow, technical "professional rules for practice"' (Manathunga 2011: 356). Moving towards a greater diversity of perspectives, then, we instead agree with Bozalek, Shefer and Zembylas (2018: 1) who suggest that employing new theories may hold the power to 'open new possibilities and provocations for the body of work in higher education'.

Postqualitative Research

Thinking with theory also offers the potential for an entirely new way of doing research. Mazzei and Jackson (2012) go so far as defining thinking with theory as a new analytic for qualitative research. Mazzei and Jackson explore the value of a process they define as of 'plugging in', where the researcher engages with theoretical texts actively, plugging in to 'ideas, fragments, theory, selves, affects, and other lifeworlds as a nonlinear movement, always in a state of becoming' (2012: 728). As such, Mazzei and Jackson identify a way of putting theory actively to work 'that functions within and against the structures of traditional forms of inquiry that have proliferated and normalized qualitative research texts and practices' (732). Thinking is doing, language is material, and research becomes nonlinear – 'always in a state of becoming'. Such an approach deviates markedly from traditional conceptions of how to do qualitative research, and has become more commonly known as postqualitative research (Lather and St. Pierre 2013; St. Pierre 2021). Mazzei and Jackson (2012: 733) contend that postqualitative research offers an

> inquiry that 'challenges the outlines' and prescriptive history of method. Inquiry that enters and exits sideways, that begins in the middle emerging from an eruption that occurs when theory and data and problems are thought together. Inquiry that does not rely on collecting data that are outside an assemblage in which we are already enmeshed. Inquiry that eschews a use of concepts for what they mean and instead puts to use concepts to show how they work, what they do, what they allow, and what they unsettle.

Here, Mazzei and Jackson describe an inquiry that speaks back to artificial ideas of linearity, that 'enters and exits sideways, that begins in the middle' and that 'challenges the outlines'. Data are understood to be as much a part of the assemblage as the researcher. Crucially, theoretical concepts are not valued for what they mean but for 'what they do, what they allow, and what they unsettle'.

Poststructuralist Perspectives

Our own interference via this book, then, is in many ways clearly influenced and indebted to a number of 'post' thinkers. Many of these writers have also been defined (albeit sometimes unwelcomely) as poststructuralist. While we are not concerned with using labels to limit, we do believe that poststructuralism, as a broad and shifting term, can serve as a useful tool to support our thinking and may provide a gateway into new literatures. St. Pierre explains that poststructuralism can be used to enable us to 'trouble both discursive and material structures that limit the ways we think about our work' (St. Pierre 2000: 477). In particular, poststructuralist theorists recurrently attend to certain key concepts: language, discourse, power, knowledge, truth and the subject, and an examination of these concepts can be useful for both pushing back against limitations surrounding the ways that we think as well as for pursuing a social justice agenda within education.

A clear goal of poststructuralism is to unsettle binary oppositions as well as to move away from taken-for-granted descriptions of knowledge, truth, rationality and subjectivity. Further, St. Pierre and Pillow write that 'poststructuralism in all its manifestations, along with other "posts" that describe continuing skepticism about regimes of truth that have failed us, has worked the ruins of humanism's version of these concepts' (2000: 1). Here, in using the memorable image of 'working the ruins' St. Pierre and Pillow evoke the idea of how theory can be put to work as well as the decay of, and dissatisfaction with, former ways of understanding and viewing the world: 'regimes of truth'. Such ideas are perceived to be the legacy of humanism, and, instead, a poststructuralist perspective enables us to reimagine this space. As Foucault contends, 'We have to dig deeply to show how things have been historically contingent, for such and such reason intelligible but not necessary. We must make the intelligible appear against a background of emptiness and deny its necessity' (Foucault 1997: 139–40).

As a result of Foucault's work in this area (1969; 1970) poststructuralism is also particularly relevant for us here in its concern with the notion of discourse. In particular, attending to the questions, how does discourse function and what does it do? How does it regulate? How can we surface its impact upon bodies, subjects, learning, thinking and acting? How can we 'make the intelligible appear'? Discourses are powerful. As St. Pierre (2000: 485) comments, 'Once a discourse becomes "normal" and "natural," it is difficult to think and act outside it. Within the rules of a discourse, it makes sense to say only certain things. Other statements and other ways of thinking remain unintelligible, outside the realm of possibility.' Discourses matter. It can be difficult to think beyond and outside them, and they impact upon and create realities. However, despite these constraints, they can be contested, as evidenced by the work of philosophers, critical theorists and feminists. As Deleuze and Guattari explain (1994: 5), the 'object of philosophy is to create concepts that are always new'.

What does this mean for those working in higher education? Discourses pervade and shape our learning spaces, relationships, curricula and interactions and it may be that we need new concepts in order to think and practise education differently. St. Pierre and Pillow suggest that such a rethinking can have broad ramifications, enabling us to 'ask questions that produce different knowledge and produce knowledge differently, thereby producing different ways of living in the world' (2000: 1). Thinking and producing knowledge differently, we suggest, may lead to different ways of thinking, working and learning in higher education.

Posthumanism and New Material Feminisms

The restlessness and scepticism of poststructuralism therefore offers us interesting opportunities to work the ruins of a humanist and positivist legacy of representation, fixed meanings and truth. Arguably, this is a legacy that has failed to deliver and has failed to offer any flexibility or agility in the face of a changing environment. Throughout this book, we draw upon poststructuralist and postqualitative concepts and writings to underpin and shape our thinking. Additionally, we also put to work contemporary ideas from writers that have been defined as posthumanist or as feminist new materialist thinkers. Although many of these ideas overlap, commonly these perspectives involve moving even further away from a humanist paradigm in order to explore what a posthuman approach to education might enable and, crucially, to consider our connections with a breadth of more-than-human actors. Departing entirely from traditional positivist conceptions of thinking that permeate higher education, such perspectives re-evaluate the impact of researchers in the research process, prioritize attention to the material as well as to the human, and advocate the notion that both the material and the human are entangled and intra-act (Barad 2007). Like poststructuralist thinking, these perspectives challenge representationalism and move towards a mobilization of meaning, and also regard that thinking with theory be considered as empirical research. Indeed, Barad's concept of intra-action (as opposed to interaction where bodies or objects are perceived as distinct) enables the blurring of all binaries and boundaries in a radical way.

For many posthuman or new materialist theorists, these directions are inextricably linked and offer potential for pursuing a social justice agenda, as well as for articulating new directions for a more ethical approach within higher education (Bozalek et al. 2018b; Taylor 2018b; Braidotti 2019; Haraway 2016). Inspired by Deleuze and Guattari, Braidotti's work introduces a number of new concepts to higher education including nomadism, cartographies and affirmative ethics. The first we explore here is nomadism. As a conceptual resource, nomadism continues Deleuze and Guattari's concept of becoming, which evokes the notion that we are all in flux, evolving, becoming, as nomadic subjects. For Deleuze and Guattari, 'a line of becoming is not defined by points that it connects … a line of becoming has neither beginning nor end, departure nor arrival origin nor destination' (Deleuze and Guattari 1987: 341–2). Braidotti (2018: xv) explains that this concept enables a focus on 'what kind of knowing subjects we are in the process of becoming and what discourses underscore this process'. This concept of the nomadic subject, whether it be student or educator, underpins our thinking throughout this book as we explore the becomings that occur throughout higher education pedagogies and practices. Crucially, such a perspective also invites a focus on the situated, localized and granular context of the individual within higher education and speaks back to universalist conceptions of experience that pervade scientific research approaches.

A further significant concept in this area is the notion of cartographies, as proposed by Braidotti. Unsurprisingly, given the significance we have seen of the blurring of boundaries between theory and practice, for Braidotti, cartographies are defined and understood as a method, a theoretical approach and also a conceptual resource, a 'conceptual off-shoot' (Braidotti 2019: 32). Offering this definition, Braidotti explains that 'a cartography is a theoretically-based and politically-informed account of the present that aims at tracking the production of knowledge and subjectivity' (33). Cartographies, then, can be understood as theoretical readings that enable us to understand how nomadic subjects experience the world. Cartographies can be understood as a gateway to new ways of thinking. Taking this framing to explore cartographies of undergraduate students' sense of belonging, Guyotte, Flint and Latopolski (2019: 2) explain that 'cartographic practices attend to the ways in which places, spaces, and discourses affect bodies, and align with critical spatial theory in that spaces and places are dynamic and relational'. The theoretical concept and practice of cartographies, then, evokes the idea of a means of reading dynamic experiences, and the production of knowledge and subjectivity (through language/discourse), as well as the significance of attending to concepts of relationality, multiplicity and complexity. Braidotti (2019: 34) explains that 'critical cartographies … entail creativity: they assist us in the process of learning to think differently about ourselves, in response to the complexity of our times'. Crucially, she also writes that 'any cartographic account is necessarily selective, partial and never exhaustive. Knowledge-production is always multiple and collective' (2018a: 33).

A cartographic framing underscores our work throughout this book as we explore the notions of relationality and plurality, as well as examining how we might surface and visualize higher education in new and fluid ways. Such ideas resonate closely with and build upon our own work in the field to date. This work has also often involved exploring the impact of concept mapping in higher education to shape theory and challenge the status quo (Kinchin 2016; Kinchin and Gravett 2020; Kinchin, Winstone and Medland 2020). Concept mapping, we suggest, offers itself as a tool to explore the overlap of traditional (often linear) structural portrayals of education that have a reductionist trend towards simplification and homogenization, with more fluid (rhizomatic) arrangements that explicitly acknowledge complexity and difference. This is explored in more detail in Chapter 8.

Braidotti's concept of affirmative ethics is also one that has informed the work of posthuman theorists and new material feminists. Braidotti (2019: 42) explains that affirmative ethics, which is again a way of both thinking and doing, offers a rebuttal 'of the accelerationist and profit-minded knowledge practices of … cognitive capitalism'. This idea is also explored by Taylor (2018b: 372) who writes that an 'affirmative critique is an opportunity to think beyond and outside dominant representations of higher education as a contemporary time-space damaged beyond repair by neoliberalism, and of HE learning and teaching as irredeemably deformed by the marketization, hierarchization and competition neoliberalism has ushered in'. Affirmative ethics, then, speaks back to the performative and neoliberal cultures that pervade contemporary higher education. It offers a space for a radical alternative: a way of thinking and acting with the belief that our world exists as an interconnected ecology that relies on our caring for it and for one another, in collegial, non-competitive, ways. Such a conception focuses on creating more affirmative spaces: finding space in life and work for joy, surprise, connections and creativity.

An affirmative ethical approach also involves attending to those 'missing people' (Braidotti 2019: 41), who have been traditionally excluded from discourse. In an interconnected world, all voices matter and people are understood as entangled with one another. At the same time, posthuman and feminist perspectives also prioritize a focus on the complex singularity and granularity of situated knowledges and experiences. Specific and accountable situated perspectives (Haraway 1988; Braidotti and Bignall 2019), encourage a move away from generalizations and an attention to the micro-moments and micro-practices of learning and working in higher education. A posthuman affirmative ethics, then, advocates a values-based, inclusive and situated approach that prioritizes the joyful within higher education and that practices collaborative, interconnected and non-competitive ways of thinking and acting. In doing so it also offers a new approach to deal with the complexity and troubles of our present times.

A Polyvalent and Patchy Inquiry

An affirmative ethical approach offers an opportunity to speak back to dominant neoliberal representations of higher education, to think and act differently, and these ideas also resonate with the work of Manathunga and Bottrell (2019), particularly their two powerful volumes: *Resisting Neoliberalism in Higher Education: Seeing Through the Cracks* and *Resisting Neoliberalism in Higher Education: Prising Open the Cracks.* In their exploration of the toxic effects of neoliberalism within the sector, Manathunga and Bottrell write that 'despite the pervasiveness of neoliberalism in twenty-first century universities around the globe, there remain significant opportunities to identify pockets of freedom for academics, professional staff and students in the academy' (2019: 293). Further, in seeking to 'prise open the cracks' within neoliberalism, Manathunga and Bottrell explore how counter-hegemonic ontologies and practices may be expanded in order to offer hope to educators and students. In order to do this they introduce the idea of 'polyvalent lines of inquiry' (2019: 309), suggesting that 'it is through polyvalent lines of inquiry that we might prise open the cracks in neoliberalism and [re]create the conditions for radical hope in the academy'. In their vision for creating spaces for radical hope in the academy, Manathunga and Bottrell define polyvalent as 'having a number of different forms, purposes, meanings, aspects or principles' (2019: 309). This notion continues poststructural and posthuman perspectives of 'mobilising meaning' and offers a useful concept for thinking about how a plurality of approaches can help to offer new directions. The authors explain that scholars enacting a commitment to polyvalent lines of inquiry require an openness as well as a certain willingness to experiment with knowledge production that lies outside their area of expertise. The idea of polyvalence also resonates with Taylor (2018b: 372), who plays with the notion of 'patchiness' in higher education. Taylor describes her method of adopting a mixed and 'patchy' approach in which 'new-old (theories, narratives, practices) jostle in entangled matterings'. Utilizing both the notion of thinking with patchiness and the idea of a polyvalent line of inquiry, we too seek to combine new-old theories, narratives and practices in this text, putting theory to work to deconstruct educational discourses as well as to consider what a new affirmative and more ethical higher education landscape might enable.

Conclusion

Taken together, our overlapping, patchy and entangled theoretical perspectives are all united in their disenchantment with the legacies of positivism, of humanism, of individualism, as well as with contemporary performative and competitive higher education cultures. Using the perspectives and concepts of the theorists considered here, this book takes a number of dominant discourses of the sector in turn and puts theory to work in order to offer new openings and possibilities. It seeks to go beyond critique and to offer hope. It examines the potential of new methods and of new ways of thinking about methodology, and it also explores transformative new ways of thinking about relationships and relational pedagogies. Ultimately, we consider how we might think and practise higher education differently. How might we move from the performative to the affirmative, how might we develop a generative and remobilizing critique, and how might we work and live meaningfully within the confines and interstices of a neoliberal higher education context.

Part 2
Putting Theory to Work

3

Positioning the Student

Introduction

Where is the student in higher education discourse? In 2010, the Department for Business, Innovation and Skills described students as 'at the heart of the system' (Browne 2010). But what do such discursive conceits actually mean and, moreover, what do discursive conceptualizations of students, of individuals, of subjects, do? A number of entrenched stories permeate higher education policy and practice, narratives that interpellate and locate students as subjects within discourse. As Charteris and colleagues explain, subjectivities are produced and often constrained within higher education discourses (Charteris et al. 2016), and work by Brooks (2018; 2021) explores how students are both understood and constructed by higher education policy documents. Words matter. In order to make decisions about how to teach, research and formulate policy for higher education we often have imagined student/s in view, and discourses which construct and locate students are reiterated and can become taken-for-granted within our thinking. However, we suggest that many of these discourses, and the assumptions that underpin both practice and policy frameworks, are often informed by humanist, individualist, conceptions that may not always bear much resemblance to the day-to-day lives of 'real' students. Such discourses, we argue, warrant further deconstruction.

In order to begin this deconstruction, we draw upon ideas from a breadth of poststructural and posthuman perspectives, for example, the work of Braidotti (2018; 2019); Barad (2007); and Bozalek, Shefer and Zembylas (2018). Bozalek, Shefer and Zembylas (2018: 1) contend that original theoretical approaches 'may open new possibilities and provocations for the body of work in higher education', while Braidotti (2019: 40) advises that it is time to generate 'new discursive practices which I call the nomadic or critical posthumanities'. Braidotti (2018: xix) suggests that posthumanism 'offers a spectrum through which we can capture the complexity of ongoing processes of subject-formation. As such, it enables subtler and more complex analyses of powers and discourses'. In this chapter, we examine some of these new possibilities and provocations for the way we think about students and their experiences. In doing so, we evaluate how students are conceptualized, and we consider what theory can offer in helping us to look again at some of the central preoccupations in higher education, enabling a move towards new discursive practices and pedagogies.

In 1989, in an article that remains powerful today, Elizabeth Ellsworth argued that

> key assumptions, goals and pedagogical practices fundamental to the literature on critical pedagogy – namely, 'empowerment', 'student voice', 'dialogue', and even the term 'critical' – are repressive myths that perpetuate relations of domination.
>
> What diversity do we silence in the name of 'liberatory' pedagogy? (Ellsworth 1989: 298–9)

Here, Ellsworth problematizes the ostensibly unproblematic: radically describing a number of concepts considered foundational to education, including empowerment, dialogue and the student voice, as 'repressive myths'. Given the prevalence of many of these 'liberatory' concepts and practices in contemporary higher education – empowerment, dialogue and student voice are widely adopted across the sector in literature and practice – such a critique makes for uncomfortable reading. Ellsworth continues to explain how many of these fundamental concepts are far more nuanced and more problematic than we might imagine. This is a bold undertaking that is still a thought-provoking read. It reminds us of how easily we can slip into forgetting about the many and diverse ways that students experience learning; how easily we can forget to critique our assumptions. However, more recently, in 2020, Macfarlane's article detailing the 'myths about students in higher education' reminds us that taken-for-granted concepts still pervade higher education, and that 'myths have an enduring verisimilitude' (2020: 1).

Reading Ellsworth's and Macfarlane's articles together diffractively, or what Jackson and Mazzei (2012) have described as a 'plugging in' to this literature, we are reminded of the need to continue to problematize taken-for-granted ideas and discourses. In this chapter, then, we attempt to think higher education pedagogy 'otherwise', moving 'towards multiplicity, complexity and emergence' (Taylor 2018b: 372), and to explore what 'diversity' of thought might we be (unwittingly) silencing within our practice. We attempt this by reconsidering some of the most prevalent preoccupations in relation to students' positioning within higher education today. We begin with one of the most pervasive goals and practices in the landscape of contemporary higher education: student engagement.

Student Engagement

Engagement, and specifically student engagement, is one of the most prominent concepts within higher education pedagogy and the focus of considerable international literature (Trowler 2010). Indeed, the notion has been described as representing 'an uncritically accepted academic orthodoxy' (Brookfield 1986: 96), a 'moral panic' (Macfarlane 2020: 12) and 'an ideology' (Gourlay 2015: 403). Certainly, it is 'amongst the most discussed and researched aspects of HE in the last four decades' (Tight 2020: 689) and is considerably influential, informing a fundamental element of institutional learning and teaching strategies and practices. Ostensibly, the desire for educators to support students' engagement in their learning appears wholly unproblematic. And yet there are problems with the way this concept has been adopted within higher education's discourses and practices, with respect to the simplistic acceptance of the term by educators (as we consider further in Chapter 7), and with respect to the conceptions of students the narratives surrounding student engagement promote.

Some of these difficulties have been exposed powerfully by Gourlay (2015; 2017) in her articles exploring 'the tyranny of participation' and building on the concept of 'learnification' (as we explore further in Chapter 5). Specifically, Gourlay contends that the notion of engagement 'relies on typological categories which tend to posit the individual as the primary site of student engagement' (2017: 1). Firstly, this conception presents the individual as the primary locus of engagement within a humanist perspective. Secondly, according to Gourlay, this conception is further problematic because it leads us to 'emphasise practices which are observable, verbal, communal and indicative of "participation"', whereas 'private, silent, unobserved and solitary practices may be pathologised or rendered invisible' (Gourlay 2015: 410). When certain practices are validated over others that are communal, observable and collaborative, other forms of engagement are devalued, 'rendered invisible', or worse 'pathologised'. Gourlay suggests that this has also fostered a further trend towards 'learnification' (2017), where the onus is placed upon the learner to learn and is held solely responsible for 'engaging'. This narrative clearly leaves little room for a diversity of learning approaches or for thinking about teaching and learning as relational activities.

Macfarlane and Tomlinson also offer a critique of contemporary thinking surrounding student engagement and specifically 'the behavioural effects of policies which promote student engagement' (2017: 2) explaining that

> particularly compulsory attendance and class participation, are beginning to be questioned ... raising concerns about the effects of neo-liberalism, and the implications for the freedom of students to learn in the face of a growing surveillance culture at university. (Macfarlane and Tomlinson 2017: 2)

Within this discourse, not only is the communal, observable and participative increasingly valorized to the detriment of other forms of engagement, but we can read this as indicative of neoliberal encroachment upon students' very freedom and leading to an 'institutionalise[d] distrust of students as learners' (Macfarlane 2020: 12).

Gourlay (2021: 55) further highlights the tensions that underpin the way that students are framed within mainstream discourses surrounding student engagement as being paradoxical: 'The human is simultaneously foregrounded, but also paradoxically made invisible and disembodied.' Discourses describe a certain kind of neoliberal student who actively performs, collaborates and engages in specific prescribed, individualistic ways. And yet, paradoxically the day-to-day actions of lived experiences of actual students are ignored. These ideas build on similar concerns voiced by Sabri (2010: 197) who explains as follows:

> 'The student experience' has become a ubiquitous phrase in higher education policy discourse and specifically in discussions of what higher education is for. It is now used as a singular reified entity. 'Student' becomes an adjective describing a homogenised 'experience' that is represented in league tables, such as that produced by the UK National Student Survey. There is no scope to problematise who is a student, where and when this 'experience' stops and starts, how it comes about, how it changes etc.

> A reified 'student experience' is wielded as a criterion for judgement about what is and is not worthwhile in higher education. It demands the exclusion and silencing of other accounts of higher education.

For Sabri, 'student' has become an adjective describing a homogenized experience. 'The student experience' has become a 'singular reified entity', that offers little insight into other accounts of students' experiences of higher education.

Agency

We can see that underpinning this prevailing conceptualization of student engagement is the assumption of a uniform and agentic individual existing independently of social or material context – depicted as 'the primary site of student engagement' (Gourlay 2017: 1). We can also see that this assumption is firmly rooted within a humanist perspective, with the onus placed upon the individual to engage and to possess agency. However, this perspective is problematic in that it offers a homogenized description of students' experiences. This homogenized description becomes reified and can result in the potential to adopt a deficit conception of student behaviour, where students are automatically problematized when they are perceived as not 'engaging' in certain idealized, ways (Gravett 2020). Such a discourse affords little attention to the myriad of broader factors, beyond the human, that may impact the learning interaction and may inhibit individuals' ability to engage. Further, cloaked in the blanket of attending to a singular, uniform 'student experience', such a perspective often fails to attend to the embodied practices and lived experiences of actual students.

Rather than understanding agency as something fixed in individuals, as something individuals possess, we suggest that agency may be more helpfully conceptualized as an embedded process of engagement and as something people (and other non-human actors) do within specific contexts. Indeed, within a posthuman or materialist perspective, agency is more usefully understood as resulting from the interconnection of individual efforts, available resources and a breadth of other contextual and sociomaterial factors beyond an individual's control. This moves us beyond conventional conceptions of student engagement, enabling us to think differently and in new ways, and encouraging a focus on day-to-day actions and micro practices. Rather, 'the posthuman knowing subject has to be understood as a relational embodied and embedded, affective and accountable entity' (Braidotti 2019: 31).

The reality of our entanglement with our day-to-day material environment and context has been brought sharply into perspective by issues resulting from the Covid-19 pandemic. The global pandemic has impacted upon all of our individual situations and constrained our agency in new and challenging ways. However, if a learner is experiencing lockdown in cramped conditions, with little space or time to themselves, with illness or caring responsibilities, then these constraints may be all the more acutely felt, and a student's ability to 'engage' will likely be severely hampered. Their experience of learning will not be the same as another student who may have greater time, energy and space to commit to their studies. Instead, bodies and actors exist in a network, or assemblage, and agency can be understood as more about the multiple elements that constitute the agentic assemblage than the individual operating independently of context. Arguably, a more nuanced conception of both the key concepts of agency and of student engagement than is commonly adopted is required if we are to fully conceptualize our 'multi-layered posthuman predicament' (Braidotti 2019: 32), and if we are to understand this predicament in ways that can help us to more effectively support a diversity of students.

Voice(s)

Closely connected to narratives surrounding students' engagement are those that emphasize the importance of listening, or attending, to the student's voice. The concern for hearing others' voices has a long and significant tradition in feminist and postcolonial work as researchers and theorists have sought overdue ways to attend to lived and diverse experiences of marginalized and often silenced others. More recently, within academic institutions, the notion of attending to 'the student voice' has become a key consideration. This notion also underpins key metrics such as the National Student Survey (NSS) in the UK and the Course Experience Questionnaire (CEQ) in Australia that evaluate institutions' performance within a marketized, neoliberal, higher education environment. However, the very notion of being able to capture or listen to one or even plural voices is highly problematic.

Recently, notions of listening to 'the student voice' have been critiqued by Lygo-Baker, Kinchin and Winstone (2019: 2). Lygo-Baker and colleagues explore how the trope of the student voice has been conceptualized 'as a single, monolithic entity'. Crucially, they argue that this conceptualization can be harmful, obscuring the divergence in experiences of students (2019: 2). Just as there cannot be a singular, homogeneous student experience, there cannot be one single student voice, so within this narrative, which voices are heard and which voices are silenced? As we have seen, the concept of a student voice has also been problematized by Ellsworth. Ellsworth further expresses her view that student voice

> functions to efface the contradiction between the emancipatory project of critical pedagogy and the hierarchical relation between teachers and students.

In other words it is a strategy for negotiating between the directiveness of dominant educational relationships and the political commitment to make students autonomous of those relationships.

Critical pedagogues are always implicated in the very structures they are trying to change. (1989: 308–10)

According to Ellsworth, no matter how much we listen to the voices of our students we cannot empower individuals to be autonomous from the hierarchical structures that remain inherent within student-teacher relationships and within institutions: 'Critical pedagogues are always implicated in the very structures they are trying to change'. The desire to surface students' voices simply functions as an attempt to 'efface the contradiction between the emancipatory project of critical pedagogy and the hierarchical relation between teachers and students'.

From another perspective, the problematic aim of attending to and capturing voices has also been explored by Jackson (2003: 702–3) who critiques even the notion of voice, specifically the existence of 'a transcendental voice that reflects a direct and unmediated consciousness of experience'. Drawing upon Derrida's (1973) critique of voice, Jackson (701) contends that:

In the metaphysics of presence, voice is living and provides access to the real … This 'absolute will-to-hear-oneself-speak' (Derrida 1973: 102) is a drive to make ourselves heard and understood, bringing meaning and self to consciousness and creating transcendental, universal truths … However, Derrida believes that language is so unstable that meaning is endlessly deferred; therefore, there never can be a transcendental Truth that serves as the foundation for meaning.

Here the concept of surfacing voice, and meaning itself, is described as being inherently problematic: meaning is 'unstable and endlessly deferred'. A student's, or students', voice/s cannot be simply represented. Likewise, Mazzei and Jackson (2017: 1091) problematize traditional approaches to surfacing and liberating voices. They contend that conceptions of 'voice as present, stable, authentic, and self-reflective … is imbued with humanist properties and thus attached to an individual (be that individual theorized as coherent and stable or fragmented and becoming). Voice is still 'there' to search for, retrieve and liberate'. Exploring the relationship between humanist concepts of agency and voice, they advise that we can no 'longer think of doers (agents) behind deeds or actions giving "voice" to an experience' (Mazzei and Jackson 2017: 1092). Taken together, these critiques offer radical new directions for thinking about voice, voices and student voice work in higher education.

Dialogue

Of course, narratives which valorize performative and communal forms of engagement and which advocate attending to student voices are also closely connected to discourses which espouse the generative possibilities of dialogue. Dialogic interactions have been offered as solutions to many of the challenges educators face in higher education – developing relationships (Ashwin et al. 2015), working in partnership with students (Jensen and Bennett 2016), and improved assessment and feedback processes (Nicol 2010). And yet, understanding both the types of dialogues that take place within learning interactions as well as the breadth of actors that impact upon human dialogue may be more complex and more nuanced than has been acknowledged. Some of the challenges of fostering dialogue are brought into focus by the concerns (and complaints) often heard across campuses regarding students' reluctance to attend academics' office hours. Finding the courage to go and seek out an academic is known to be difficult for students, as evidenced by this quotation from a student participant: 'I mean they say go and see your personal tutors, like that's your problem if you don't want to go and see them but it's still a scary thing' (Gravett and Winstone 2021: 1584). In this research study, students discussed their day-to-day experiences and described the challenges of navigating staff–student relations, as apparent in the quote above. For students, approaching an academic to discuss their work may not be straightforward. Indeed, the very space, an academic's office, may be problematic. Ellsworth explains this clearly:

> Acting as if our classroom were a safe space in which democratic dialogue was possible and happening did not make it so. Dialogue in its conventional sense is impossible in the culture at large because at this historical moment, power relations between raced, classed, and gendered students and teachers are unjust. (1989: 315)

Again, we are reminded of the agentic assemblage and the complex interplay of power, bodies, space, time and material objects – 'acting as if our classroom were a safe space in which democratic dialogue was possible and happening did not make it so'. These ideas also translate to the online space or Zoom room, where most, if not all, teachers will know the familiar feeling of wholeheartedly encouraging students to engage in dialogic approaches only to be met by a resounding silence. As a result, the multiplicity of factors impacting upon dialogue can be seen to underscore many contemporary discussions surrounding students' remote learning, with educators often querying: why do students not speak in my online classes? Why do they not turn on their cameras? Why do they not 'engage'? Often there is limited consideration of other factors that may inhibit dialogue, for example, poor equipment, a lack of confidence with learning online, poor internet connections, feelings of tiredness related to being online or embarrassment regarding the student's learning space being displayed to all. In recommending dialogic approaches uncritically, there also often lies the assumption of the homogeneous student, who learns and behaves in uniform ways, and who has the power to make individual choices free from the constraints or affordances of non-human tools, spaces, materials and power relations.

As Ellsworth suggests, within the well-intentioned recommendations of educators lies a failure to acknowledge some of the most crucial issues of classroom practice:

> Often the term critical education has been used to imply but also to hide positions and goals of anti-racism, anti-classism, anti-sexism and so forth.
>
> We need to unlearn key assumptions and assertions of current literature on critical pedagogy and training to recognise, name and come to grips with crucial issues of classroom practice that critical pedagogy cannot or will not address. Strategies such as student empowerment and dialogue give the illusion of equality while in fact leaving the authoritarian nature of teacher/student relationship intact. Empowerment treats the symptoms but leaves the disease unnamed and untouched. (1989: 303–6)

Here, Ellsworth unsettles the 'illusion of equality' which may reside within our liberatory classroom practices. She explains that empowerment strategies espoused by educators may not really impact upon the structural inequalities that critical pedagogies seek to address. Of course, we are not suggesting we do away with dialogic approaches, or that dialogue should not remain a valued cornerstone of pedagogical practice. However, rather than expecting to be able to empower others through dialogue, perhaps instead educators need to be cognizant of the multiple forces and actors that exist within student-teacher interactions. Engagement with this complexity can be supported by work that explores students' situated, day-to-day experiences of higher education, and with artefacts such as concept maps that help to visualize the nuances and uniqueness of each interaction (see Chapter 8). Hierarchies, systemic and structural inequalities cannot be removed through dialogue. Rather, it may be more appropriate see the power and resistance as inherent and fluid within all relationships, assemblages and institutions. More honesty is required, as

Ellsworth advises, regarding those fundamental issues of classroom practice that critical pedagogy 'cannot or will not address', as well as a greater understanding of the heterogeneity of students' lives.

Plurality and Partnership

One alternative to move beyond the problematic trope of the student's voice and to foster dialogue is to seek ways to engage with a plurality of voices. Lygo-Baker, Kinchin and Winstone (2019: 320) suggest that pluralism, grounded in dialogue, may offer a solution to allow us to engage with a wider variety of voices. However, Ellsworth (1989: 312) argues that the situation may be even more nuanced than this: 'Pluralizing the concept of voices implies correction through addition. This loses sight of the contradictory and partial nature of all voices.' Likewise, as we have seen, the idea that voices can be listened to and represented may be problematic. Jackson (2003: 706) contends that 'to only pluralize voice remains focused on units of voice rather than dimensions of voice'. Rather, following a poststructural perspective, all voices can be conceptualized as partial, contradictory, evolving and becoming. While moving from voice to voices is arguably a move in the right direction towards the goal of greater inclusivity, perhaps we still need to remain mindful that even a multiple of voices may only offer but a partial perspective. Instead, in order to consider the fluidity and rhizomatic nature of voices, Jackson (2003: 707) adopts the term 'rhizovocality': 'Rhizovocality, in its multiplicity and contingency, is difference within and between and among; it highlights the irruptive, disruptive, yet interconnected nature of positioned voices.'

Another potential solution for disrupting binary relationships, power structures and conventional assumptions within higher education is the pervasive move within the sector towards working with students in partnership (Cook-Sather, Bovill and Felten 2014; Healey, Flint and Harrington 2014; Gravett, Yakovchuk and Kinchin 2020). Student–staff partnership practices have been shown to have the potential to disrupt entrenched institutional cultures (Matthews, Cook-Sather and Healey 2018), to enable students to move beyond identities as customers within the neoliberal university (Gravett, Kinchin and Winstone 2020b), and to foster genuinely transformative learning (Healey, Flint and Harrington 2014). Of course, solutions to entrenched challenges cannot be simple, and as we have seen, power and dialogue are complex. In particular, others have challenged how far partnership can limit opportunities for equitable engagement (Mercer-Mapstone and Bovill 2020) as well as how far partnerships simply operate within the neoliberal forces shaping current higher education policies (Matthews et al. 2019). Another important consideration will be the extent to which the partnership is meaningfully engaged in by both student and teacher (Ali et al. 2021). As Ellsworth (1989: 311) advises, without critique of the educator's own 'voice' – their assumptions, biases and positionality, engagement in such practices may become simply 'voyeuristic':

> Grounding the expression of and engagement with student voices in the need to construct contextualized political strategies rejects both the voyeuristic relation that the literature reproduces when the voice of the professor is not problematized, and the instrumental role critical pedagogy plays when student voice is used to inform more effective teaching strategies. (Ellsworth 1989: 311)

This view resonates with Freire, who asks 'how can I dialogue if I always project ignorance onto others and never perceive my own?' (1970: 63). Recently, Kinchin (2021: 191) also advocates the potential utility of the concept of parallel states of becoming in order to surface the dual processes of becoming that both student and teacher experience within partnership: 'While we can never argue for student–staff equality in being, we may offer a more persuasive argument for equality in becoming.'

Belonging

Intertwined with notions of students as positioned at the heart of their university communities, and with ideas pertaining to students' engagement at university, is the concept of belonging. The assumption that students can and need to belong to a higher education community has also become a taken-for-granted narrative within higher education policy and practice, and the positive outcomes of belonging are oft-cited, for example, as explained by Ahn and Davis: 'Students' sense of belonging is known to be strongly associated with academic achievement and a successful life at university' (2020: 622). How to ensure institutions create inclusive environments, remove 'barriers to belonging', and are able to foster a sense of belonging for marginalized groups is also a key preoccupation within research, policy and practice (Meehan and Howells 2019). Certainly, for many students belonging represents perceptions of acceptance and connection, and it is known to be 'associated with student wellbeing, academic attainment and retention' (Winstone et al. 2020: 2). But is this concept as transparent as it might appear? Can belonging be experienced differently within different times and spaces? And what about those students who do not wish to belong?

Recently, a new conceptualization of belonging has been offered in work by Gravett and Ajjawi (2021) and by Guyotte, Flint and Latopolski (2019). Reminding us that 'belongingness is not inherently positive', Guyotte and colleagues (2019: 14) argue for the need to ask more provocative questions when attending to the concept of belonging in higher education, such as 'what are we wanting students to belong to? Why? When might belonging be undesirable? … What does belonging do to/with students? What does it make possible? How might it constrain?' In their discussion of the importance of extracurricular activities upon students' experiences, Winstone et al. (2020: 3) explain that 'many clubs and societies are inherently social spaces, with engagement in these activities forming a social practice that may be uncomfortable for some students'. Again, Gourlay's critique of engagement and participation is relevant here, as Gourlay warns of a 'reification of the notion of "participation" which – although appearing to support a "student-centred" ethos – may serve to underscore restrictive, culturally specific and normative notions of what constitutes "acceptable" student practice' (2015: 403). Gravett and Winston (2020: 11) examine how often 'students desire the individuality of their experiences to be recognised'. This resonates with Derrida's critique of the concept of community. This critique is considered by Mann (2005: 45–6), who, drawing upon Derrida's discussions with Caputo (1997), argues:

> The ideas of sharing in common and belonging, which the word 'community' presupposes, suggest a requirement to homogenise one's identity, purpose and value in order to be a member … What seems at first glance to be an inclusive and welcoming term contains within it the very opposite.

Understanding the significance of non-belonging, then, may also be important if we are to understand students' experiences. Indeed, a concept of non-belonging, of being an outsider, has been important to feminist and postcolonial writers who have for many years put to work concepts of displacement and otherness (Woolf 1938). In his work *The Location of Culture* (1994: 200) Bhabha explores the concept of the 'locality':

> Locality is more around temporality than about historicity: a form of living that is more complex than 'community'; more symbolic than 'society' … more hybrid in the articulation of cultural differences and identifications than can be represented in any hierarchical or binary structuring.

Evidently a more nuanced reading of some of these concepts may be helpful for educators and could lead to a deeper understanding of students' experiences within higher education. But how are we able to disrupt such persistent narratives and move beyond binary conceptualizations and dominant discourses? Instead, Gravett and Ajjawi (2021) argue for a more nuanced understanding of 'belonging as situated practice'. Likewise, Guyotte, Flint and Latopolski (2019: 1) contend that one positive direction may be to reconceptualize belonging as ongoing and evolving: 'As nomadic subjects, students are perpetually in motion, in transition, and in relation, which shifts our analysis from the fixity of being, to dynamic narratives of becoming in higher education.' Such conceptions articulate belongingness as a situated and nomadic process, echoing Braidotti's (2019: 52) notion of 'process-ontology'. Belonging is not a bounded, fixed or achievable state, located in fixed or neutral places and spaces, but processual and fluid.

Becoming-Subjects

A generative new direction, then, may be for educators to look beyond humanist, individualist and universal conceptions of agency, engagement, interaction and voice – to move beyond universal or fixed conceptions of students' experiences altogether. Instead, through adopting a poststructural or posthuman perspective we move towards an understanding of the day-to-day, messy, fluid, evolving and situated nature of individuals' entanglement with the learning environment. Barad (2007) explains that such a perspective involves an awareness of the entanglement of the individual with their (both human and non-human) surroundings: 'Matter and meaning are not separate elements' (Barad 2007: 3). Rather, 'individuals emerge through and as part of their entangled intra-relating' (Barad 2007: ix). Barad explains that 'what is needed is an analysis that enables us to theorize the social and the natural together, to read our best understandings of social and natural phenomena through one another' (2007: 25). Drawing upon ideas from sociomaterial theory, Gourlay (2017: 15) puts these ideas into context in relationship to student engagement:

> In order to capture the messy, complex nature of contemporary student engagement in material and digital spaces we may profit not only from a move away from the dominance of constructivist theories of learning, but towards a sociomaterial framing (Fenwick et al. 2011). This sees engagement as

radically distributed across a range of actors, including nonhuman actors more conventionally viewed as 'tools' or elements of 'context'.

Similarly, Haraway (1988) introduces the theory of 'situated knowledges' where individuals are understood as situated knowers who construct knowledge through their lived and contextual experience. Likewise, Braidotti (2019: 1–2) 'stresses the importance of specific and accountable perspectives'. Such situated 'perspectivism' can offer up the opportunity to look at learning and teaching from alternative values and counter-perspectives. It asks, how can we read this from a new, more nuanced, contextual and situated perspective, one that considers the human and the nonhuman elements that impact upon learning?

In explaining her posthuman perspective further, Braidotti (2019: 52--3, 38) also writes:

> The posthuman subject ... is less a concept than a *conceptual persona*, a navigational tool that helps us illuminate contemporary discursive and material power formations ... Instead of new generalizations about an engendered pan-humanity, we need sharper focus on the complex singularities that constitute our respective locations.
>
> The aim is to track the multiple, grounded and hence specific and diversified ways in which we are becoming knowing subjects. (Emphasis in original.)

Here, Braidotti argues for 'sharper focus on the complex singularities that constitute our respective locations'. Our understanding of key concepts such as engagement, dialogue, agency and interaction can thus be enriched by attending to the multiple, specific and diversified ways in which we are becoming knowing subjects. We might want to consider the following: how are our day-to-day experiences different? How can we look again at the micro practices of students' experiences of higher education? How can we avoid representing others' voices as fixed or singular? What differences do students experience in terms of their context, learning environment and ability to engage?

Engaging ideas from posthuman or poststructural perspectives, then, can help us to avoid the assumed localization of agency as existing within individuals. These ideas remind us of the partial, rhizomatic, evolving and fractured nature of voices, and evoke the situated nature of learning and experience. This has been described by Bozalek et al. (2018a) as leading us towards a 'pedagogy of response-ability' where we become accountable, responsible and entangled. This leads us to think differently about the concept of relationality: what it might mean and what it might mean that we should do. Posthuman perspectives also mean that we can more helpfully understand the subject as a nomadic process.

Concepts of becoming, of nomadism, and of diversity are therefore generative for a rethinking of the assumptions and narratives that dominate higher education as considered in this chapter. Not only can we practice a problematization of received narratives, but we can also reconceptualize individuals more generatively, beyond normative models of subjectivity. Such a perspective moves us beyond the human, embracing both matter and context to understand subjects as in process and as interconnected. How different might the narratives which pervade higher education look should we adopt such an approach?

Conclusion

In this chapter we have offered a re-reading of some of the most prevalent assumptions and discourses that inform discussions surrounding students and their learning within higher education policy, research and practice today, engaging with and building upon these narratives. We have 'plugged in' (Jackson and Mazzei 2012) to a breadth of texts in order to look more closely at key issues such as student engagement, student voice, dialogue, partnership and belonging. Such a critique is not intended to close down debate, to be overly critical or negative or to lead to apathy. Rather, we are excited about the potential for new ways of thinking and doing. Inspired by Braidotti (2019) who suggests that critical cartographies are not negative but foster creativity, assisting us in the process of learning to think differently about ourselves and learning to think differently about the complexity of our times, our thinking too is evolving. Our thoughts and writing have changed over time and will continue to change. A process validated by St. Pierre who, speaking with Guttorm, Hohti and Paakkari (2015: 16), writes that thinking differently can be understood as 'rigorous scholarship':

> If we can't think outside what we studied 20 years ago as doctoral students, how can we keep moving, keep thinking, keep inquiring? I think the mark of excellent scholarship is changing our minds and being willing to do that. I tell my students how precarious our work should be, that we should understand that the next article or book we read might very well upend everything we believe and that that is mark of 'rigorous' scholarship'. Patti Lather said something about the value of 'rigorous confusion', and I really like that.

But thinking differently can be daunting, and confusion is often uncomfortable and even frightening. As a result, we follow Bozalek, Schefer and Zembylas

(2018) who propose fearlessness in our teaching and thinking, and (referencing Haraway's 2016 work) advocate an on-going process of staying with the trouble. In this chapter, then, we have explored what thinking differently might do to our understanding of some of the most pervasive narratives relating to how students are positioned and conceptualized in higher education. In the next chapter, we turn this rethinking to attend to some of the prevalent narratives regarding our university environments today.

4

The University Environment

Introduction

What are the dominant discourses in higher education that we use to describe and understand our university environments: the structures, spaces and cartographies of higher education? Where do these discourses come from, and most importantly – what do they do? In this chapter we focus on three broad discursive points that pertain to the university environment: participation and inclusivity, time and transition. We consider how narratives surrounding these ideas pervade higher education, policy and practice. However, we suggest that these narratives often emerge from neoliberal ideologies that exist in tension with imperatives of social justice, creating discordances and tensions in how we enact our practice and support our students. We explore what an unravelling of such narratives might achieve with respect to offering a richer understanding of the experiences of both staff and students in higher education, and in terms of creating new spaces to think differently about our higher education contexts.

Widening Participation and Inclusion

The areas of widening participation and inclusion have been fundamental to higher education discourses and practice over the past thirty years. The terms widening participation and inclusion have evolved from government policies and targets for universities to achieve in relation to the number of students recruited from under-represented social groups. Introduced in the late 1990s, the UK's widening participation policy focused on the aim to reduce social exclusion across the nation as a whole and included the target of achieving 50 per cent participation in higher education of all eighteen to thirty year olds by 2010. This intended move towards a fairer, more equitable society was also underpinned by a neoliberal logic. As Gale and Hodge (2014: 689) explain, 'expansion in the current period originates with governments in response to changing global economies and where they want their nations to be positioned within these'; being 'fairer' is interwoven with being 'stronger'.

As we write this chapter, the university sector (and the world as a whole) is experiencing a period of radical upheaval. Across the globe, the Covid-19 pandemic is still making itself felt with far-reaching impacts for all sections of society, but particularly for the most vulnerable, bringing with it new and significant implications for universities and for issues of equity, widening participation and inclusion. Within the UK, other more local decisions have had direct impacts upon the widening participation agenda. The present Conservative government have recently reorientated their widening participation policies, announcing that they no longer uphold a target of 50 per cent (Donelan 2020) of society to enter higher education, suggesting that social mobility should not be interpreted as about recruiting more people into university. In the UK, 2020 witnessed the fallout from the situation where an algorithm employed to allocate students' grades following the Covid-19 pandemic was shown to actively discriminate against students from less privileged backgrounds (Duong 2020), exposing the entrenched systemic inequalities within society. And this is just one of the far-reaching effects of the Covid-19 pandemic upon students and staff. Indeed, the pandemic is rapidly being shown as exacerbating the inequalities that persist within society and that these inequalities are widening. What, then, has been achieved during recent years with respect to advancing issues of social justice and participation, and what can we learn from the dominant discourses surrounding the narratives of widening participation and inclusion?

Today, while recent policies have delivered increases in representation for students from more diverse backgrounds, Black students are under-represented in many of the most elite higher education institutions, women are under-represented in some disciplines, and there exists increasing sectoral concern about Black, Asian and minority ethnic students' outcomes and about gender gaps in attainment and outcomes (Cotton et al. 2016; Mowat 2018; Bunce et al. 2021). Moreover, recently researchers have exposed that widening participation narratives themselves are underpinned by recurrent, yet problematic, ideas. In particular, often widening participation discourses and narratives evoke a simplistic conception of the role and scope of individual agency.

One example where we can see this narrative appear is within the speech of the Universities minister, Michelle Donelan (2020). During this speech, Donelan explains her view that 'true social mobility is about getting people to choose the path that will lead to their desired destination'. Even within this short extract there exist a number of key and powerful ideas. Firstly, the emphasis is firmly placed upon an individual's agency, their ability and responsibility to choose the correct path 'that will lead to their desired destination'. Students are expected to follow their 'desire', which again reiterates the agency and choice available to the individual, and the explanation is given that such choices are indicative of 'true' social mobility. Within this narrative, the appeal to notions of choice, desire and truth interpellate the student into a discursive position where they are imbued with individual agency and possibility. Such a freedom is seductive, they are responsible for their own fate. The implication is that any deviation from the 'correct' path would be the responsibility, fault or choice of the individual.

Wilkins and Burke explain that such narratives are located in discourses of consumerism, contending that students have become positioned as 'an empowered consumer in pursuit of individual desires' (2015: 440). They explain that such conceptions have become 'canonical' to widening participation discourses:

> Canonical concepts that are particular to WP discourses (including choice, empowerment, aspiration and achievement, to name a few) are sometimes abridged through government texts and policies into a single governing norm: the creation of students of consumers ... students as self-governing, 'willing selves' (e.g. active, managerial, self-improving, aspirational, engaged, etc.), but also therefore acting within a pre-determined horizon of thinking and behaviour. (Wilkins and Burke 2015: 436)

We can see, then, that neoliberal and humanist discourses of individualism and rationality underpin the widening participation agenda, forming a 'single governing norm' that constructs students as 'self-governing, willing selves'. And yet, as we have explored in Chapter 2, such discourses which centre on an agentic individual, free from social or material contexts, have been exposed by poststructural and posthuman scholars to be false, limiting and exclusionary. Just as discrimination and inequalities remain within society, widening participation and inclusion narratives remain problematic: aspiration is offered 'in ways that adhere to the hegemonic neo-liberal ideal of the entrepreneurial competitor-individual, de-meaning and de-valuing "other" personhoods' (Lumb and Burke 2019: 215). For those who do not achieve, the assumption is simple: the wrong choices were made.

Such narratives can be seen to be firmly entrenched within the 'ethical cul-de-sac' of humanism (Taylor 2018a: 82). Taylor articulates that what is problematic is 'the relation humanism sets up between the individual and the universal.

Humanist ethics locates moral conceptions in individual human bodies while, at the same time, positioning ethics within abstract, universalising and human rights-based discourses' (83). We can see such an 'individual-universal duality' within the widening participation discourses examined here. Such discourses place the onus entirely on the individual to succeed, regardless of the contextual and more-than-human factors that impact upon and constrain human agency and conflict with ideologies of social justice. Such discourses can also be viewed as being ground in 'hegemonic middle-class values' (Lumb and Burke 2019: 222). One impact of this is that they produce a 'poverty of aspiration' discourse, conflating material poverty with that of assumed 'aspirational poverty' (Lumb and Burke 2019: 222). Such a framing therefore forms hegemonic widening participation narratives that offer little consideration of the structural, cultural and more-than-human factors that impact upon choice and aspiration. Such a failure to articulate situated inequalities that impact upon students' experiences is an increasing concern as we see the global context exacerbate the challenges experienced by the most vulnerable.

However, Wilkins and Burke (2015: 448) also explore how 'the language of WP is a contested terrain open to revision and translation'. Discourses are not static, and openings for disruption and reframing do exist. Acknowledging that neoliberal discourses compete and conflict with progressive ideologies of social justice, Wilkins and Burke (2015: 449–50) explain that

> WP initiatives and strategies can be conceptualized in contingent terms as arenas where there is struggle over meaning and where the ideological dilemmas of policy-making reveal themselves ... neoliberalization never fully constitutes the performative capacity of those it directly addresses and seeks to constitute in its own image.
>
> A corollary of this is that policy enactments can be understood as terrains for the struggle over meaning and where concepts can be re-imagined, resignified and transformed to suit new discursive terrains and structures of feeling.

Despite the ideological dilemmas described here and the dominance of limiting neoliberal narratives within widening participation discourses, there remains scope for concepts to be 're-imagined, resignified and transformed to suit new discursive terrains and structures of feeling'. This is hopeful, and one powerful reimagining is offered by posthuman scholars who are beginning to explore new ethical ways of understanding concepts of relationality and agency. Haraway's (2016) concept of 'response-ability' exposes the interrelationship of individuals, and more-than-human actors. Similarly, Barad's (2007) concept of 'entanglement' rejects self-centred human individualism and proposes new ways of thinking about concepts such as individual agency, responsibility and relationality within communities. What new openings are created if we shift the discourse beyond its tropes of individualistic choice, aspiration and desire? This question is attended to by Bozalek et al. (2018b) who follow Haraway in their articulation of 'a pedagogy of response-ability'. This includes a focus on 'attentiveness', where learning from the other and becoming with the other (103) become fundamental, as well as a focus on the notion of responsibility where 'being accountable means seeing yourself as entangled and part of the world' (106).

Likewise, speaking back to discourses of meritocracy and equal opportunities, and in a similar play with concepts of relationality, Morley (2016) also draws upon Barad's concept of intra-action in order to disrupt the problematic conception of individual agency at the heart of participation narratives. In doing so, Morley (2016: 30) (and Barad 2007) remind us of the complex interdependent factors that influence an individual's ability to act: 'Intra-action signifies the mutual constitution of entangled agencies. Agency is the ability to act. Intra-action is the mingling of people, objects and other materialities' abilities to act.' The notion of intra-action and of finding ways to promote non-competitive and collaborative ways of learning and working in higher education offer a new space within higher education for thinking and doing differently. This idea is also explored in earlier work (Gravett and Kinchin 2020) that seeks to problematize individualist discourses of teaching excellence and focuses instead on understanding teaching in higher education as a relational practice, underpinned by non-competitive and collegial values.

It is not only the narratives surrounding students' entry into higher education, then, that can be perceived as limiting. Because these discourses fail to attend to the more-than-human, the structural or cultural factors that inhibit agency, these discourses also often fail to acknowledge the constraints experienced by individual students when they do embark upon a programme of higher education. Thinking beyond widening participation, about what an inclusive education might look like, also involves an increasing awareness of the pressures upon students to assimilate into higher education when they do gain entry into their desired institution. For example, Hutchings (2014) contends that for students, developing key skills such as academic literacies at university can be an unsettling experience, existing as a 'strange discourse' that can foster 'a sense of self-as-intruder in the new institution's space' (2014: 313). Likewise, Wilkins and Burke (2015: 435) explain that 'students are summoned to adjust their behaviour and learning to fit with culturally implicit norms and pedagogical demands. To be legitimated and rewarded is to inhabit and perform requisite skills and roles'.

Increasingly the relationship between inclusion and participation into higher education, and whether institutions are genuinely offering an 'inclusive' higher education experience for students from under-represented groups, is beginning to be researched and better understood (Reay, Crozier and Clayton 2010; O'Shea et al. 2016; Bunce et al. 2021). O'Shea et al. (2016: 333) examine a pervasive deficit discourse in universities, and they contend that crucially, 'creating an educational environment that does not perceive of diversity in deficit terms begins with exploring the nature of this culture and the underpinning beliefs of its members'. Likewise, Bunce et al. (2021: 535) report that a significant factor in limiting Black and minority ethnic students' experience of university is that students report that they 'experience a sense of "otherness"' and describe 'teachers as underestimating their abilities and having low expectations'. Even more concerning are voices that contend that, for institutions, issues of inclusivity and equity have become subsumed with a neoliberal logic and that such issues are not treated seriously as ethical practices of care. For example, Blackmore (2020: 1) contends that 'gender, ethnic and racial diversity policies are encouraged because they increase productivity and not because of socially inclusive universities being a good thing in a democracy. Equity becomes an institutional asset, a brand, rather than a matter of rights and an ethical practice of care'.

Such policies being treated as institutional assets, brands and sources for productivity jar uncomfortably with the excellent and transformative work of many educators 'on the ground' within institutions. Thinking about what an inclusive education might look like means that educators have also begun to rethink what is on the curriculum and whose knowledge matters, leading to an increasing interest in decolonizing the curriculum. Notably, Bunce et al. (2021: 544) argue that treating students 'as individuals could help to build rapport and establish relationships of trust' improving outcomes for under-represented students as well as all students. While Gravett and Winstone (2020) also found that students desired to be understood as individuals with diverse experiences. In addition, a great deal of work has been done in the sector in recent years with regards to thinking about whose voice matters and what difficulties the concept of student voice might create (Robinson and Taylor 2013; Lygo-Baker, Kinchin and Winstone 2019), how students can work with academics as partners in their learning, and how curricula should be designed (Gravett, Yakovchuk and Kinchin 2020; Matthews et al. 2019; Cook-Sather, Bovill and Felten 2014; Mercer-Mapstone and Bovill 2020).

Of course, participation and inclusivity are not only critical issues with respect to students' experiences but are also fundamental to the experiences of those working within universities: academics and professional staff. Despite inclusivity and community being central values as stated on the mission statements and websites of higher education institutions across the globe, an alternative perspective is that twenty-first-century academia still remains an exclusionary space for many colleagues. Taylor (2020: 259) explains this starkly: 'The representation of higher education as a meritocratic system in which the "best" and the "excellent" get the rewards for their labour promotes an ideological cover story for the perpetuation of gender, race and class and other inequalities.' Similarly, Morley (2016: 32) argues that 'the neo-liberal academy, while not essentially male, can reinforce particular masculinities, producing a virility culture which values people in relation to how much money they make'. The reality of this 'virility culture' sits in tension with the 'ideological cover story' as articulated by Taylor; the perpetuation of gender, race and class and other inequalities is opaque within the academy, masked beneath the myth of meritocracy. As a result, Taylor (2020: 256) suggests that instead we urgently 'need new ways of attending to what matters and who counts'.

Participation, Inclusion and the Resilient Individual

Discourses of individualism can also be seen to underpin a recent sectoral interest in concepts of resilience, 'grit', 'academic buoyancy' and well-being, with such terms featuring within institutional learning and teaching strategies, policies and initiatives, and in the literature. However, increasingly, discourses of resilience are experiencing a harsh critique within the education (and wider) literature (and among colleagues, as we explore in Chapter 7). In this extract, the academic and author Sara Ahmed powerfully exposes the conservatism underpinning the increased interest in resilience as a concept:

> Resilience functions as a command: be willing to bear more, be stronger so you can bear more. We can understand how resilience becomes a deeply conservative technique ... resilience is the requirement to take more pressure; such that the pressure can be gradually increased. (Ahmed 2017: 89)

Here, Ahmed describes how resilience discourses may operate as a command to 'take more pressure', to 'be willing to bear more'. For Ahmed, these messages form the insidious subtexts beneath discourses that appear at first glance to be superficially benign, even helpful. In other recent literature too, discourses of grit and resilience have been shown to be complicit in the continuation of exclusionary, neoliberal narratives of achievement in higher education. Such ideas have been powerfully critiqued by Zembylas (2020). Zembylas (2020) contends that 'the narratives of psychologized and neoliberal resilience make us – educators, scholars, administrators in higher education institutions – complicit in the reproduction of social inequalities' (2020: 10). As with the discourses surrounding widening participation, the recurrent focus of such narratives is upon the notion of individual responsibility, meaning that responsibility becomes divorced from its social and political context: the onus is placed upon the individual. And yet, as we do not begin from an equal starting point, we cannot equally bear more, we cannot equally take more pressure. As a result, Zembylas (2020: 2) explains how resilience 'normalizes the ongoing oppression of already disadvantaged groups of students … the combination of neoliberal governmentality and psychologization frames resilience in essentialized and individualized in ways that have many theoretical and political limitations'.

Similarly, in his exploration of the implications of popular ideological positions that drive teachers' and teacher educators' understandings of poverty and injustice in schools, Gorski (2016) offers a radical critique of grit ideology. Gorski (2016: 381) explains that 'the most obvious trouble with grit ideology is that, of all the combinations of barriers that most impact the educational outcomes of students … not a single one is related in any way to students' grittiness'. Likewise, recent work by Webster and Rivers (2019) explores how such narratives promote self-help ideologies in higher education as the 'solution' to complex social and political problems, missing the complexities of interdependent social, material and political factors as well as the role of socially unjust structures. For Zembylas, this forms part of a wider problem: 'The growing preoccupation with psychological categorizations, emotional well-being, and emotion-based explanations of "vulnerability" and "risk" has come to dominate education discourses … emphasizing the need to work on changing the self rather than transforming the institution' (2020: 5).

How, then, can we reprioritize the role of structural inequalities and social injustices in higher education that such discourses obscure in their emphasis on changing the self? As we have suggested, one approach is to turn our attention in new ways to rethink the relationality of individuals to one another and to the wider university and societal landscapes that institutions operate within, considering how we each intra-act with one another and with our surroundings. Attending to the ecologies, communities and systems that individuals are situated within enables a broader discussion that shifts the gaze from the individual's desires, attributes or psychological traits. Crucially, such a perspective has the potential to enable instead 'a new set of discourses and practices that abolish neoliberal ones by identifying and nurturing those entangled relations of materiality-immateriality and nature-culture within and outside of higher education institutions that do not rely on psychologized resilience' (Zembylas 2020: 10).

Such an approach is revitalizing and exciting. It prompts us to go beyond critique and to consider new questions. These might include asking the following: How can we reinterpret university spaces as networked, entangled, communities? How can we consider how we relate to others, including developing an awareness of both the human and the more-than-human? What can we do to enable staff and students to develop within this context? What active steps can we take to destabilize power relations, to employ new discourses and practices, and to offer sources of support to all individuals within higher education? How can we stop speaking for the Other and work in partnership with others?

Time, Temporality and Transition

Another key and interrelated area to our understanding of contemporary institutions are the dominant discourses surrounding time and temporality within higher education. Time can be conceptualized in different ways, and in recent literature, the way that time has been treated in higher education discourse has been exposed as problematic. In their work examining the higher education context in Chile, Guzmán-Valenzuela and Barnett (2013) argue that the university as an organization has its own 'timescapes'. They associate the concept of time with a backdrop of marketization and argue that the marketing of academic time is 'a strongly contingent feature of the marketized university' (2013: 1133). Similarly, in her work on doctoral education, Manathunga (2019) argues for a reconceptualization of doctoral 'timescapes' and presents the need for making space for individuals' epistemic, lived and eternal temporal rhythms. These authors draw upon Adam's (1998) notion of timescapes. Adam's concept of timescapes disrupts conventional understandings of time as uniformly experienced, as well as alerting our attention to the significance of time within experience – equally as significant a concept as space, or landscape. Rather, time can be understood as experienced in heterogeneous ways, although timescapes can be artificially constricted and constrained by institutions or other forces. This is explained by Manathunga as the idea of 'multidirectional flows of time rather than a one-way linear, chronological progression of time so associated with the clock time of modernity' (2019: 1232). Like Guzmán-Valenzuela and Barnett, Manathunga also contends that politics of higher education in Australia have become dominated by neoliberal agendas of efficiency, profitability and managerialism, altering the timescapes of higher education and individuals (2019: 1227). Crucially, she explains that hegemonic, neoliberal approaches to measuring time fail to acknowledge the ways in which time is experienced differently by individuals from diverse backgrounds such as different genders, classes and ethnicities (2019: 1230).

Common linear conceptualizations of time in Western higher education have also been unsettled by Bennett and Burke (2018). They argue for the need to attend to the relational aspects of time and the different study trajectories individuals may experience, and contend that 'as socio-political, economic and cultural contexts change over time, and institutions and students' lives change, with due consideration and care, the measurement and construction of time-lines that are more responsive and flexible should be attempted' (922). A reconceptualization of time has also been proposed by Taylor (2020: 255) who examines academics' experiences in higher education and who contends that 'the contemporary university privileges speed, precarity, competition, and performativity; it operates through modes of accelerationism, work intensification and productivity; and it is oriented to producing academic subjectivities rooted in self-commodification'. Student and staff experiences and the way we think about concepts and practices of time are interlinked.

This rethinking of time also has implications for our understanding of students' trajectories and transitions into and through higher education. To date, hegemonic approaches to supporting students' transition into and through university have often encouraged a focus on short term, practical strategies to promote success, for example, pre-entry, induction and welcome week initiatives, and have operated within a linear conception of a student journey or lifecycle. Such a focus has been described by Quinn as a 'fetishisation' of certain time frames and activities (2010: 123). However, such a homogeneous, universalist focus leads to an approach that may fail to be able to support the diversity of students transitioning into and through university today (Gravett 2021). For students, transition and its associated concepts of learning and change are unlikely to be experienced uniformly in a linear manner and are more likely to be messy, fluid, ongoing and rhizomatic (Gravett 2021). Within student transition too, the intense focus on fixed time frames and outcomes can also be seen to alter the 'timescapes' of higher education, presenting a view of time and of transition that may be unhelpfully fixed, and that may exclude individual lived temporal rhythms (Gravett 2021). What is missing from these narratives then are the multiplicities and granularities of students' experiences: those stories that exist in the gaps and margins of a narrative and that deviate from preconceived expectations and homogeneous, linear pathways. Instead, we may need to reimagine both time and transition as something more heterogeneous, more rhizomatic, with students experiencing ongoing becomings as they evolve throughout higher education.

Such a view that disrupts dominant discourses pertaining to time, change and transition has implications for the way we might understand success. As Manathunga explains, success in higher education is often understood as a linear process; dominated by neoliberal agendas of efficiency, profitability and managerialism, hegemonic, neoliberal approaches to measuring time often fail to acknowledge the ways in which time is experienced differently by individuals from diverse backgrounds, such as different genders, classes and ethnicities (2019: 1230). As a result, there is little room for alternative conceptions of what it means to achieve and to be successful within higher education. For example, the Higher Education Academy's 'What works? Student retention and success programme' (2017) frames 'drop out' in no uncertain terms: 'Every student that drops out of their higher education course is a loss: a loss to their university or college, a loss to the future economy and, above all, a loss to that individual' (Higher Education Academy 2017: 7). While it is clear that retention is a key priority for institutions, what success might mean for different students is highly subjective and such an unforgiving perspective is simplistic and potentially harmful. An alternative view is proposed by Quinn, who in her chapter 'Rethinking Failed Transitions to Higher Education' (2010) explores the value of ruptured transitions and non-linear understandings of what learning lives are (126). Quinn argues that a 'turn-stile conception of transition' can be problematic for students for whom 'drop out' can be perceived 'not as a failure but as a rational decision based on circumstances that meant that this was not the optimum time, place or subject to study' (124). Ultimately, if time is understood as a uniform homogeneous experience, interpreted according to institutional priorities, and if success is conceptualized within a binary frame of progression and retention, this contributes to the telling of a deficit narrative of attrition that can be seen to be both unjust and unhelpful for our understandings of students' experiences.

Conclusion

In this chapter we have examined some of the dominant discourses in higher education pertaining to participation, inclusion and achievement within the university environment. We have explored how these discourses, despite their prevalent nature, are often problematic. At best they are simplistic. But at worst they can be seen as perpetuating systemic and structural inequalities, and a culture of self-centred individualism, beneath an ostensibly benign narrative of agency, choice and aspiration. We have advocated a need to look more widely at institutional landscapes and societal forces beyond institutions in our consideration of key issues such as participation, inclusion, resilience, time and transition, moving entirely beyond a focus on the individual, or on notions of meritocracy, and instead finding new narratives and practices to reimagine higher education differently.

We suggest that a new focus on relationality can offer a way forward for thinking differently. Relational pedagogies involve a broader focus that recognizes that attending to the multiplicities and granularity of staff and students' situated experiences is essential in enabling us to seek alternative perspectives. As Braidotti (2019: 53) argues, we contend that 'instead of new generalizations about an engendered pan-humanity, we need sharper focus on the complex singularities that constitute our respective locations'. Such a refocusing on the singularities that constitute our situated experiences unravels generalizations and assumptions about homogeneous experiences. This unravelling has implications for both students and staff and creates openings for radical new questions. As Taylor (2020: 255) asks, 'What constitutes a liveable life as a feminist in the accelerated university?' Further, relational pedagogies also promote a new focus on the entangled relationality of staff, students, with one another and with their situated contexts. Adopting a view that explores how we each intra-act may, we suggest, offer a powerful counterview to the discourses of consumerism and individualism that limit and oppress.

Such a rethinking is not easy. Bozalek et al. (2018a: 110) articulate that moving towards a pedagogy of response-ability is both challenging and risky. However, they advise that our teaching strategies ought to promote fearlessness. In writing together and apart we help each other become less fearful. Reconsidering our teaching and research practices, we have all felt the tensions in shifting from traditional individualistic approaches towards making relationships matter in a democratising manner. In our becoming-with students, stories, learning materials and socio-political events, we have needed to and continue to adjust our thinking and doing to patterns of relationality. As our thoughts move away from ourselves as discrete entities separated from those (human and non-human) around us, there is an on-going process of staying with the trouble.

Both the troubling of dominant discourses then, and the adjustment of our own thinking, is an ongoing project. Reconsidering our teaching and research practices can be uncomfortable, destabilizing and even frightening. However, there is also energy and excitement in new ways of thinking and doing and staying with the trouble that accompanies thinking differently. This might include experimenting with new teaching practices, for example, working in partnership with our students to design curricula, assessment practices or to carry out research. It might mean engaging in more collaborative and creative learning opportunities that offer students greater agency in the classroom and disrupt traditional student-teacher relationality, for example, storytelling, concept mapping or playful learning approaches including Lego or Playdoh or collage. Ultimately, we suggest that a troubling of dominant discourses and an experimentation with new ways of thinking about our university environments is necessary if we are to create liveable lives for a diversity of students and staff in higher education.

5

Ecologies of Teaching and Ecosystems of Learning

Teaching and Learning

In this chapter, we explore the discourses that surround the key activities of teaching and learning and how they have been conceptualized within the university context. We consider how the common usage of the compound formulation of teaching-and-learning has obscured the role of the teacher and how this has overwritten the importance of pedagogy as a foundation for our teaching. The reductionist tendencies of the neoliberal university divert our focus towards measurements and outcomes and contribute to the pathology of the institution. We explore how an ecological view of teaching can help to avoid an oversimplification the classroom environment by refocusing on a relatively small number of dynamic processes with the teaching ecosystem rather than on an unmanageable number of objects. This reflects the systems thinking promoted by Capra and Luisi (2014) and promotes an underpinning philosophy of becoming (Deleuze and Guattari 1987).

It has been noted that the distinct activities of teaching and learning are rarely considered independently in the current context of enhancement within the university (Buckley 2021). A number of commentators have teased apart the conjoined notion of teaching-and-learning to offer a greater appreciation of the impact of this compound formulation and the possible implications for the separate concepts of 'teaching' and 'learning'. Biesta (2015: 233) argues that 'there is no necessary conceptual connection between teaching and learning' – the so-called medical model (Biesta and van Braak 2020) – and in trying to force the connection, the idea of learning has been hijacked to pursue a specific political agenda that positions learners to serve the global economy. Biesta (2015: 231) has endeavoured to create some distance between teaching and learning so we can 'stay away from the mistaken idea that teaching can be understood as the cause of learning'. This is also explored by Opdal (2020: 459), who is clear that 'teaching sometimes leads to learning, and learning is possible without teaching at all'.

In recent years, the singular focus on the needs of the student has resulted in the increasing invisibility of the role of the teacher (Biesta 2013). This has been accompanied by a clear demarcation of status between teaching and research within higher education, with the term, 'teaching-only staff' seen by many as a pejorative term reflecting the hierarchy of research over teaching (Young 2006). The widespread perception of over-regulation and standardization of teaching practices has resulted in the emergence of the notion of the 'teacher-proof curriculum' that implies that anyone can teach any subject. Indeed, some of the linear teaching practices that are commonly observable in the university classroom, such as the ubiquitous reading out of bullet points to students from PowerPoint slides (Kinchin, Chadha and Kokotailo 2008), require little in terms of either disciplinary expertise or teaching expertise to deliver content to a passive student audience. This reinforces the idea that teaching is little more than a technical exercise in which expertise is trumped by competence – the latter being more amenable to evaluation using simplistic, quantitative metrics for the purposes of performance management. The general contempt felt by many academics for the idea of the measured university (Manathunga et al. 2017) has been summarized by Giroux (2014: 5):

> These are the tools of accountants and have nothing to do with larger visions or questions about what matters as part of a university education. The overreliance on metrics and measurement has become a tool used to remove questions of responsibility, morality, and justice from the language and politics of education.

Teaching and Pedagogy

Giroux (2010a) talks about the rise of 'bare pedagogy' within higher education. He sees this as a practice that is constructed within a market-driven rationality that abstracts economics from ethical considerations, and where compassion is a weakness. An imbalance has therefore been created between the needs of students and the needs of academic teachers as a result of the commodification of higher education (Manathunga et al. 2017). This can be seen in the overemphasis of the economic function of the university that has placed pedagogical practice as a technical exercise, and where higher education is framed in 'a corporate-based ideology that embraces standardizing the curriculum, supporting top-down management, and reducing all levels of education to job-training sites' (Giroux, 2010a: 185). To step back from market-driven policies and to recognize the professional values espoused by many academics requires a recalibration. As articulated by Mahon et al. (2019: 497), 'what is needed in higher education is a restored sense of balance. This requires a re-emphasis on universities as ecosystems of learning rather than merely sites of production'.

There is confusion about what is meant by 'learning' within 'learning and teaching'. As Biesta (2015: 232) points out, '"learning" is used both to refer to the process and to the outcome of the process'. He goes on to argue that policy makers often expect too much of teachers in terms of outcomes, suggesting that it implies 'students are merely willing objects of intervention, rather than thinking and acting subjects who carry responsibility for their part of the educational process' (Biesta 2015: 231). Rather, teachers should focus more on the process of learning, which might be referred to as 'studenting' (Biesta, 2015) or 'studying' (Buckley 2017). In addition, the hegemonic discourse of 'teaching and learning' depletes the emphasis on teaching and the teacher to the extent that 'the teacher is an increasingly absent presence in the discourse of education policy' (Ball 1997: 240). This is an indicator of the 'learnification' of educational discourse (as discussed in Chapter 3). A discourse that has collapsed the understanding of pedagogy into a 'technist' view of effective teaching techniques which are often seen simplistically as 'the didactic strategies employed to ensure that learning is acquired, and the bureaucratic gathering of evidence of acquisition' (Malcolm and Zukas 2003: 148).

Rather than focus on the 'teaching' or on the 'learning', Edwards (2006: 121) has focused on the 'and' of 'teaching and learning', to ask, 'What type of link is being suggested in the use of this conjunction?' By considering the nature of teaching and learning as part of a larger rhizomatic assemblage (Bacevic 2019; Mooney Simmie et al. 2019), 'The multidirectionality of the "and" and its rhizomatic movement points to a range of further connections' so that 'we should be open to further conjoinings rather than to seek to root ourselves in teaching and learning alone' (Edwards 2006: 131) – with the two activities potentially being seen as an unhelpful binary of 'I teach, you learn'. These conjoinings should include disciplinary and vocational practices; personal and political values and beliefs; national and institutional issues as part of a fuller ecology of our pedagogic identities (Edwards 2006; Malcolm and Zukas 2003).

Teaching and learning may be viewed unproblematically by some as 'teaching→learning' (implicit in the chain of concepts on the left of Figure 5.1). This reflects the comments made by some educators that 'we teach, they learn'

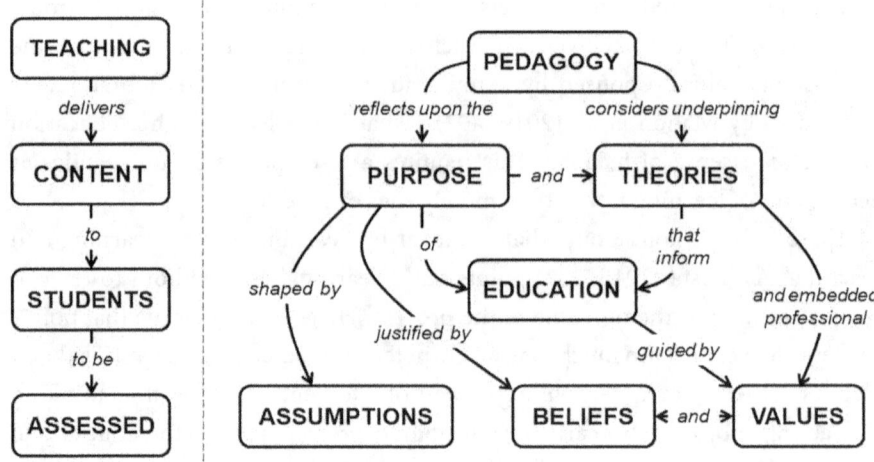

Figure 5.1 The chain of practice that comprises the basic act of teaching as content delivery (as perceived by many academics) alongside the elements of pedagogy that invite the teacher to make connections and construct a pedagogic identity.
Source: Kinchin (2012).

(as reported by Biesta 2015), emphasizing a passive learning role for the student to the extent that the idea underpinning the Teaching Evaluation Framework (TEF) is that 'we teacher better, they learn better'. The traditional thesis underpinning the Deweyan assumption that teaching always entails learning (Dewey 1910) rules out the idea of *attempting* to teach (Buckley, 2017), and hence the idea of '*becoming teacher*' (*sensu* Strom and Martin 2017a). A closed, linear, sequence of concepts presupposes no reason for reflection on practice or the need for the scholarship of teaching (Kinchin 2009). So long as the sequence remains intact and uncontested, it will proceed without inhibition. However, in a changing context, practice needs to be able to develop and evolve in response to new demands. For this to occur in a purposeful and scholarly manner, teaching practice needs to be supported by an appreciation of the underpinning pedagogy.

Using the 'and' to open up the assemblage and view teaching with a rhizomatic lens (*sensu* Deleuze and Guattari 1987) allows us to make the further connections to pedagogy (Figure 5.1) so that teaching is more than the competent delivery of content to be assessed. The concepts that relate to pedagogy require further exploration (theories, assumption, values and beliefs), and may take the teacher in a variety of directions. In such a complex structure, reflection on practice is required and the scholarship of teaching will offer mechanisms to integrate and develop the components in various ways that are context- and discipline-specific. The linking of the underpinning network of knowledge to practice in this way is essential if we are to achieve expert practice (Kinchin and Cabot 2010) that can evolve in a scholarly manner, rather than through trial and error. This has been referred to by Roberts and Johnson (2015) as applying 'the thinking behind the doing'. The notion of the rhizome presents an additional conceptual challenge to staff engaged in teaching, which reflects the need for adaptive expertise:

> Deliberately designing pedagogy rhizomatically, as though the brain were a grass and not a tree, requires pedagogical mettle. Lacking the security of predetermined trajectories and known outcomes, one must operate with flexibility. (Walker 2014: 355)

In this way we are challenged to 'treat pedagogy as uncertain and heterogeneous assemblages – not as identifiable or prescribable events, and certainly not as the exclusive concern of a teacher' (Fenwick and Landri 2012: 5). Walker's idea of 'pedagogical mettle' might be underpinned by a clear sense of coherence about teaching in a pedagogically healthy environment.

Learning Outcomes

While there are often valuable teaching moments that occur beyond the confines of the formal curriculum, it is nevertheless within the boundaries of the curriculum that we focus our teaching efforts. The curriculum has been conceptualized in various ways, as the 'curriculum-as-written' in comparison with the 'curriculum-as-delivered' and the 'curriculum-as-experienced'. All these viewpoints share a static depiction of learning, usually dominated by a catalogue of content to be covered. As such, it might not be a surprise that students are then seen as passive recipients in the process of curriculum delivery. In an effort to move away from this underlying passivity and to place students as active agents of learning, Pinar (2019) has coined the term, *currere* – the verb from which 'curriculum' is derived. The concept of currere turns attention away from what constitutes *the course* of education (i.e. a track to be followed) towards recognizing learning as *coursing* (i.e. a process of active exploration), and so shifts the curriculum concept from an object to an experience. To experience currere, the learner needs to be active. Active learning is a mindset and is not dependent on teaching in rooms with 'funky furniture' or with the level of noise being generated by students. We have observed active learning taking place even in the most traditional of settings including steeply raked, Victorian anatomy lecture theatres. Likewise, one can observe passive learning (or non-learning as described by Kinchin, Lygo-Baker and Hay 2008) taking place in the most stimulating surroundings, but where connections have not been formed between teacher and students.

There are significant implications that stem from a shift in the consideration of the course as an object towards *coursing* as an experience. For example, the outcomes approach to curriculum focusses on the start and end states of the student (a binary comparison between 'A' and 'B' from which change can be deduced after following the course) leaving the learning as a black box (Opdal 2020). This can be depicted as follows:

$$\text{Outcomes} = A \rightarrow \boxed{\text{BLACK BOX}} \rightarrow B$$

$$\text{Currere} = A^1 \rightarrow A^2 \rightarrow A^3 \rightarrow A^4 \rightarrow A^5 \ldots\ldots A^n$$

A focus on learning outcomes places no value on the personal route the student has taken to get from A to B as it is assumed the track followed is that of the set curriculum. In adopting the concept of currere (Pinar 2019), the path taken is that of the learner, 'lost in the curriculum' (Wang 2015: 1556). In this case mapping the journey is seen as a part of the learning experience and will be peculiar to the student and how they understand that journey. The currere approach (drawing on the rhizomatic grammar of 'and, and, and …') offers greater consideration to the process of learning ($A^1 \rightarrow A^n$) and is less concerned with reaching a predefined end state (B). However, in current practice we find that universities cling to the idea of a curriculum as a set pathway designed by experts in the belief that this confers rigour and prestige to those who follow it:

> For institutional education, the image of the track has come to constitute an homogenizing territory. Taken as a transcendent ground for experience, the course to be run constrains the potential becomings of a pedagogical life. Instead of thinking through the active powers of currere to traverse boundaries, produce anomalies, and unfix identity, the course to be run assumes the givenness of a well-tread path or course of life. (Wallin 2010: 3)

When designing a curriculum track, the unit of focus is often what we want students to achieve or how we want them to be changed by the experience – irrespective of their starting position. This is codified within the curriculum in the form of learning outcomes. Hussey and Smith (2010) provide a concise summary of the pathway that has led higher education to its current addiction with learning outcomes. Initially, many of the decisions that led us along this road appear to be based on good and common sense, and few would argue with the idea that, 'it is wise to decide what we want our students to learn and it seems prudent to let the students in on the secret' (Hussey and Smith 2010: 55). However, the sub-plot to this ambition for clarity has always been about the management of teaching and justification for spending money rather than ensuring the quality of the learning experience. Hussey and Smith suggest that one of the first steps along the road towards the universal adoption of learning outcomes was the influence of Hirst (1974: 16), who commented that a shift from 'aims' to 'objectives' offered a more technical term that would allow educators to be more specific about what it is that students should achieve. Again, the common-sense argument offered meant that the distinction between aims and objectives has become part of the orthodoxy of teaching. However, while we may discuss at length the best verbs to use to explain the objectives that we insert into our programme documentation, and 'while we might specify them with laudable exactness, they still seemed tainted with subjectivity' (Hussey and Smith 2010: 57). Hence the addition of 'learning outcomes' to the lexicon to accompany 'aims' and 'objectives'. Over the years, this terminology has been the subject of numerous staff development workshops and helpful guides to ensure that colleagues teaching in the faculties could adopt the right word at the right time (Moon 1999) and ensure that there was consistency across the disciplines so that when the paperwork was audited it gained approval from those whose job it is to assess such things. Too often it is the paperwork that takes centre stage (rather than the practice in the classroom) and policy and practice appear to have lost their connection with the underpinning educational theory (Loughlin, Lygo-Baker and Lindberg-Sand 2021). In these circumstances, those involved in academic development gain a clear (often forcefully articulated) sense of cynicism among some colleagues. It also meant that energy that could have been expended on productive, scholarly investigations of teaching and its improvement was diverted to developing a technical language that was no one's mother tongue. Hussey and Smith (2010: 58) conclude:

> Very soon the auditors impressed upon universities that they must pepper their paperwork with the right terminology. Not only must teachers list their intended learning outcomes for each and every teaching session, these must correspond to the to the learning outcomes enumerated in the booklet for each module, and these in turn must cohere with the learning outcomes listed in the

documents describing the whole degree course. It hardly needs adding all must be written in the language of precise descriptors. But this is not all: the teachers and academics must demonstrate how their assessment scheme exactly tests the extent to which the learning outcomes have been achieved by the students. The students must also understand precisely what is expected of them, so they must be given 'assessment criteria' which exactly reflect the learning outcomes of their modules. The result is the most perfect paper trail leading up, down and around about, ornamented by diagrams with more arrows than Agincourt.

While paper trails might impress auditors, it may not actually have the expected impact in the classroom. Within the numerous structured teaching observations we have undertaken in university classrooms in various disciplines, it is not unusual to see staff try to toe the party line and demonstrate a form of symbolic compliance (*sensu*, Teelken 2012) by displaying the learning outcomes for the session as a list of bullet points in the opening slide of a lecture. However, these typically utilize the precise language of the auditors, entangled with the specialist terminology of the discipline such that only the most alert and well-prepared students could have any idea of the learning journey they were expected to embark upon in the following fifty minutes. The ubiquitous format of the bulleted list creates additional problems that fails to support student learning by implying a false sense of linearity and isolation between the learning outcomes (Kinchin, Chadha and Kokotailo 2008). While there may be some common-sense reasons for using outcomes in education, Fawns, Aitken and Jones (2021: 68) have warned that

> outcome measures … are dangerous when taken as isolated proxies for quality. They neglect the value of exploration and critical thought, as well as the process of education, and how this fits with a student's … current needs. They tend to be orientated towards short-term goals rather than long term stability and the potential to adapt to shifting and unpredictable contexts.

Numerous commentators have highlighted problems with learning outcomes, particularly when they are introduced predominantly for managerial purposes (Havnes and Prøitz 2016), where they are seen to establish a ceiling for student ambitions (Erikson and Erikson, 2019) and work against a pedagogy for social justice by promoting conformity (Postma 2016). In response to the question, 'are learning outcomes providing all the benefits they were supposed to deliver?' Holmes (2019) states bluntly, 'clearly not'. Even within a single disciplinary area, Morcke and Eika (2009: 647) have shown that learning outcomes will mean different things to different teachers as they integrate the concept into their personal philosophies of teaching and assumptions about curriculum design:

> The role changes from learning outcomes as essential, to learning outcomes as unimportant, to learning outcomes as incompatible with higher education. Medical faculty who find learning outcomes to be unimportant or incompatible can put up a strong resistance to outcome-based education, because their opinions are rooted deeply in their (tacit) models.

Despite the weight of argument, the inertia to institutional change means that learning outcomes still dominate most institutional quality assurance regimes and provide a framework against which to assess teaching excellence.

It has been suggested that in striving towards excellence, teachers should develop a personal philosophy of teaching (Skelton 2009). Unless these personal philosophies are cloned from a restricted, approved selection, they will be diverse and idiosyncratic. As such they will be enacted in the classroom as a variety of teaching approaches, each with their underpinning values and beliefs. As such, they will interact with the current policy initiatives in a variety of ways that will also be influenced by the teacher's academic discipline and their current status within the university hierarchy. How teachers see themselves and how they reflect upon their career development are essential elements that inform their interaction with the policy discourse, particularly those staff with sufficient professional agency to determine their priorities and how they play out in the classroom. Such personal narratives can be found in the literature and may be seen as examples of how to thrive within the neoliberal university, rather than just survive. For example, Adcroft (2018: 88) says:

> I have always been reflective and have tried to learn from experience, sometimes through keeping journals and records, sometimes through discussions with colleagues and peers, sometimes just by musing myself on what has happened. I cannot say that my career has happened, or my identity as an academic has been established, by design as there is as much accident and happenchance in there as there is a plan, but I can see how my experiences as an early career researcher, as a management researcher, as an academic leader and manager, as a teacher have all left some imprint on the academic I now am.

Such comments are highly context dependent. A contrasting view from within the same institution is offered by Ogden (2018: 56), who says:

> I can see how others may struggle with a number of tensions that arise as they negotiate university systems, new developments, management strategies, and

the pressures of academic life. But writing this has made me realise that I am quite resilient and just determined to do what I do well and not only enjoy it but make it enjoyable for others. If I had been on the miner's picket line in the 1980's I may not have been so thick-skinned then, but watching them on the picket line at an impressionable age seems to have helped to make me thick-skinned now.

By comparing reflective narratives from successful academics, we can get a picture of the patchy nature of the teaching ecology within a university. An understanding of this ecology may be more easily achieved if we can move from the description of large number of objects towards an appreciation of a much smaller number of processes.

The Ecology of Teaching

There has been a long-standing tendency to draw upon ecological analogies within education research that help to articulate the complex relations that are seen to occur within classrooms and, more widely, across whole institutions (Svenkerud et al. 2020). The attraction fuelling this tendency was summarized by Toulmin (1972: 316), who stated as follows:

> What makes it worthwhile to extend ecological terminology from organic to intellectual evolution is, simply, the extensive parallels between the ecological account of organic change and the disciplinary account of intellectual development.

An ecological perspective recognizes the interconnected nature of concepts and the importance afforded to those connections. However, exaptation of systems of ecological concepts into the educational research literature (rather than mere appropriation of the term) requires an appreciation that ecology is part of the wider assemblage of biology – itself an interconnected web of complex concepts that are all related to each other by the unifying (threshold) concept of evolution (Dobzhansky 1973). And so, reference to ecology cannot be conceptually disentangled from the rest of biology (particularly from evolution) if the concept label is to retain any deep understanding of the field. As Deleuze and Guattari (1987: 249) have put it when referring to multiplicities such as ecology, 'it is not divisible, it cannot lose or gain a dimension without changing its nature'. Therefore, to 'use' ecology in isolation from the rest of biology would be to lose its nature and make the term meaningless. Exaptation of the concept, is therefore, also likely to require a degree of ecological literacy on the part of the user requiring development beyond novel descriptions using colourful metaphors because, 'real ecological literacy is radicalizing in that it forces us to reckon with the roots of our ailments, not just with their symptoms' (Orr 1992: 88). This has been elaborated by Molina-Motos (2019: 5):

> Ecological thinking is now genuinely ecological not because it accounts for the biological or economic interrelations in an ecosystem, but because it understands the term 'ecological' as the indissoluble systemic union of these with the social, cultural and mental. In short, the foundation of the real ceases to be simplicity and becomes complexity.

Within the concept's home discipline of biology, the understanding of ecology is placed within a constellation of other concepts and is influenced by the appreciation of genetic variation (i.e. diversity within the environment) as the engine of change for the disciplinary threshold concept of evolution (Walk-Shannon et al. 2019). The concept of variation may also have a similar role in the development of teaching in the university. Whereas more arborescent and restrictive thematic analyses of teachers and teaching will tend to emphasize 'sameness' or uniformity in a population (Mazzei 2016), the acknowledgement of the central role of variation (and the need to foster it in a healthy teaching ecosystem) requires a rhizomatic analysis of difference. In the teaching assemblage, this is exemplified by the ecological analysis of the variation in academic narratives in the context of pedagogic frailty (Kinchin and Winstone 2018), where difference has been explored using concept mapping. This foregrounding of difference may form the basis of an ecological literacy of teachers and teaching that could in turn support an appreciation of the ecological university.

The influential perspective of the ecological university developed by Barnett (2017) is centred around the idea of the seven ecosystems that he recognizes within the university – summarized as knowledge, social institutions, persons, the economy, learning, culture and the natural environment. Therefore, it seems sensible to clarify what we mean by 'ecosystem' if it is to form the centre piece of the ecological university. In order to achieve this, we first need to be clear whether we are searching for a realist definition that claims to make a statement about an external 'truth', or a nominal definition that functions as an abbreviation for a complex statement (Jax 2007). The idea of a universal truth would be a difficult idea to sell within the contested landscape of the university and so we are looking at a nominal definition. In addition, we argue that in the context of the university we are considering 'ecosystem' as a perspective that offers a way to deal with a problem, rather than as an object that is realized in space and time. The former seems to fit better with Barnett's seven ecosystems, in which case, as it is argued by Jax (2007: 352): 'An ecosystem concept that serves as an organizing scheme should even be rather vague and conceptually open to stimulate research and concept development'. The traditional teaching of biological ecosystem structure offers the promise of a linear progression (ecological succession) towards the false promise of a sense of stability (Schön 1971), provided by the dynamic equilibrium of *being* a climax community. The rhizome never makes such a promise. Within the rhizome, the final state is one of *becoming* (May 2003). This is a more authentic promise, and places authenticity at the centre of any claim towards teaching excellence (Nixon 2007).

Contrary to Barnett (2017: 121), we do not see the concept of the rhizome as inhibitory. Barnett's critique of the limited perspective of the botanical rhizome as being rather slow in its development does not acknowledge the wider perspective embraced by Deleuze and Guattari (1987) who also refer to the 'animal rhizome', and consider the behaviour exhibited by a pack of rats or a colony of ants as rhizomatic. Rather than using rhizomatics as 'a cover for our ignorance and for a current antipathy for firm structures' (as suggested by Barnett 2017: 57), we use it here to embrace and explore our ignorance and our need for further scholarly exploration and learning, and to acknowledge the complexity and fluidity of the elements involved. This is consistent with a philosophy of becoming in teacher development (Clarke and Mcphie 2016; Strom and Martin 2017a), and with Braidotti's ideas about process ontology (2006: 197) in which 'subjectivity is understood 'as a complex and open-ended set of relations'. Indeed, we can learn from research into ecosystems from the natural sciences that firm structures are not always forthcoming, and reductionist, static representations of ecosystems may not be the most authentic. Ecosystems are always in a state of becoming, and rather than focusing on their structural elements and geographical limits, they are increasingly represented in terms of their dynamic processes and cycles. A promising tool to help explore the nature of ecosystems (both biological and social) is the adaptive cycle (Hollings 2001).

As a metaphor for dynamic change in socioecological systems (SESs), the adaptive cycle links sequential phases of growth, conservation, release and reorganization (Figure 5.2). Over time the SES will develop increasingly rigid structures and complexity as it progresses from the growth phase to the conservation phase. Increasing inertia will slow adaptations and reduce agility in the conservation phase. In the case of a university, this might also be seen as a phase of complacency, where a single hegemonic discourse (e.g.

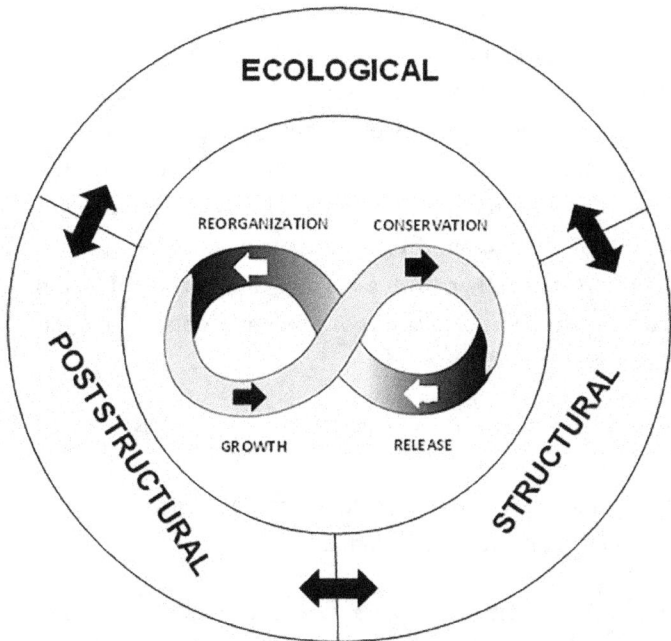

Figure 5.2 The adaptive cycle of ecosystem maintenance set within a variety of mutually supportive philosophical positions.
Source: Based on Holling (2001).

neoliberalism) may inhibit creativity and innovation. More positively, this may be viewed as a period of stability. The test of a system is in the release stage, as it is here where the capacity of the system to survive an extreme disturbance is tested (Fath et al. 2015). A system (such as a university) must maintain vital functions throughout the crisis. This has been demonstrated by the ways in which universities have coped with the global health emergency created by the Covid-19 pandemic of 2020 (Giroux and Proasi 2020). Where institutions have coped with relatively minor prior disturbances to the resilience of the system by cultivating resources to draw upon (e.g. robust e-learning strategies), they have been better prepared for the emergency migration to online learning (Watermeyer et al. 2021). The growth phase is a relatively rapid period of re-assembly of system components and provides an opportunity for novel recombination. This is a time 'for academic leaders courageous enough to disrupt longstanding patterns of behaviour [*sic*], to challenge opinions and organizational norms, and disrupt the status quo' Fernandez and Shaw (2020: 41). It is also here that an openness to interdisciplinary research and epistemological pluralism may have the greatest impact on the development of a system (Miller et al. 2008) and where there may be greatest opportunity for creativity and innovation.

The adaptive cycle (Figure 5.2) is seen by Sundstrom and Allen (2019: 9) 'to reflect the inevitable dynamics of complex adaptive systems as a result of the internal processes of self-organization and evolution over time'. The 'lazy eight' adaptive cycle reflects the argument offered by Hollings (2001) that the complexity of SESs emerges not from a random association of a large number of interacting factors, but rather from a smaller number of controlling processes. He argues that any theoretical framework that attempts to integrate these ideas needs to satisfy the following criteria:

- Be 'as simple as possible but no simpler' than is required for understanding and communication.
- Be dynamic and prescriptive, not static and descriptive.
- Embrace uncertainty and unpredictability.

The adaptive cycle heuristic provides a fundamental unit that contributes to the understanding of the dynamics of complex systems. The depiction of the adaptive cycle in Figure 5.2, in which the ecological perspective may be seen as a bridge between structural and poststructural perspectives, draws on the recognition of the value of epistemological pluralism (particularly in the reorganization phase), and an appreciation that such pluralism can lead to a more integrated study of SESs (Miller et al. 2008), and this has been seen as a helpful descriptor of sociological systems (Varey 2011).

Paradoxically, by mining the scientific literature that examines the structure and function of ecosystems, we can find support for the inclusion of other (non-scientific) viewpoints such as those offered by poststructuralist and posthuman philosophers – creating a conceptual consilience (*sensu* Wilson, 1998). Carpenter et al. (2009) argue that we can fail to perceive the full complexity of SESs because of the way we filter out inconvenient information. This occurs as a result of the tendency to focus exclusively on the measurable – something that can be observed in the managerial culture that dominates higher education. In addition, there is a tendency to believe dominant models, even where they are incomplete and provide only partial evidence to support a particular course of action. They argue that a healthy ecosystemic approach benefits from a diversity of viewpoints:

> Although the benefits of a diversity of viewpoints seem obvious, there are good explanations for why diversity is so often lacking. The payoffs from efficiency,

rationality, and the standardization have resulted in an emphasis on 'best practice' and a tendency toward monoculture or the dominance of the few. (Carpenter et al. 2009: 2)

The 'best practice' mantra, and the associated 'evidence-based' mantra, therefore come under scrutiny when considered as part of the ecology of teaching. For example, Stratford and Wals (2020) have shone a light on the limits of evidence-based policy in which critical messages can be lost and a monocular view provided by dominant models can end up supporting the status quo rather than encouraging transformation. They also highlight the irony that developing evidence-based policy is assumed to be a best practice in itself, despite the lack of evidence to prove its worth.

Ecological Resilience

Within the current teaching and learning university context there is concern over the welfare of students and their teachers. However, rather than re-evaluate the university environment, the academy has turned to the idea of developing resilience among the stakeholders to help them cope with the stresses and strains of the system we have 'designed' for them to operate in – a bit like giving everyone an umbrella rather than fixing the leak in the roof! Although resilience has become a *mot du jour* in recent times, it remains a contested concept within higher education. A number of authors highlight the failure of the dominant discourses to do anything other than promote compliance and complicity rather than support social transformation to address social inequalities (Evans and Reid 2013; Webster and Rivers 2019; Zembylas 2020). We have already commented on the concept of resilience in Chapter 4, but here we look specifically at ecological resilience and its significance in the teaching ecosystem.

In reviews of resilience, commentators note a lack of consensus on the definition of the term along with a range of other factors that make it difficult to draw conclusions from the literature (Brand and Jax 2007; Brewer et al. 2019). By investigating interventions targeting student resilience within higher education, studies have generally paid insufficient attention to the pathological nature of the environment in which students are working – assuming a deficit in the individual that can be overcome or remedied through guidance or instruction rather than an issue with the wider context. In addition, Walker, Gleaves and Grey (2006: 255) have suggested that some interventions in higher education that address student resilience and claim to raise self-esteem 'are possibly addressing only a superficial "feel-good" notion' that may leave more fundamental issues unaddressed'. Ungar notes that focus of resilience research should not be exclusively on characteristics of individuals, but that social and physical aspects of the ecological conditions of the environment also impact upon resilience at a systemic level (Ungar 2008; 2011). This is reiterated by Ainsworth and Oldfield (2019) who have shown that while individual factors (e.g. self-esteem, motivation, etc.) have an impact on resilience levels, the impact of environmental factors (e.g. management support, workloads, institutional culture) are at least as important, and need to be included in any institutional drives to increase resilience. System resilience can be put at risk as a consequence of a focus on optimization of resources and maximization of efficiency. The dangers to the development of resilience have been commented on in ecological terms by Kinchin and Francis (2017: 66–7):

> Resilience of the department depends on redundancy of expertise and role in particular. Staff tend to be appointed based on research ability and 'fit' within the department, complementing other research interests, rather than on ability to cover key aspects of the Geography curriculum (which is after all quite flexible and heterogeneous). This does tend to result in a community of specialists rather than generalists, and as an ecologist might observe, a community composed of specialists is usually far less resilient in the face of disturbance than one of generalists. Academic generalists tend to be undervalued – I would consider myself a generalist and have been told several times during my career that having a wide range of teaching and research interests is a sign of a lack of focus (the 'jack of all trades' model), rather than representing an important functional role within the department. Sometimes individual academics are responsible for running key modules or directing entire programmes and their sudden absence and the need to find alternatives creates stress across all levels of organization, from students to the Head of Department. Greater redundancy of role within the department (e.g. through more generalization) allows much better integration of material and ensures quality of delivery.

This redundancy (mentioned above) is an important aspect of ecosystem health and relates to the adaptive capacity of institutions to changes in context. It resonates with the redundancy of biodiversity in biological ecosystems in which species that have little influence under normal conditions have the capacity to absorb disturbances that challenge the core functions. Without such a 'buffer', systems may be prone to catastrophic collapse.

In relating the concept of resilience to the adaptive cycles that maintain ecosystems, Holling and Gunderson (2002: 27–8) have attempted to add clarity to terms by separating the overarching concept of resilience into *engineering resilience* and *ecosystem resilience*. This is an important distinction that has implications for the ways in which resilience is described in universities to support conflicting agendas. Engineering resilience is seen as focusing on efficiency, control, constancy and predictability – characteristics that are a feature of university managerialism. In contrast, ecosystem resilience is seen as focusing persistence, adaptiveness, variability and unpredictability (Holling 1996). The characteristics of ecosystem resilience embrace an evolutionary or developmental perspective and are consistent with a philosophy of becoming. The interplay between stabilizing and destabilizing properties within the adaptive cycle need to be actively engaged within the context of ecosystem resilience and are suggestive of a dynamic teaching environment. In the context of engineering resilience, these factors are more likely to be damped down by managerial interventions to try to maintain a steady state, even when this preserves a maladaptive system. This type of resilience can be seen as the 'enemy of adaptive change' (Holling and Gunderson 2002: 32). If different communities within the university ecosystem are using the same terminology (i.e. resilience), but this represents different concepts (i.e. engineering resilience or ecosystem resilience), then the conditions are set for the development of pedagogic frailty (Kinchin and Winston 2017), where tensions in the system impede the development of teaching. The ecological university needs to embrace ecological resilience in order to maintain some consistency in thinking.

We also need to ensure that *resilience* is not confused with *resistance* (i.e. a reluctance to change at all). To move the terminology on even further, and to avoid any confusion created by varying uses of resilience, it has been suggested by Taleb (2012) that we should adopt the term 'antifragile'. This describes the category of things, people or phenomena that improve with stress and disorder, and is seen as less of a neutral descriptor than resilience: 'The resilient resists shocks and stays the same; the antifragile gets better. This property is behind everything that has changed with time: evolution, culture, ideas' (Taleb 2012: 3). The adoption of an antifragile stance towards the university ecosystem is seen as a way to counter the neoliberal efforts to crowd out diversity in education and to provide students with a better preparation for a future that is largely opaque and unknowable (Polowy 2016; Fortunato 2017).

Conclusion

Within the rhizomatic development of the becoming teacher (Strom and Martin 2017a), and positioned in the wider fluid assemblage of university teaching (Bacevic 2019), it would seem unreasonable to expect associated concepts such as resilience to be fixed in a state of being. They will also be in a parallel state of becoming (alongside the becoming teacher), as expressed by Waller (2001: 290): 'Resilience is an ever-changing product of interacting forces within a given ecosystemic context.' As such, rather than wrestling with continual refinement of the definition of resilience (that has become a distraction for community) and the listing of attributes and development of indices of resilience, energy should instead be focused on analysis of how the concept works (*sensu* Deleuze and Guattari 1987), and exploring the links between associated concepts within the assemblage, as it is the links that convey meaning with a network of concepts rather than refinement of the concept labels (Kinchin 2016). The literature on resilience in the natural sciences is far more developed than in the field of education. However, even after seventy years of research there is still no single universal definition of ecological resilience to which the academic community subscribe. The education community can learn from this and realize that process does not always rely on constructing definitions. In addition, a critical characteristic of the resilience literature is the way in which authors have explored the connections between key concepts such as vulnerability, adaptive capacity and transformability (Walker et al. 2004; Gallopín 2006; Folke 2006; Folke et al. 2010). It is understanding the nature of this wider network of concepts within particular contexts that is likely to offer utility in going forward and developing a healthy teaching ecology.

6

Expertise in Context

Introduction

Universities have positioned themselves in relation to the wider social context, with government policies keen to stress the link between higher education and employability. Many of the other moves within academia have reinforced this alignment and so learning outcomes, learning gains and digital literacy are often considered within the suite of graduate attributes that our ideal students should have gathered as they make the transition into, through and out from higher education (Oliver and Jorre de St Jorre 2018). This outcomes-led approach to education often seems to miss the point that university is an experience in its own right rather than just a passage onto something else. This creates issues of identity (student vs. future worker) and creates a tension between competence frameworks and professional expertise. The ownership of these tensions often falls through the gap between education and employment. The key concept within all of this is that of expertise – what it is and how it can be conceptualized within the university. Here we consider how the literature on expertise has been used in the context of student learning. While the literature talks about forms of knowledge, this is usually considered within a single epistemological framework. In this chapter we take this forward to include a consideration of how a more dynamic epistemological cartography may contribute to a more polyvalent consideration of expertise as a process of becoming, and what impact this will have on satellite discourses such as 'employability' and 'learning analytics'. We argue that academics involved in educational research and teaching practices within the disciplines need to develop some epistemological flexibility in order to navigate disciplinary borders.

The Search for Expertise

The higher education literature in the area of expertise development has been dominated by the models presented by Patricia Benner (Benner 1984) and Hubert and Stuart Dreyfus (Dreyfus and Dreyfus 1986). These models offered a linear perspective on professional development (describing sequential stages from novice to expert), though the pedagogic interpretation of these models often appears to deliberately arrest student development at 'competence' (Brooks 2009; Talbot 2004) – a tendency that is seen by some to provide a barrier to higher education (especially for nursing students [Watson 2002]). The linear protocols that relate to competence (sometimes 'competency' – Teodorescu 2006) and the linear knowledge structures that represent them exhibit low levels of recipience (Kinchin, Winstone and Medland 2020) and are seen within the professional literature of the clinical disciplines as a fixed 'state of being' (Pijl-Zieber et al. 2014), rather than a fluid state of '*becoming*' (May 2003). The idea of the expert as achieving a fixed or permanent state is challenged by the more nuanced descriptions of 'routinized' versus 'adaptive' expertise (Salmon and Kelly 2015; De Arment et al. 2013), with the former tightly linked to the idea of efficiency, and the latter more closely aligned to the concept of innovation and ongoing change. The consideration of expertise in these ways has implications for professional development of teachers as well as for curriculum development and development of the 'expert student' (Kinchin 2016).

Linear thinking (as introduced in Chapter 1) and non-learning (Kinchin, Lygo-Baker and Hay 2008) will stifle students' process of becoming as their associated knowledge structures do not invite formation of links with new knowledge and are context specific. This effectively inhibits growth of the rhizome. This precludes the development of extra links (Massey 2005) and so restricts the development of powerful knowledge among these groups of learners (Wheelahan 2010). The persistence of dominating competence frameworks for teaching, even in the context of contrary evidence (Watson 2002), is an example of 'the mumpsimus' at work, where professionals can be seen to exhibit an escalating commitment to a failing cause, particularly where they have made a personal investment towards the status quo (Chambers 2003). The dangers of teaching practices that dislocate chains of practice from networks of understanding are illustrated by the anecdote reported by Kinchin (2020: 19):

> A clinical colleague who had been teaching in a developing country had found that whilst the clinicians there had the means to sterilise their surgical

instruments, they did not have the means to sterilise the trays on which the instruments were placed during use. As a compromise she got the nurses to line the trays with a clean piece of paper between patients so that the instruments were always placed on a clean surface. The paper was then disposed of between each patient to prevent any cross contamination. When she returned some months later to see how they were getting on, she found that they were still lining the trays with paper, but instead of using white paper they were now using Christmas wrapping paper as they found that it "stayed clean for longer", as it was dark coloured and so didn't show up the marks and accumulated drops of blood. So now the paper was dirtier than the tray it was supposed to be protecting the instruments from. The nursing staff had completely misunderstood the concept of 'clean' and had no understanding of 'sterile', or the reason for changing the paper liner between each patient. They had grasped the chain of practice, but it was not linked to an underlying network of understanding.

Much of the literature on expertise has been based on assumptions about the structure of knowledge (Kinchin, Cabot and Hay 2008), in particular:

1. Expertise is a structured phenomenon that may exhibit stability within a timeframe which is sufficient to permit it to be measured, recorded and compared with exemplars.
2. The structural nature of expert knowledge is universal and will exhibit the same physical attributes irrespective of context.
3. Expertise may be assessed within a community of practice by those presumed to possess a 'goal' structure, which may be perceived as the end point of development.

The structural model of expertise (Figure 6.1) that relates linear chains of practice with underlying networks of understanding (developed by Kinchin and Cabot 2010), has been used by Roberts (2016) to consider 'the thinking behind the doing', particularly in the context of curriculum development and also in scientific research more broadly (Roberts and Johnson 2015). Roberts's work provides a good example of how development of a concept map can help in the visualization of related knowledges, and the subsequent development of theory and expert practice – particularly for those working within a structuralist paradigm. Kinchin, Cabot and Hay (2008) have suggested that rather than attributing expertise to a certain level of sophistication and integration within a knowledge structure, that expertise may be characterized by an individual's ability to navigate between underlying networks of understanding and chains of practice that are appropriate to the context. However, as these

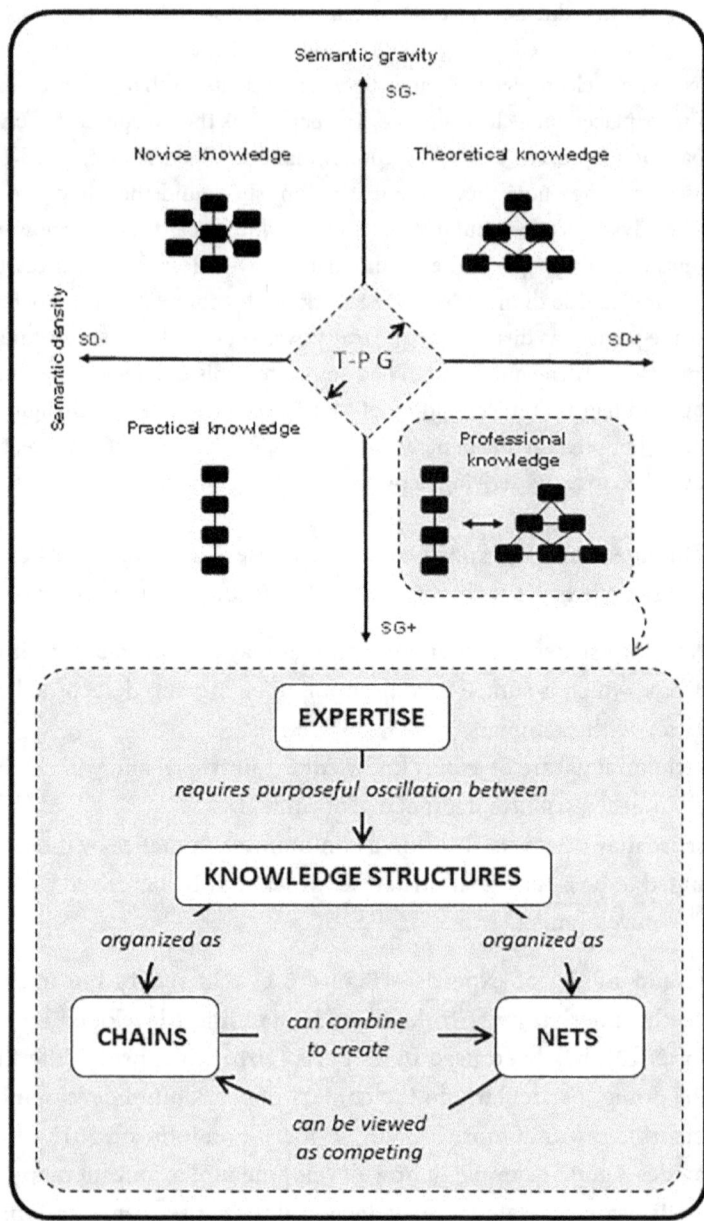

Figure 6.1 The dominant knowledge structures that are seen to inhabit the quadrants of the semantic plane (after Kinchin, Winstone and Medland 2020), with (inset in the greyed box) the dynamics of professional knowledge and expert practice, featuring purposeful oscillations between chains of practice (indicative of competence) and networks of understanding (indicative of knowledge) (based on Kinchin and Cabot 2010). T-PG = Theory-Practice Gap

chains and networks will be continually evolving within a professional setting, the oscillations between them occur between two moving points and will necessitate a continual state of becoming. The structural assumptions given above start to break down under the challenge initiated by the visualization of expert practice as being rather fluid and become problematic when considered across disciplinary boundaries. Underpinning the binary logic of the theory-practice gap is the assumption that both theory and practice are each unitary constructs. However, if we acknowledge the pluralism of the ecology of practices (Kemmis et al. 2012) and the ecology of knowledges (Santos 2014), we need to consider the theory-practice assemblage in a more complex (non-binary) manner as a multiplicity of non-linear interactions within a complex network (*sensu* Capra and Luisi 2014). The structuralist view of expertise is further disrupted by our consideration of 'theory-*as*-practice' that we elaborated in Chapter 2.

Post-Abyssal Thinking and Knowledge Ecologies

The structural depiction of expertise in the preceding section draws from the dominant literature in the field. This work has contributed greatly to the understanding of expertise and the way in which it can be related to professional practice and curriculum design. The processes of expert practice can be directly related to the knowledge structures that need to be manipulated. However, observers have been critical of the narrowness of the perspective offered. For example, Healy (2003: 700) comments:

> Expert culture is currently a bastion of 'epistemic sovereignty' that impedes not only non-expert involvement in knowledge creation [of the sort promoted by the students-as-partners movement] but also the development of the inter- and trans-disciplinarity 'epistemological pluralism' requires.

It is clear that epistemologies drive presumptions about the researcher/subject-of-study relationship while shaping how researchers set about answering questions. This is well known in the sciences, where, for example, Heisenberg (2000: 25) has stated that, 'we have to remember that what we observe is not nature in itself but nature exposed to our method of questioning'. A crossing of epistemological divides offers a broader range of methods of questioning, and is required between the fixity of science curricula and the comparative fluidity of the arts and humanities if we are to engage in interdisciplinary research, such as that required in the study of social-ecological systems (Miller et al. 2008), as explored in Chapter 5.

It is important for the application of the field of education to develop weak disciplinary boundaries and strong overlaps with other disciplines (*sensu* Wignell 2007) so that it may interact with other disciplinary discourses, whether or not that discipline has strong boundaries (e.g. physics) or weak boundaries (e.g. sociology). Therefore, in order for the educational researcher to be able to relate to and engage with a variety of other disciplines through a process of repeated border crossings (Mignolo 2000), it is important, not only to recognize different structural models of disciplinary content (Donald 2002), but also different ways of knowing – different epistemological frameworks – to ensure that education does not become dissociated from other disciplines, but becomes actively integrated with other disciplinary discourses so educational research can permeate practice. The entrenchment of epistemologies and the ways in which they can divide communities has been the subject of study by Santos (2007). While Santos focuses on the hegemonic epistemologies of Western Science (typified by the Global North), over the richness of indigenous knowledges (typified by the epistemologies of the Global South), we can recognize a homologous tension between the sciences and the arts across an individual campus, and the ways in which academics in the sciences will react to alternative perspectives:

> In the field of knowledge, abyssal thinking consists in granting to modern science the monopoly of the universal distinction between true and false. The exclusionary character of this monopoly is at the core of the modern epistemological disputes between scientific and non-scientific forms of truth. … On the other side of the line, there is no real knowledge; there are beliefs, opinions, intuitive or subjective understandings, which, at the most, may become objects or raw materials for scientific enquiry. … In the great domain of science – the divisions carried out by the global lines are abyssal to the extent that they effectively eliminate whatever realities are on the other side of the line. … The other side of the line comprises a vast set of discarded experiences, made invisible both as agencies and as agents. (Santos 2007: 47–8)

This range of perspectives is described by Santos as 'an epistemological cartography', and 'the other side of the abyssal line is the realm of beyond truth and falsehood'. The idea of 'this side' and 'the other side' of the line is entrenched in our disciplinary tribes. Overcoming this traditional stance requires effort and a respect of 'the other side'. While the rewards of post-abyssal thinking may be significant, it poses a considerable challenge for academics:

> Post-abyssal thinking can thus be summarized as learning from the [other side of the abyssal line] through the epistemology of the [posthumanists]. It confronts the monoculture of modern science with the ecology of knowledges. It is an ecology because it is based on the recognition of the plurality of heterogeneous knowledges (one of them being modern science) and on the sustained and dynamic interconnections between them without compromising their autonomy. The ecology of knowledges is founded on the idea that knowledge is inter-knowledge. (Santos 2007: 66)

It needs to be emphasized that 'the ecology of knowledges, while forging credibility for non-scientific knowledge, does not imply discrediting scientific knowledge' (Santos 2007: 70). Indeed, a post-abyssal view may be enhanced by a broader application of scientific knowledge through an epistemologically plural lens (as was explored in Chapter 5). Learning to navigate the epistemological cartography may not only be a useful strategy, but may also be a requirement of expertise in educational research. As an initial step, Andreotti, Ahenakew and Cooper (2011: 46) suggest:

> becoming (consciously) bi- or multi-epistemic or operational in two or more ways of knowing, involves understanding different social and historical dynamic processes of knowledge construction, their limitations and the social-historical relations of power that permeate knowledge production. It also involves being able to reference, combine and apply the appropriate frame of reference to an appropriate context.

The idea of an epistemological cartography (*sensu* Santos 2007) opens up the prospect of a fresh lens to focus on the notion of student expertise. Viewed within a singular epistemological perspective, Kinchin (2011: 187) defined the expert student as 'one who recognizes the existence and complementary purposes of different knowledge structures and seeks to integrate them in the application of practice'. Adopting an epistemologically plural lens, to not only view but to also actively interrogate knowledge, could offer a new level in the analysis of expertise. Expertise, particularly in cross-disciplinary fields such as educational research, could now be seen to include the ability to contextualize the arborescent knots (*sensu* Deleuze and Guattari 1987) of disciplinary domain knowledge within the wider rhizomatic assemblage. As such, the definition of the expert student offered above could simply be amended to describe, 'one who recognizes the existence and complementary purposes of different epistemologies with an ecology of knowledges and seeks to integrate them in the application of practice'. For this to be applicable to students, one would need to include epistemology as a topic within the curriculum, at least to recognize the epistemological underpinnings of the traditional curriculum hierarchy (Bleazby 2015). The idea of an epistemological cartography offers the potential to consider anew the ten instructional principles proposed by Elvira et al. (2017) for the promotion of expertise development:

1. Support students in their epistemological understanding (and abyssal crossings)
2. Provide students with opportunities to differentiate between and among concepts
3. Enable students to experience complexity and ambiguity
4. Enable students to understand how particular concepts are connected
5. Target for relevance
6. Share inexpressible knowledge
7. Pay explicit attention to prior knowledge
8. Support students in their problem-solving strategies
9. Evoke reflection
10. Facilitate metacognition.

The 'epistemological understanding' suggested in point 1 takes on a new dimension if we are considering these principles through Santos's post-abyssal lens and requires students to 'traverse the abyss' that may be found between one discipline and another or between 'academic' and 'life' knowledge. Osborne, Anderson and Robson (2021) see students as 'active epistemological agents' who experience tensions between 'knowledge arising from their life experience being ignored or treated as non-academic'. This type of epistemological flexibility will be increasingly important as the need to address cross-disciplinary issues (such as education for sustainability) become more significant elements within the higher education research agenda in the coming years (Miller et al. 2008; Suri 2013). Once the first point is amended (as above) to consider the existence and the value of epistemological pluralism, the other nine principles, as expressed by Elvira et al. (2017) will be seen to broaden their meaning.

Recognition of the variety of knowledges in terms of structure and function allows students to develop understanding that has utility beyond the immediate strategic goal of passing the exam. This more nuanced appreciation of knowledge goes beyond the simple deep-surface dichotomy that is described within the literature on learning (Marton and Säljö 1976). It not only relates to 'acquisition-of-the-known', but also grants possible access to the 'yet-to-be-known' (*sensu* Bernstein 2000), and new ways of thinking that 'frees those who have access to it and enables them to envisage alternative and new possibilities' (Young and Muller 2013: 245). Traditional transmissive teaching approaches tend to emphasize the contents of the 'nodes' of information that are seen as the objects of learning. Teaching to support the development of powerful knowledge also needs to emphasize the nature of the links between the nodes, that is, the relationships that are characteristic of systems thinking (Capra and Luisi 2014). This is where students can generate an appreciation of the explanatory power of their knowledge. To support the development of powerful knowledge and develop student expertise we need to

> provide students with access to the relational connections within a field of study and between fields, and students need access to the disciplinary style of reasoning to move beyond a focus on isolated examples of content. Unless students have access to these relational systems of meaning they will not be able to drive the production of knowledge, or to determine the criteria they need to evaluate knowledge. (Wheelahan 2010: 84)

Students will need guidance in the evaluation of knowledge as they will not have access to the whole disciplinary picture. This guidance is unlikely to emerge by accident and requires intentionality on the part of the teaching team who need to appreciate the ways in which different forms of knowledge are brought to the curriculum by their colleagues. This is reiterated by Winch (2013: 128) who considers as follows:

> A key feature of good curriculum design is the ability to manage the different types of knowledge in a sequence that matches not just the needs of the subject, but also that of the student, so that the different kinds of disciplinary knowledge are introduced in such a way that the development of expertise is not compromised.

For this to be effective, it is not just the students who need to be aware of the types of knowledge and their relationship. Teachers also need to be working with a clear conceptual map related to appropriate ways of learning the relevant subject matter. However, mastery of one aspect of the subject is not enough. Students need to grasp the conceptual core within a discipline. Teachers need to ensure that this is not 'scrambled' as a consequence of disciplinary fragmentation or modularization of the programme (Muller 2009), or allow the curriculum structure to obscure the structure of the discipline (Kinchin 2016). Clear conceptual links across a programme of study are not just desirable but are also a necessary condition for students to construct powerful knowledge which 'comprises not one kind of knowledge but rather mastery of how different knowledges are brought together and changed through semantic waving and weaving' (Maton 2014: 181). These comments by Maton, highlight how dependence upon a single theoretical perspective on educational research (e.g. sociological or psychological) or on a single disciplinary context (e.g. arts or sciences) or a single methodological perspective (e.g. quantitative or qualitative) is unlikely to generate a complete picture of learning in higher education. Maton's 'waving' and 'weaving' needs to encompass an acknowledgement of epistemological pluralism within the university (Miller et al. 2008) to help generate a more integrated understanding and avoid the creation of competing bodies of powerful disciplinary knowledge – which would then (paradoxically) not be powerful at all.

Being versus Becoming: A Fundamental Philosophical Tension as a Potential Source of Pedagogic Frailty

In distinguishing between being and becoming, Trifone (2019: 11) offers the following: 'A state of being is static and unchanging, like a stagnant puddle; a state of becoming is dynamic and changing, like water flowing down a river toward an unknown point downstream'. As we follow Guerin's rhizomatic researcher principles (Chapter 1), we are committed to a dynamic focus on becoming (rather than a static focus on being). However, we have to acknowledge that different discourses within higher education focus differentially on being or becoming depending upon their epistemological maturity and on the political drivers that are directing policy. In consequence, there may be a tension between discourses of being and discourses of becoming that separate students and staff within a university and contribute to an environment exhibiting pedagogic frailty (Kinchin and Winston 2017). When talking about learning as partnership between teachers and students (Gravett, Yakovchuk and Kinchin 2020), there are evident power differences between teachers and students that may inhibit the learning process. It has been suggested that this inequality may be reduced by considering students and staff as occupying *parallel states of becoming* (Kinchin 2021). Key elements of a potential range of states are summarized in Table 6.1. Here, we would describe those who are becoming teacher (Strom and Martin 2017a) alongside those who are becoming students – even *expert students* (Kinchin 2016). These parallel states of becoming challenge unequal states of being. Whether we are looking at students through a linear lens

Table 6.1 The Contradictions between 'being' and 'becoming' can be seen in tensions between competing discourses

Becoming and being	Graphic interpretation	Detail	Tendency along the pedagogic health continuum
Simultaneous states of being	[BEING / BEING]	Identities: singular and fixed as expert-novice Pathways: linear and predictable (tracks) Focus: on product Emphasis: quantitative metrics (management)	Frailty
Becoming vs. being	[BEING / BECOMING]	Identities: conflicted Pathways: unrelated or incompatible Focus: confused communication Emphasis: contradictory	Frailty
Parallel states of becoming	[BECOMING / BECOMING]	Identities: fluid, plural and complementary Pathways: rhizomatic and unpredictable (coursing) Focus: scholarship Emphasis: qualitative enhancement	Resilience
Divergent states of becoming	[BECOMING / BEING crossed]	Identities: fluid, plural and contradictory Pathways: rhizomatic and unpredictable Focus: confused communication Emphasis: diffuse	Frailty

or a rhizomatic lens, they are becoming, or transitioning (Taylor and Harris-Evans 2018; Gravett 2021). However, there is a perception that students are not becoming scholarly or critical (in parallel with the aspirations of their teachers), but becoming consumerist and employable (O'Leary 2017). Learning outcomes and assessments that consider being may be the source of tensions with teachers who are working within a philosophy of becoming – a condition that exhibits *divergent states of becoming* rather than parallel states of becoming. Conflicts between being and becoming may be a source of pedagogic frailty (Kinchin and Winstone 2017).

Borrowing from Cristancho and Fenwick (2015: 128), we are interested in investigating the complexities of professional practice where 'becoming' has no endpoint:

> In contrast to notions of rugged individuals who achieve definitive status as experts, 'becoming' is a continuous emergent condition. It is often a process of struggle and is always interminably linked to its environs and relationships.

This view of teachers as a constant work in progress (Adams 2021), resonates with the perspective on students offered by Guyotte et al. (2019: 1): 'As dynamic subjects, students are perpetually in motion, in transition, and in relation, which shifts our analysis from the fixity of being, to dynamic narratives of becoming in higher education.' This is in contrast to the whole 'excellence' discourse that is seen to commodify academic practice as part of the neoliberal hegemonic agenda by focussing on static quantitative expressions of creative and dynamic educational processes as part of a simplistic governance by numbers (Sellar 2015, Brink 2018). Academics who maintain strong professional values and who challenge the status quo might be considered as 'subversives' – working counter to the prevailing stasis in the system, engaged in 'acts of resistance' against the inertial forces of neoliberalism (Tomlinson, Enders and Naidoo 2020). In rhizomatic terms (Strom and Martin 2017a; Guerin 2013), these academics are following disruptive 'lines of flight', in a constant, dynamic state of 'becoming'. In the current higher education environment, university teachers are expected to be rugged individuals who have achieved expertise. Whether they are novice teachers who have only recently gained their PhDs and gained their first lectureship or experienced academics who have been teaching in various contexts for a number of years, they are evaluated together (e.g. within the NSS) in a situation where there is an expectation that 'excellence comes as standard' (Clegg 2007) – where the focus is firmly kept on *being*.

Satellite Discourses

When we start to consider the issues surrounding the ideas of being or becoming expert, there are various other narratives that operate as satellite discourses, which show how universities operationalize the idea of expertise. The role of universities in developing graduates for employment (as mentioned in Chapter 5) has had a fundamental influence on what and how we teach. Rather than employability arising as a consequence of a sound education, it is now seen by many as a goal in its own right. However, this may have deflected our attention from what it is to learn (to be a thinking person who is ready for employment) to what should be learned in order to address the short-term needs of employers. Such a goal-oriented and strategic stance can miss out on learning for enjoyment and tends to focus on routinized over adaptive expertise (as explored above). While the development of graduate attributes for employment follows the path of good and common sense, they also tend to fragment learning into itemized measurables. Such a fragmentation can make the goal of developing adaptive expertise or powerful knowledge more difficult by creating a tension that need not exist. In line with the arguments offered by Wald and Harland (2019: 371):

> we argue that rather than constantly changing education to meet contemporary employment demands, universities would be better to address the quality of foundational knowledge and skills. To do this, we have argued that GAs [graduate attributes] and GAFs [graduate attribute frameworks] should be abandoned by universities and suggested powerful knowledge as a theoretical framework for learning outcomes that are both reasonable and legitimate.

It also comes under the heading of common sense that we monitor our students' development and offer support for their learning that is tailored to their individual needs. As the development of a mass higher education system with large numbers of students has made it impossible for academics to follow all the students they teach on a one-to-one basis, universities have employed digital systems to monitor student performance and highlight individuals who may need additional support. This is often achieved through the use of learning analytics that has been made possible by the increased use of virtual learning environments which can record student participation in various ways.

As digital learning platforms can be used to harvest user information, there is a danger that we can fit the questions we ask to the data available. Such an approach would drive us towards the use of large sets of quantitative data that are ripe for the development of sophisticated dashboards to facilitate complex statistical analyses, with the result that we embed the discourse on one side of the abyssal line, losing sight of individual stories and personal experiences that shape learning (Hamshire et al. 2017). While the instigation of learning analytics may be motivated by the common-sense notion of wanting to improve the student learning experience through a better understanding of student activity, the danger of 'mission-creep' in being co-opted as a tool for the surveillance of broader managerial objectives has been discussed in detail (Selwyn 2019).

Selwyn considers how the application of learning analytics is likely to adopt a reductive stance that focuses on proxies for learning that may be widely misunderstood as direct measurements. In addition, the core claims of learning analytics to apply clarity and precision to the observation of student learning is at odds with the uncertainties that are inherent in a systems view of learning (Capra and Luisi 2014).

A second satellite discourse has grown around the use of learning analytics to describe student learning trajectories, particularly in the sphere of online learning. However, the ways in which learning analytics have been developed in many scenarios also appear to be at odds with other discourses in higher education, in particular the idea of learning in partnership. Broughan and Prinsloo (2020: 617) have commented on this, stating:

> The exclusion of students in much of current learning analytics practices, as well as defining categories of analysis and making sense of (their) learning, not only impoverishes our (and their) understanding of the complexities of learning and assessment but may actually increase vulnerabilities and perpetuate bias and stereotypes. In acknowledging the voice and agency of students, and recentering them as data owners, rather than data objects, learning analytics can realize its transformative potential – for students and institutions alike.

Indeed, the application of learning analytics tools need to be explored and developed with students as it really doesn't matter how sophisticated a system is, it only matters how the system is used and how it supports the development of learning networks and dialogue between stakeholders:

> This need is aligned to the theory of value-in-use (ViU) that argues that value is created through usage, and it is the value that the students or the teachers place on learning analytics that is the actual value of the software. Therefore, within the ViU concept, learning analytics' value cannot be predetermined, but rather is dynamic and changes as the students and/or teachers adopt and use the service. The idea that value is created not through a product but through an interaction or a process is also a factor in successful student and staff partnership as well. By applying concepts that stress the importance of relationships and interactions between students and staff, learning analytics can begin to break down the barriers that often exist in highly technical fields by facilitating continuous dialogue. (Dollinger and Lodge 2019: 9)

In other words, any system that monitors learning needs to be a part of that learning process rather than a passive observer of it. Learning analytics need to be used to support a process of *becoming* rather than as a tool for the assessment of *being* so that there is alignment between the philosophy of teaching and the accompanying analysis. Systems that are fixed in place and built on assumptions of the compliant student offer no space for the inclusion of 'counter-script' discourses (such as that discussed by Charteris 2014) that may challenge teachers' perceptions of learner agency and the way such instances might offer learning moments for teachers. By increasing the distance between student and teacher, learning analytics dashboards can obscure the learning that is happening behind the proxies that are recorded.

Conclusion

The implicit discourses of expertise are rarely raised for examination in open fora, for either students or academics. Therefore, the application of a philosophy of *becoming* is difficult to determine in this context, even though there are hints at this within the supporting literature. A conflicting philosophy of *being* is exposed through the enactment of satellite discourses that emerge from the assumptions of expertise in practice (e.g. employability and learning analytics). These discourses impose a reductionist perspective that have the potential of reducing expertise to the level of competence – a perspective that is more in line with the neoliberal university. The consideration of expertise within the context of Santos's Epistemologies of the South and Ecology of Knowledges brings the discussion of expertise to the fore and identifies the convergence between Santos's framework and professional knowledge – particularly in the caring professions (Lussi 2020, Cassiano et al. 2021). This highlights the deficiencies in the philosophical assumptions of being within the satellite discourses of employability and learning analytics. These discourses need to be re-evaluated to avoid tensions within the policy patchwork within higher education that may contribute to an environment that promotes pedagogic frailty (Kinchin and Winstone 2017).

Part 3
Emerging Polyvalent Lines of Flight

7

Contested Concepts in Higher Education

Introduction

In this chapter, we draw upon a selection of dialogues exploring dominant discourses in higher education, in order to offer further perspectives on some of the issues we have addressed so far throughout the book. The dialogues involved discussions among a small team of teachers and educational researchers. The series of discussions were loosely focused on the broad topic of 'contested concepts in higher education'. Each of the conversations took a recent higher education article as a starting point and stimulus for debate and focused on a specific area of higher education discourse. The topics were chosen as we felt they represented some of the most prominent, and often most troubling, narratives affecting our work, signifying specific 'contested concepts' in higher education. These debates were audio recorded and later transcribed. Below, we present anonymized extracts from the dialogues, together with a reflective analysis of some of the key themes and questions that surfaced from the discussions, drawing connections to concepts that we have surfaced elsewhere in the book.

As a method of research, we were interested in the affordances of critical debate for exploring our teaching and for challenging our thinking. We were conscious that, as academics, everyday pressures mean that we often perceive that while we become busier and busier, there is actually very little time spent to explore and discuss our teaching in a scholarly manner. We were also conscious that as a team we came from a diversity of backgrounds including linguistics, political sciences, English literature, biological sciences and psychology, meaning that our experiences, career trajectories, epistemological and ontological positions may be vastly different. We were intrigued to explore what a dialogue involving colleagues' diverse perspectives would expose and uncover. What new questions might it create? In this chapter, we examine these dialogic interactions and reflect further upon the key concepts examined in the debates.

Dialogue One: The concept of Teaching Excellence

In this discussion, we read the paper written by Daniel B. Saunders and Gerardo Blanco Ramírez (2017), 'Against 'Teaching Excellence': Ideology, commodification, and enabling the neoliberalization of postsecondary education', *Teaching in Higher Education*, 22(4): 396–407. Taking the paper as a loose starting point, we explore the contested concept of teaching excellence and its implications for praxis. Please note, participants have been anonymised and given pseudonyms.

Extracts from the Dialogue

P1 It makes us think about why we've even got this notion of teaching excellence in the first place and I think it is good to question where it's coming from. Again, about all the subjects we've been discussing recently, the concept, it means different things for different people at different times again, so it's not static at all.

Lots of things I agreed with and I like reading it from an intellectual point of view, but I don't agree with the idea of excellence and how it's pushing forward the metrics and measuring things. At the same time, if I were a student and I were paying lots of money, I would want there to be some accountability. What can we have instead of this word, excellence? Is it quality?

P2 I think for you to even say the phrase, for students who are paying an amount of fees will expect something like that, is pushing forward that neoliberal lens already. We've already been conditioned to think in that particular way without thinking about, what do we want to give our students? How do we want to develop our students? Not so much about, what do they expect from it? I think we need to, perhaps, change the way that we think about it because I think governments, etc., and the executive committees of boards have told us that is what students want, but not necessarily what universities need to do.

P1 I agree, but having had two children go through university, I think it's one thing to have these principles of, yes it is about developing the mind and becoming a better person and all of these sorts of things, but there is a reality as well. The reality is, for both of my children, they needed jobs when they left university. I don't think we can hide from that. However, we look at this, there's got to be something … I don't think it's okay, regardless of what students pay, for teachers to go into the classroom and not care and not do as best job they can, I really have a problem with that. However, we look at that, I think it's something that has to be looked at.

P3 I think those two things are different. I think saying people should care, and my kids need a job are two totally separate things. It's interesting how ideals, in any political system, change when people have an experience. Prior to having children, you may have said, it's a space for people to think, now you want them to get a job. I've got two children, I want them to have a space to think. I don't care whether they get a job, but that's me.

P1 But why does it have to be an either or? Either a space to think or get a job. Why can't it be both? We're always thinking in dichotomies, either it's about excellence or it's about absolutely nothing and there's no measurement or no accountability at all. I know it sounds really liberal, but there's got to be something that can embrace both perspectives to a certain extent.

P4 I would argue in that case then that they're attempting to measure the wrong thing. I don't have a problem with the idea of excellence in teaching as an idea. When people go to university I think there should be quality to it, not in a measurable way, just in terms of the fact that there actually is some kind of, they're coming in a certain position and they leave in another position, they have some kind of change there, through that process.

Labelling it as teaching excellence and then trying to measure that, metrics, is really problematic because it's too complicated a thing and then they boil it down to a number which makes it even more basic. It wouldn't even work with multiple numbers, it feels like it's too complicated because it's not a thing that exists outside of the context and the discipline.

How do you measure that in a general sense, when excellence in one domain means something else completely different to excellence in another domain? I think it's just the familiar, the way that it's used does fit with a neoliberal university because that is all about metrics and measurement and therefore they turn it into metrics and measurement. I'd say they're incompatible because I just don't think that you can measure it.

P3 Do we have to have either or, no we don't have to have either or, but we've gone from one extreme to the other and I think that's the danger, and I think it's that creep towards, again for me it's an ideological thing. I think we've crept from allowing people a space in university … we didn't negate them getting a job because lots of people left university and got a job, but we've now gone into, that is the overriding thing and that's what the students coming in are fed and therefore that's what they respond to. We, in academia, I think have to take also responsibility. We've agreed that, we haven't fought at it, we've allowed that to happen.

It depends what we're measuring, doesn't it? And what kind of questions we ask our students. I hear a lot in the press, and also in our own universities, we talk about student satisfaction. I don't necessarily want my student to be satisfied. It depends partly on your own individual style, doesn't it? I know I'm happy when I disrupt and cause uncertainty in people. Well that doesn't make them necessarily comfortable and that may mean, well I tend to get these evaluation scores, which are polar opposites, people either love it or hate it.

Does that mean I'm a bad teacher or I'm not excellent? In the minds of those people, yes, but I've actually fulfilled what I wanted to do, which was, get under their skin and make them think. They may have thought something I didn't want them to think, but ultimately, I may have achieved what I wanted to achieve. According to the university, that's a disaster if I get ones and twos. I don't necessarily see it as disastrous, it just seems flawed in the system, in what you're seeking.

P4 I think that student satisfaction is the perfect encapsulation of that. They use the NSS (National Student Survey) to measure student satisfaction but there's no real evidence that it actually measures this construct of satisfaction and that then gets transformed into a measure of teaching excellence. It's now moved from being, almost like a Tripadvisor type thing, as a measure of satisfaction to then being teaching excellence. At no point is that really actually capturing learning in any kind of way, which is really what we're meant to be there, to make people learn, to make students learn. We're not really there just to satisfy them, like you say. I think it's all the wrong things that are being picked up that are all connected, or aren't connected, but are being made to connect with each other.

I think it's the difference as well, potentially in my mind, that the excellence, or quality is something that's looked at from outside into you. I think that integrity is an internal thing. We, for example, when you talk about teaching observations, that part becomes from that person's integrity because it's a dialogue about their teaching. Rather than me merely imposing, well I didn't think that was very good, or I thought that was good, it's a dialogue which should start from their integrity.

This is what I was trying to achieve. I might not agree, but if they can justify that, why should I be the one to say, it's not excellent? If they can justify why they chose that. We're not going to tell you how to teach. We're not going to force you to teach in a particular way. It's up to your integrity to say why you've chosen to take the direction you have. If you can justify that, and that may be context specific, maybe your own personal values, who am I to say that it's wrong? I might have a different interpretation of that, but that's open for discussion and debate and I think that's the value of doing it.

Analysis

In this discussion some important issues are raised. Notably, the participants explore the fluidity of discourses. Participant 4 powerfully describes 'that creep towards' a changing understanding of teaching excellence, suggesting the subtlety of discourses and how ideas may become entrenched and 'creep' into our thinking, and considering how discourses and understanding of practices change over time. Crucially, this participant argues for the need for academics to accept their complicity in the continuation of certain problematic discourses and practices: 'We, in academia, I think have to take also responsibility ... we haven't fought at it, we've allowed that to happen.'

This dialogue also evolves around the complex tension between a conception of teaching excellence that can be measured, and internalized understandings of excellence and integrity. As one participant explains,

> I think it's the difference as well, potentially in my mind, that the excellence, or quality is something that's looked at from outside into you. I think the integrity is an internal thing. We, for example, when you talk about teaching observations, that part becomes from that person's integrity because it's a dialogue about their teaching. Rather than me merely imposing, well I didn't think that was very good, or I thought that was good, it's a dialogue which should start from their integrity. (P4)

For this participant, the concept of excellence as an internal value associated with integrity sits in juxtaposition to something measurable, situated outside the teacher. The relationship between internal values-based approaches to teaching as opposed to externalized conceptions of quality resonates with explorations of teaching excellence in earlier work, for example, Gravett and Kinchin (2020). Here, for this participant, an internal model clearly offers a further means to disrupt dominant discourses that may be imposed upon teachers from the outside, and which potentially pose a threat to individual teacher integrity.

Dialogue Two: Student Engagement

In this discussion, we began by reading the paper written by Ella R. Kahu (2013), 'Framing student engagement in higher education', *Studies in Higher Education*, 38(5): 758–73. Taking Kahu's work as a loose starting point, we then explored the broader narratives surrounding student engagement and its implications for our practice. During the discussion we also draw upon the work of Bruce Macfarlane (2020) as well as the work of Lesley Gourlay and Martin Oliver (2018).

Extracts from the Dialogue

P1 Why does student engagement matter?
P2 To whom?
P3 I think that was a really useful qualification, wasn't it? About to whom. We need to look at where student engagement as a concept sits now. And I think I would argue it's become a really pervasive narrative within HE, upon a par with narratives like student experience, and all those really key discourses that are important in shaping the universities that we work within. And I think as a concept it's almost lost its usefulness. On the surface of it, it seems very positive, something that we all want to do, we all want to engage our students, and ensure that they are learning and enjoying their time at university.

But I think it's been almost hijacked by institutions to mean something slightly dissimilar from what we would perhaps want it to. So, for example, in Gourlay and Oliver, and also Macfarlane's work, they talk about some of the problems with student engagement as a term. And they argue that it's become quite performative. So, how students are engaging in their learning is something that can be monitored, can be observed, it's something that we can analyse and record and there's a negative implication of that, I would argue.

P4 I think the problem is talking about it as a concept. It is not a concept, it is many things that different names. And I think to talk about it as a concept suggests that it is measurable, as this is a level of student engagement someone has because it's multifaceted. I think really it needs to be disentangled a bit more, and I think we need to maybe stop using that term because we're not talking about anything.

P3 Yes, I'd agree. And part of the critique of the way student engagement is discussed and understood at the moment in HE is perhaps the emphasis that has happened about student engagement being something that only the teacher has to do, or has to enable in their students. I think that puts a lot of stress and strain upon the teacher. But also, I think importantly it misses that whole part of learning that is the quiet, introspective, more individual elements of learning that cannot not necessarily be monitored or observed.

P1 I think there's also a risk, when we're talking about levels of engagement, of assumptions we might make about what data the institutions might collect tells us about engagement. So, for example, if you look at common measures of engagement that are used in dashboards, for example, like number of times a student has swiped into the library, or the number of hours they've spent using the VLE (virtual learning environment). They could have swiped into the library and gone and had a sleep, they could have opened up documents on the VLE and done nothing with them, but it looks like they've been on there a long time. Whereas, as Catherine said, you could have a student who doesn't show up as being highly engaged according to those metrics, but is doing quite in-depth study somewhere else. So, we can miss deep engagement because it's not on the radar. But we can also think that something is deep engagement when in fact it's just surface engagement hidden by data.

P2 This relates to Bruce Macfarlane's comment, doesn't it? When he says, he just wants to sit at the back and listen and take notes. He's totally engaged, but he doesn't want to be the person who stands up and shouts and remonstrates with the lecturer because that's not the type of learner he was. But in many ways in which we look at engagement there, he would have been a non-engaging student. He just rocked up and did the exam. But why should we expect any more?

P2 I think part of the problem is putting the word student in front of it. So, if we have got academics who are not engaged, either … Well, they're probably cognitively, but not emotionally, engaged, why would we expect students to be engaged? And if we've got management who are not engaged on the shop floor, how do we expect engagement to percolate through?

P3 Yes, I would definitely agree, and going back to this book (Gourlay and Oliver 2018) they talk about one way forward is to actually go back to looking at the detail of day-to-day practices of how students or academics or anyone engages with learning. So, they use some journaling methods in terms of actually looking at what engagement might mean in practice. And they argue that we can talk about engagement as something that goes beyond the cognitive, as a sociomaterial assemblage. I think this is an interesting idea in terms of thinking about the material things that impact on our learning, in our environment. But also, the spaces and moving beyond it just being an internal, humanist, approach to learning.

P1 Just a little thing, do we even need the word engagement? Never mind student. Why have we got the word engagement? The things we've been talking about, are students learning the material, are they happy, are they interested, are they well? These are not new things, these are not new questions.

P3 I was just going to pick up on Catherine's point about the sociomaterial within student engagement. Because I think there's a lot of criticism in students today in the way in which they learn, the way in which they study. One of the things we see a lot in the media, and even in the research literature, is students' notetaking via laptops. And they're often a quite deficit-orientated view of students, that look out at the lecture theatre and I just see a sea of laptops. And they're all in their laptops, they're not engaging with me, they're engaging with their laptops. And almost an assumption that they're on Facebook or something, rather than doing something meaningful. I can remember a year or so ago, doing an observation in the Vet school, and it's quite useful when you sit behind students because you see what goes on, on their screens. And I was fascinated by this student who had the lecture slides and was doing the most amazing annotation of them as she was going. And she was almost taking what was up there on the screen and transforming it into her own representation of that topic in real time. Which I thought was a brilliant example of some really quite deep learning that was going on there. But if you just assume that because their head was in their laptop she wasn't engaged, then you'd be making quite a dangerous assumption.

P4 What I was going to say is, when I think of student engagement, I think of behavioural engagement. So, I think that those sorts of things are kind of easy shorthands for us all to say, my students aren't engaged because they're not paying attention in the class, or they're not turning up. Which I suppose is another form of behavioural engagement. But I think what Sam said is right, I think the term itself is unhelpful.

P2 We have a tendency to do that, don't we, in the sector. We find easy ways of labelling things and we simplify things for whatever reason. And we lose all the nuance, and we lose all the purpose of being.

P6 And I think what we, and we're all partly guilty of this, but when you … I think what we do is we create sides, and the sides are there's a student side and a teacher side. And I wonder if we reframed it as the fact that we're all learners, we don't need to talk about student engagement and lecturer engagement. We'll create this us and them, therefore we have to measure one side against what the other has done. Rather than seeing it as an encounter where we're all doing this together. I don't know, all the learners in there, I may happen to know different things to some of the other people, but so do all of those. And therefore, if we reframe it as actually, it's an encounter in which we all offer things in our different ways. Because then inevitably what then happens is we set up this us and them, and then somebody says, so we can now measure what you've done for or to them. And that creates this notion, therefore there is a student engagement which is the responsibility solely of the teacher. And I don't think it is, I think it's a responsibility of everybody in the room to enact that, it's a social environment, let's say.

P2 If you say that engagement is an encounter, it's a two-way thing, then as you say student engagement is nonsense as a phrase. But also, if my students are not engaged, then by definition I am not engaged with them. The encounter hasn't worked.

P4 I think that the overall thing we've all got an issue with is the concept, and maybe what we should be looking at is why this term is so prevalent and what maybe is a better way of framing.

P4 I'm just going to say, I mean, I've made the point a few times but when people use it, I think they need to question themselves what they actually mean by that because we all mean different things. So, I think it's just about getting them to unpack it themselves. The term's not going away and it will continue to be used by universities.

Analysis

A number of points are raised in this detailed debate on the topic of student engagement. One key theme that is considered is the responsibility for engagement and for developing 'engaged' learners – does this lie with the student, the teacher, the environment, or are a multiple of elements complicit? Participant 3 comments that these kinds of discourses can often be used as weapons to blame teachers: 'And part of the critique of the way student engagement is discussed and understood at the moment in HE is perhaps the emphasis that has happened about student engagement being something that only the teacher has to do, or has to enable in their students.' Rather, the participants discuss the value of conceptualizing engagement as a shared endeavour needing to 'percolate through' the institution in a more holistic manner.

Another key theme is the notion of the need for a broader understanding of student engagement, moving beyond humanist, behavioural conceptions of the term that may limit and constrain. This resonates with theoretical ideas explored in Chapters 2 and 3, for example, ideas emerging from sociomaterial and posthuman approaches to understanding relationality and pedagogy. It continues the discussions surrounding the need to move beyond overly simplistic conceptions of learner engagement that might centre solely on data derived from learner analytics, or upon teachers' observations of 'active' modes of learning in the classroom. Ultimately, in this discussion, the participants close with an interesting reflection regarding the durability and power of embedded, yet contentious, discourses in higher education: 'So, I think it's just about getting them to unpack it themselves to change the notion. The term's not going away and it will continue to be used by universities' (P4). Arguably, a thoughtful approach to using and engaging with concepts, with reference to the literature and to research, can be helpful in avoiding simplistic interpretations of key aspects of higher education praxis.

Dialogue Three: Resilience

This dialogue draws upon the following paper as a starting point: David R. Webster and Nicola Rivers (2019), 'Resisting resilience: Disrupting discourses of self-efficacy', *Pedagogy, Culture and Society*, 27(4): 523–35.

P1 I'm glad that I read it, so thank you for choosing this one, but I was left a little bit at the end going, okay so you've deconstructed everything and what do you suggest instead?

P2 I thought it was an excellent paper. I have read quite a lot about resilience in the last couple of years and most of it comes from the same stable, if you like. Talking about students can't cope, and we need to do something about it. Which is the discourse that's been picked up by the university I think. Students can't cope, therefore we need to fix them. And it has the focus on the individual which is the various managerial neoliberal type, the individuals can't cope, what do we do. It doesn't focus on the system that they're working in. What seems to be the case is, talking from my own experiences, when you see students who are not coping they go somewhere else and suddenly they cope in a different environment. So, it's not necessarily the weakness of the student, it's the fit of that student in wherever they are. So, it's the system that is problematic rather than the individual being problematic. And that's sort of what Webster and Rivers were saying.

P1 And so, then it occurred to me that maybe it isn't such an issue because the neoliberal agenda is focusing very much on that individualist type of culture. Whereas in a collectivist culture, would there be more support from the people? So, you say that the structures, or university structures or whatever.

P2 Yes, the community.

P1 Yes, exactly, the word community. I was thinking that would have been a really interesting divergence or perhaps part of this paper would be, rather than the individual, looking at how people as collective together can support resilience.

P3 I think there's a really important point about the context that you've both discussed there, which is the idea that if we say we need to develop resilience, you're actually saying the individual is at fault and so there's nothing wrong with the culture and the environment … You think about it in work and how people valorize over working: 'Oh, look at me I've only had an hour off this weekend, how terrible!' But it's actually bragging. And I thought there's a really important point in here about how if you encourage people to say, well you just need to adjust, cope with this. It's suggesting that the conditions are fine, rather than us maybe questioning the kinds of pressures, and the kinds of environment. Resilience is a requirement to take more pressure, such that pressure can be gradually increased.

P2 And I think there's a lot of things that the university does implicitly which adds to the stress. So, for example, having the library open 24/7 to allow students to learn and do whatever they want, whenever they want, sort of implies, why aren't you working at three o'clock in the morning, because you can because we make it possible.

P1 I would actually disagree with that. I think the fact that the university library is open 24/7 acknowledges the fact that students work very differently. I mean, just taking my son, for example, when he was living close to campus he would often study until three, four o'clock in the morning because that's how he likes to study. And had he not been able to do that, I think that would have caused him some stress. But back to the earlier point about it being the conditions, or the institution rather than the individual, just to play devil's advocate a little bit, I do also think the individual has responsibility. I don't think it's entirely the institution. So, little bit of both.

P4 I agree with a lot of the central thesis of this paper in the sense that I like the way it's moving away from the deficit perspective. But I do have similar issues to what Sam raised, which is that I do think that if you are deconstructive of that whole narrative … if you're suggesting that the structures that are in place are causing the issue not the individual, and that any kinds of interventions in that are pointless because then you're putting the emphasis on the individual, then there needs to be some kind of solution that then deconstructs the structure to actually deal with that issue.

P1 Can I just pose a question then, is there a risk in throwing the baby out with the bath water? Is there a useful concept here, and the challenge is one of semantics, is it resilience? Is it bounce-back-ability, academic buoyancy, whatever? Is it useful to have a concept within higher education which represents the capacity to manage and deal with challenge?

P5 I think resilience itself is not necessarily a bad thing. We need to have some kind of resilience about how we deal with situations. But I think it's a separate discourse itself from how the system, the structure is constituted. I think we need to think about it more in an ecological way. Not just what individuals need, but how does everyone react or how do they situate it in this ecology. So, I think if you're working or studying in a bad department with a horrible climate, you either have to change your ecological system, get out of it or figure out how you're going to change part of yourself so you can deal with that sort of ecological system until you have the tools or prospective of leaving it. So, I think there is a need for resilience to figure how do you manage and negotiate these things. But also recognize that you can leave as well.

P2   And I think this idea of the ecological system is absolutely vital because students are part of that system. And I think what the traditional resilience discourse does is see students as something separate. They're not coping, the system's fine and they're coming in. Well, they're part of the system, so the system is failing if the system is failing. So, you can't just say, well what's wrong with the students?

P1   And this idea that students are less resilient than they used to be, there's a real ... They call it student shaming, but there's a real discourse around snowflakes. Students lacking resilience, an anxiety epidemic, all of these kinds of things. So, are students less resilient than they used to be? Or do we need to draw on these issues of ecology and context to understand why?

P1   So, if we see these problems with the term resilience and things like mindfulness and resilience training, what should we be doing to support students? Whether we're thinking about their time at university or what they're going on to do next, what is a useful approach to supporting students to get the most out of their time at university? Whether that's wellbeing, academics, the whole range of things really? If we're not supporting them to develop resilience, what should we be doing?

P1   Something that Martin said earlier, and that is talking to people. You can't undervalue, undermine, whatever, underestimate the power of students knowing that they can go and talk to somebody. Be it about their grades, be it about the assignment they've got to do.

So, yes when you have cohorts of 500 students, that's simply not going to happen. And until that structural element changes I think you can put on as many mindfulness classes as you like, there needs to be that personal interaction. I think that's absolutely key to it.

P5   I think if we reframed the idea of resilience as being able to take back your autonomy, I think that's more important. Because you're saying, I have control of what I can do within this system, and I understand how I work within the system. I think that's more important to a person, because if they realize that they can control to some extent, what they can do. And that includes being able to go talk to people, etc.

P4   But I think the important factor is that while universities across the country continue to pile more and more students and increase the size of programmes, you reduce the chances of that. I think until there's some kind of top down change, I think it becomes really hard.

And I guess, yes these … I don't think, when they put on these sorts of things like having counsellors, mindfulness training, all those sorts of things, I don't think it's necessarily … It is plugging the wound.

P3 A band-aid.

P4 Putting a band-aid over the wound.

But I think ultimately, unless there is some kind of change from the top, some kind of sense that this is the problem and we need to be doing something on a larger scale, I don't see how we can really deal with it. And that's why I think maybe this paper ultimately doesn't come to a firm solution because maybe there isn't one that really works within the way universities are at the moment.

P1 Not answering your question, but just going back to something that I made a note on earlier is, also resilience isn't a state, is it? So, it's presumably fluid. There are days I feel more resilient than other days, and so resilience must also be a kind of task-related activity as well, or a situational dependent feeling or disposition. I don't know, what is resilience?

P5 I'm going to go with disposition.

P1 Yes, so it's fluid as well, so I suppose it's recognizing that. When you name something it becomes a problem, doesn't it? So, before we had resilience, what was it? Was it just, oh students are struggling, or students are having a problem? I just think by naming it we've created a monster in itself to be honest, I'd love to just get rid of the word completely.

P2 Universities love to name things because then you can put it on a shelf somewhere, can't you?

P4 I think it's what I was saying earlier about when they like putting these labels on young people. It's like this group of people are all going to be like this because they're all … I don't know, this is the thing that's in common, when you know very well that's not how it works.

P1 Couldn't it be called having a good day, having a bad day …

P3 So, it comes back to relationships doesn't it?

P2 It comes back to relationships and knowing people.

P1 And having the opportunity to talk.

P1 Interaction. Face to face, not even on the phone, but somebody is available, I can go and talk to them.

P4 So, how do you achieve that with such large student numbers?

P2 Well, that is the problem. And the question is, I guess, why do we have such large student numbers? Why do we have a growth policy? Is that the best thing? Is it money that is driving this institution or is it the good of society? Interest in our disciplines? What is this driving?

Analysis

The debate here surfaces some significant themes and questions pertaining to the contested concept of resilience. Underpinning the discussion is the tension between humanist discourses of the agentic and resilient self, as opposed to ecological discourses which instead critique systemic inequalities and seek a wider view of the institution as a space that supports those who learn and work within it. As Participant 2 comments, traditional resilience discourses 'focus on the individual which is the various managerial neoliberal type, the individuals can't cope, what do we do. It doesn't focus on the system that they're working in'. The participants identify how, as such, resilience discourses represent an insidious requirement to take more pressure. Participant 2 comments further: 'And I think this idea of the ecological system is absolutely vital because students are part of that system. And I think what the traditional resilience discourse does is see students as something separate.' These tensions and their impacts are explored further in Chapter 4 of this volume. Crucially, in this debate the participants discuss the need to move beyond critique. One participant memorably states that 'universities love to name things because then you can put it on a shelf somewhere, can't you?' (P2). While, notably, another comments, 'I was left a little bit at the end going, okay so you've deconstructed everything and what do you suggest instead? So, while I enjoy reading critiques, I do feel that there's some sort of obligation to provide a way forward at the very least' (P1).

Conclusion

This series of debates proved interesting and useful as a means to surface ideas and to explore some of the dominant discourses occurring within contemporary higher education. Through the discussion of different perspectives upon the contested concepts, and reflections upon our own practice, we were able to explore the issues in a generative way. Ultimately, the participants reflect that there is a need for teachers to pause our practice and to take time to question normative narratives. They suggest that we can use the research and theoretical literature to do this, as a means of interpreting key concepts anew and applying them to our own praxis. They also suggest that there is a need to provide a way forward from critique, a belief which resonates with the goals that underpin this book. Through this scholarly reflection, we aim to adopt a thoughtful, situated approach that emerges from our own integrity and values as teachers.

8

Concept Mapping

Introduction

The idea of mapping is one that appears in various guises within this book in the form of explicit visual representations and also as more implicit ideas embedded within concepts – such as social cartographies. Mapping implies some degree of exploration, coupled with the suggestion that links or directions are needed to navigate between different points. Massey (2005: 109) has pointed out that maps can be used to 'tame confusion and complexity' and so provide a tracing (*sensu* Deleuze and Guattari 1987) that serves as a static representation. However, Massey goes on to explain how maps can also be disruptive and used to provoke a novel view from an unaccustomed angle. This latter perspective fits with a more active view of mapping (*sensu* Deleuze and Guattari 1987) and with our purpose here to exploit mapping as a tool to support the process of becoming and to move away from the reductionist tendency of measuring. Capra and Luisi (2014) see mapping as an element of systemic thinking to focus on relationships rather than on isolated objects. As such, mapping is an essential element of the ecological university that is needed to visualize theory and explore complexity, rather than gloss over it.

Mapping, Tracing and Becoming

Novakian concept maps (Novak and Cañas 2006; 2007) have been seen as a powerful tool in the armoury of the university teacher (Kinchin 2014; Machado and Carvalho 2020). Although concept maps are sometimes confused with other graphic organizers (such as mind maps), they are very different in their function (Eppler 2006). Whereas mind maps are often constructed as a quick way of collating related ideas, concept maps need to be constructed more slowly, often requiring interrogation by a third party to encourage revision and refinement to explain the complex connections between ideas. Concept maps are two-dimensional, hierarchically arranged graphical representations of relationships between concepts. The concepts are typically presented within boxes. Labelled arrows drawn between the boxes represent cause and effect relations in the form of propositional phrases allowing the map to be read from concept to concept. The important feature of concept maps to enable them to support reflection and meaningful learning is the quality of the links between the concept nodes. The arrow signifies the existence of a relationship, but the verb included in the linking phrase provides the explanatory power by revealing the nature of the link. The example of a concept map in Figure 8.1 shows the typical arrangement of concept nodes and linking phrases on arrows between the nodes.

Concept maps have been key to the development of a structuralist view of learning (Kinchin, 2016). One of the key revelations of this line of research is to expose the various forces that act upon university teachers to force the trend towards linearity (Kinchin, Lygo-Baker and Hay 2008) and placing constraints on creativity. The dominant view of concept mapping within the research literature has been of a tool to assess prior learning, that is, to provide a visual summary of what has already been learned. While this may represent a valuable approach to assessment, it fails to look ahead at a student's potential learning trajectory or to support a philosophy of becoming. The concept mapping literature has been described as being caught in a linear (arborescent) developmental pathway that is a product of its origins in educational psychology and science education (Kinchin 2020). We have chosen to consider concept mapping within the context of this book to demonstrate how a change in perspective (from *being* to *becoming*) can change the ways in which we might use tools like concept mapping. Rather than fixing what has been learned, concept maps can be used as an indicator of pathways for future learning.

The constrained arborescence of the field is exemplified by the methodological conservatism observed in review articles that routinely adopt *systematic review* protocols with strict exclusion criteria. This appears to be a default methodology, without offering any consideration of the other types of review that could be conducted or the difference in perspective they may bring (Grant and Booth 2009). As an example, the exclusive focus by Yue et al. (2017) on papers that published quantitative data from randomized control trials (RCTs) resulted in analysis of only 22 of the 180 possible papers in their sample. This is despite criticism of RCTs as having 'zero practical application to the field of human affairs' (Scriven 2008: 12), and that such methods have been seen to reflect the reporting needs of the researcher rather than the needs of students or practitioners (Clegg

Concept Mapping 117

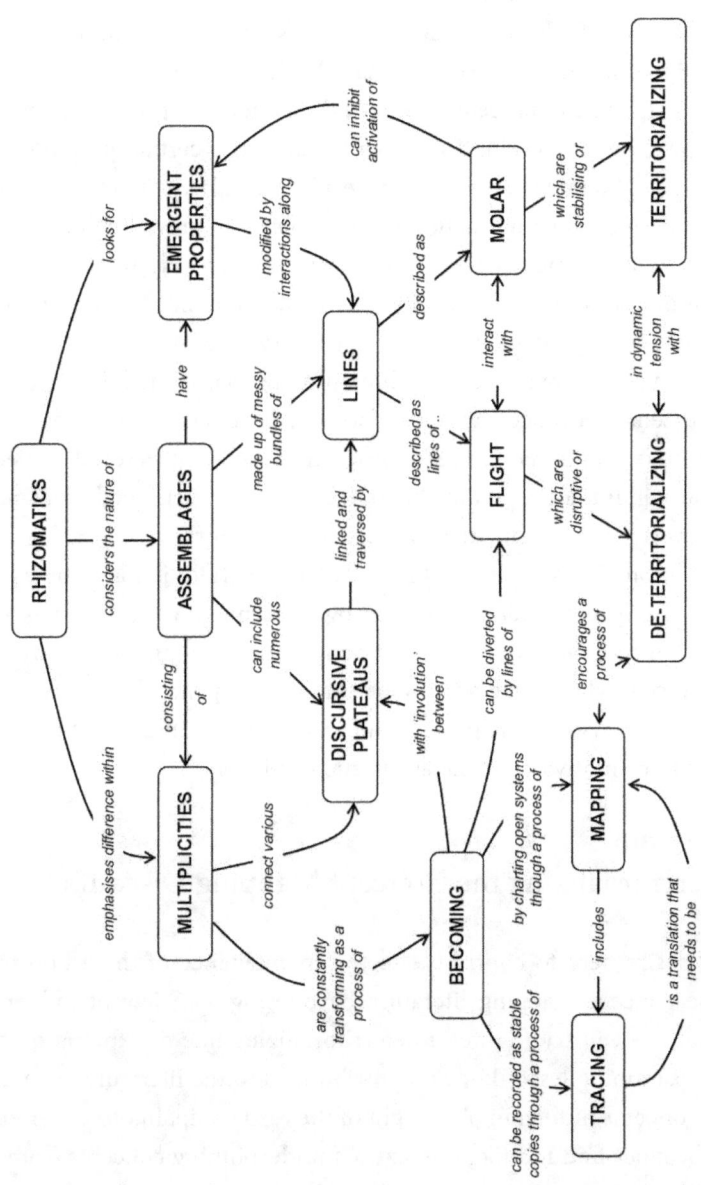

Figure 8.1 The language of rhizomatics presented using the grammar of the concept map.
Source: Modified from Kinchin and Gravett (2020).

2005; Hanley et al. 2016). This methodological conservatism ensures the linear maintenance of a particular view of research and effectively excludes studies that might be seen as outliers and which may present the research community with unexpected challenges. The rigorous provenance of concept mapping, growing from its roots in STEM education, has been an asset in the development of the tool (Schwendimann 2019). However, it has also limited the scope of concept mapping research and the range of theoretical positions that have contributed to its evolution (Kinchin 2020). This has perpetuated a certain gaze on what concept mapping should be able to achieve in an ideal world. However, this ambition is often at odds with practice, for example, with prevailing assessment regimes that can encourage strategic, rote learning resulting in a downward misalignment of assessment (as described by Leber et al. 2018) that can block the meaningful learning intended by mapping interventions.

There is also a section of the research literature that has treated the classroom as a standardized, controlled laboratory in which concept mapping can be viewed as an intervention that can be 'done to' students as if it were a therapeutic treatment that will initiate a predictable outcome (e.g. as critiqued by Mintzes et al. 2011), or even as a vaccine that can produce a uniform change among the student population (Nicoara et al. 2020). This unhelpfully ignores the active, personalized role of the students in their own learning. We think it is self-evident that a concept map without student engagement (as an inert entity) can no more enhance learning than a textbook that is not opened, or a lecture that is not attended. The map simply provides an arena for potential activity, and the student needs to be motivated to engage in such activity.

Deterritorializing the Concept Mapping Discourse

We have no desire here to contribute to the maintenance of the arborescent nature of the concept mapping literature by offering a review of influential papers. Rather, we will try to offer a deterritorializing line of exploration that is offered by examining lesser-known contributions to the literature, where we can find key concepts hidden in plain sight of the readership. In our experience, academic colleagues find it difficult to extract underpinning concepts from the context in which those studies are carried out. For example, colleagues working in engineering look for concept mapping studies of engineering content and focus on how the content is displayed, rather than concentrating on any principles of teaching that might be applied to their experience. To illustrate the value of the 'outlier literature', we explore two papers that offer helpful insights to the mapping process and to student learning that need to be excised from the contextual frames in which they are presented. Neither of these papers – set in mathematics education (Jin and Wong 2010) and nursing education (Drach-Zahavy et al. 2017) – are included in recent reviews of the literature (Machado and Carvalho 2020), and are published in specialist disciplinary journals that are unlikely to attract a generalist readership or have an impact on the wider concept mapping research community.

The first paper, by Jin and Wong (2010), is published in a mathematics education journal and has a title that suggests that it would only be of interest to teachers of geometry. However, the authors explore the contentious issue of training research participants to use concept mapping. It has been stated by numerous authors that students can learn how to produce concept maps with a few minutes of training. While this is true, the first maps that students produce are unlikely to be conceptually rich or to offer valuable research insights. The quality of maps improves with practice and with feedback from knowledgeable peers. This is explored in detail by Jin and Wong who note that brief training is not enough to prepare students with sufficient mapping skills to produce data to inform research projects on the structure of knowledge. They also note that different students will acquire mapping skills at different rates, so that research protocols in papers that offer a standardized training session of a given length to their participants will not be preparing participants in an equitable manner. Jin and Wong break down the training of their students into stages that involve 'statement transformation' (converting ideas into diagrammatic propositions), 'free-association' (linking and arranging concepts on the page), and 'discussion' (to enable the interrogation of maps and enhancing their explanatory power). This provides the basis of a protocol to ensure that students know what is expected of them when they start to produce concept maps. In addition, the purpose of the map, to support rather than assess learning, changes the focus of this training from producing a response that approaches the 'correct' response to exploring a tool that is personally valuable by becoming part of the learning process.

The second paper, by Drach-Zahavy et al. (2017), is published in a nursing education journal and has a title that emphasizes a key component of nursing practice (shift handovers) that masks the wider implications of the authors' findings. The communication that occurs between nurses at shift handovers could be viewed as a particular teaching moment, where critical information is passed between professionals about the patients and their treatment regimes. In such instances, the accuracy of information is seen as paramount to avoid any mistakes in patient care. The authors describe how the outgoing information (analogous to that being presented by a teacher) contains errors when summarized as concept maps. These errors ranged from missing information to redundant or even contradictory information. When the incoming information (analogous to that being received by a student) was then mapped, it was evident that there was an information gap. The knowledge received was transformed by the personal motivations of the recipient and then re-coded so that a concept label might include several different concepts, processes and associations. It was clear that in the minds of the nurses involved, the 'information received' did not have to be scientifically accurate but did have to be functional in meeting the demands of daily practice. To be practical, the received information that was mapped was a simplification, and data might be missed (or dismissed) in order to get tasks completed. From this, we can see that the information passed in a concept map cannot always be taken at face value. Other sources of information are required to test the understanding embedded within a map. The paper addresses the key issue of information transfer and the way it is shared within a community of practice. This is something that needs to be considered in other contexts when considering the information that research participants or students include (or omit) from a concept map.

The issues raised by these two papers are important and challenge the tacit assumption that there is a direct correlation between the mental models held in the minds of students and the concept maps they may construct during their learning. While it is seductive to imagine concept maps as offering a window into the minds of our students (Shavelson et al. 2005), this is probably oversimplistic with the representations produced by students being moderated by numerous environmental factors that vary with time and context. In addition, many concept mapping studies take the map as a product to be evaluated, indicative of a state of *being* rather than mapping as a process of *becoming*. When the mapping process is recognized as the more significant element (over the product), then other factors, such as the talk generated during the mapping activity, also take on added significance (Heron et al. 2018), and might help to fill in some of the information gap identified by Drach-Zahavy et al. (2017).

In recent years the focus of concept mapping studies has started to shift away from simplistic organization of agreed curriculum content towards the exploration of the more contested theories and values that underpin academic practice (Lygo-Baker, Kingston and Hay 2008; McNaughton et al. 2016; van den Bogaart et al. 2017; Reimann and Sadler 2017; Gravett et al. 2020).

In consequence, the nature of the knowledge being mapped has changed, particularly regarding the certainty of the knowledge being mapped (known → yet-to-be-known), with the gaze shifting from the content being mapped towards the changes in those creating the maps (Kinchin and Winstone 2018). Such maps might be considered as precursors of the learning-yet-to-happen among 'people-yet-to-come' (Hroch 2014). For Hroch, thinking about students in this way means, 'valuing learning as a process of transformation, the process of students' coming to think differently, thereby becoming other in the process, and supporting thinking differently from the norm' (57). Of course, if teachers prefer not to complicate their lives by initiating the promotion of difference, they can take action to restrict their students' learning to the acquisition of inert chains of information. This has been observed to be the case when universities act as centres of non-learning (Kinchin, Lygo-Baker and Hay 2008). This happens when teachers focus only on dispensing information to satisfy the curriculum documentation by disclosing unanchored fragments of their discipline (as chains of knowledge) without helping students to make connections to the underpinning understanding that is required to construct powerful knowledge (Wheelahan 2007) or expert knowledge (Kinchin and Cabot 2010). This, along with other contextual factors that can put pressure on staff to be complicit in cycles of non-learning that involve the transaction of chains of information, acting as a selection pressure to maintain linearity – in presentation of content, in teaching approaches and in assessment. (see Figure 8.2)

Mapping and Rhizomatics

Rhizomatics (see Figure 8.1) is a philosophical position created around the non-linear figuration of the rhizome by Deleuze and Guattari (1987). This has been developed as a reaction against predominantly linear thought processes, described as 'tree thinking' or 'arborescent thinking' that has driven higher education along a detrimental, neoliberal route. This trajectory has been observed to be 'detracting from the knowledge project that was once the central function of universities' (Charteris et al. 2016: 32), by providing simplistic 'causal relations that policymakers and others have assumed exist between students and test, teaching and learning' (Strom and Martin 2017a: 5). The rhizomatic exploration of the assets for learning in the salutogenic university (Kinchin 2019a) seeks to cultivate 'brave spaces' to engage in challenging dialogues (*sensu* Arao and Clemens 2013) and to face up to the dominant culture in higher education:

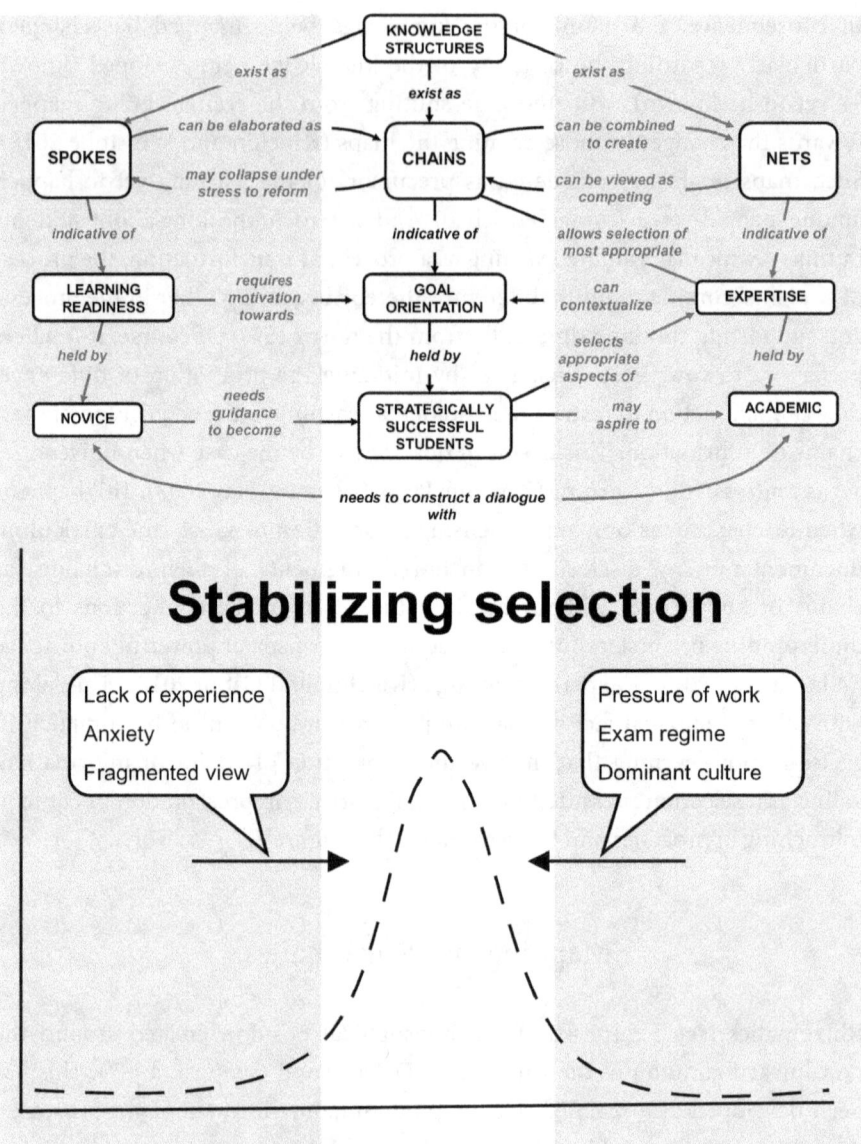

Figure 8.2 The stabilizing selection pressures that contribute to the maintenance of linearity within the university as exemplified by chains of understanding. *Source*: After Kinchin, Lygo-Baker and Hay (2008).

> Resisting the flows of neoliberalism is different from past struggles. For now it also encompasses resisting our own practices, it is about confronting oneself at the centre of our discomforts. (Ball and Olmedo 2013: 93)

Whereas linearity maintains the status quo, the rhizome encourages the destabilizing examination of difference. The image of the rhizome has not yet led to extensive cartographic analysis of knowledge despite what appears to us as obvious overlaps as described by Ruitenberg (2007: 17–18):

> Because of their multiple connections, rhizomatic knowledge structures are difficult to represent in traditional, more linear text. Cartographically, however these multiple connections can both be represented and questioned. When one attempts to map rhizomatic processes or texts, one may discover other nodes and connections not previously realized.

Therefore, we anticipate that an exploration of this overlap will widen, deterritorialize and develop the (currently) separate discourses of concept mapping and rhizomatics. Initial reading of Deleuze and Guattari's work exploring the rhizome immediately suggests overlaps between rhizomatic thinking and concept mapping. For example, the versatility and malleability of concept maps resonate with Deleuze and Guattari's description of the rhizome:

> The map is open and connectable in all of its dimensions: it is detachable, reversible, susceptible to constant modification. It can be reworked by an individual, group or social formation. (1987: 12)

A number of observers have critiqued the validity of the rhizome analogy and the ways it addresses the needs of the twenty-first-century learning community that is so heavily influenced by the unstructured nature of the internet. For example, Knysh and Kochubey (2017) suggest that the analogy of the fungal hypha might be a more appropriate metaphor to consider the nonlinearity, inter-connectedness and complexity of networks. However, as the literature that exploits the figuration of the rhizome is now well established, it might be unhelpful to introduce a division in the use of terminology here. We have to acknowledge the holes in any analogy, and discussion of these issues maintains a healthy level of critical scrutiny. Therefore, we have used 'rhizome' throughout this book, even where others might prefer 'hypha'.

When referring to the artefacts of learning, Novakian maps can be understood as Deleuzian tracings. Whereas within the process of learning, Deleuzian mapping and Ausubelian meaningful learning are synonymous activities of active exploration and discovery. By adopting a Deleuzo-Guattarian lens, it is not our intention here to develop a line of thought that might actually exclude anyone from applying concept mapping in any way they want to. We are not attempting to develop a perspective to constrict or inhibit thinking – such an exclusionary mechanism would itself be anti-Deleuzian by preserving high theory for the use of a select few (Strom 2018). However, from a rhizomatic perspective, a concept map is always 'provisional' and open to a multiplicity of interpretations. This has not always been made explicit in the concept mapping literature, especially when the application of scoring protocols reinforces the idea of the map representing a fixed reality. Rather, we adopt the view, as described by Wilson, Mandich and Magalhães (2016: 1154):

> Concept mapping is a medium through which people come to understand more about an event and about themselves. This change of self, re-shapes the meaning of the phenomenon that is being studied, and offers the participants an opportunity to 're-see' the significance the experience and the mapping process offers them. Through this process of 're-seeing', participants develop an artistic expression of self-discovery (the concept map).

As a concept map of the 'yet-to-be-known' is a moving construction of converging and diverging lines and their connected practices, we need to acknowledge that a Deleuzo-Guattarian inspired cartographic exercise is not about representing a final structure, but rather it is about constructing a map as a field of play to experiment on (Lenz Taguchi 2016). That is, the process of mapping is more important for learning than production of the artefact – the tracing. However, when maps address the yet-to-be-known (including tacit knowledge), they 'render visible forces that are themselves invisible; to cause those who might categorize for the sake of social conventions *to look* and then *look again*' (Clarke/Keefe 2014: 112; emphases in original). The value of concept mapping will, therefore, vary with context and purpose. There seems to be agreement that for most purposes, the most detailed image is not necessarily the best. Zdebik (2019: 41) states that from a Deleuzian perspective, 'the tracing does not reproduce, repeat, or copy a map; instead, it selects, isolates, restricts part of the map'. A parallel view is expressed by Hine (2013: 1162) that 'representations in science are inherently selective, showing particular aspects of the phenomenon being studied, for specific purposes', with 'distracting noise' deliberately excluded from the final drawing. The concept mapping literature has been slow to adopt this idea of focus, and the notion that 'bigger is better' is tacitly supported by the continued adoption of additive scoring protocols that rate larger maps more highly than smaller maps, irrespective of the sophistication of the ideas presented.

It is clear that we could be setting up a potential tension by aligning the poststructuralist notion of the rhizome with the concept mapping tool that has been explicitly linked to the tree-like structural representation of knowledge (Kinchin 2016). This would be the case if we suggested that there was a mapping/tracing duality, with one superior to the other. However, Deleuze and Guattari do not adopt such binary conceptualizations and neither do we. Rather, we are interested in the generative possibilities of a blurring of the boundaries between these two seemingly opposed perspectives. In his analysis of Deleuzian theory, Harris (2016: 230) highlights a way in which we can produce concrete visualizations of assemblages, and considers the use of concept maps, noting that:

> The intriguing possibility arises that those concept maps can themselves be seen as figures cut from or sliced through a more complex rhizomatic multiplicity as a cross section.

By analogy, the concept map may, therefore, be considered as a view of a section of the rhizome at a 'vascular level' (Bell 1980). While a concept map might be seen as an artefact, fixed in time, such a static representation of understanding is of value to the observer trying to ascertain the active links developing in the conceptual rhizome – offering an imperfect window into its workings.

Concepts to Be Mapped

We must be clear that concepts are often complex, and that any graphical depiction will almost inevitably offer a simplification. Paradoxically, this simplification is a helpful way to start to access and appreciate the underlying complexity. Deleuze and Guattari (1994: 15) write:

> There are no simple concepts. Every concept has components and is defined by them. It therefore has a combination. It is multiplicity, although not every multiplicity is conceptual. There is no concept with only one component. Even the first concept, the one with which a philosopher 'begins', has several components, because it is not obvious that philosophy must have a beginning, and if it does determine one, it must combine it with a point of view or a ground ... Every concept is at least double or triple, etc. Neither is there a concept possessing every component, since this would be chaos pure and simple.

For Deleuze and Guattari (1994: 18), every concept has a history, but at the same time it also has a becoming 'that involves its relationships with concepts situated on the same plane'. They see a concept existing in relation to the problem it addresses: 'A concept requires not only a problem through which it recasts or replaces earlier concepts but a junction of problems where it combines with other coexisting concepts.' It is the relational nature of concepts that offers a trajectory for future learning:

> There are different conceptual 'bits', each initially introduced in relation to a particular problem, then reintroduced into new contexts, seen from new perspectives. The coherence among the various bits shifts from one work to the next as new concepts are added, fresh problems addressed; it is not given by 'logical consistency' among propositions, but rather by the 'series' or 'plateaus' into which the conceptual pieces enter or settle along the web of their interrelations. (Rajchman 2001: 21)

An ecological perspective (Chapter 5) may provide a helpful point of overlap between structuralist and poststructuralist literatures, as we can discern similarities in understanding of the connectedness of concepts. However, different academic tribes often employ different languages and may also have different assumptions when referring to 'representations' about the existence (or not) of any pre-existing reality. For example, within the science education literature Pines (1985: 109) has stated that 'one might describe a specific concept as the hypothetical meeting place of all propositional relations in which that concept participates. There are an infinite number of such relations and a concept is a summary of all those relationships'. Hodson (1998: 52) has asserted that, 'concepts cannot be "evaluated" separately from their relationships with other concepts and the roles they play within conceptual structures'. When we compare these comments with the discussion of 'what is a concept?' by Deleuze and Guattari (1994: 15–34), we can see the overlap. They settle on three key points in their description of the nature of concepts:

- Every concept relates back to other concepts, not only in its history but in its becoming or its present connections.
- What is distinctive about the concept is that it renders components inseparable within itself.
- Each concept will therefore be considered as the point of coincidence, condensation, or accumulation of its own components.

Deleuze and Guattari (1994: 21) conclude:

> The concept is therefore both absolute and relative: it is relative to its own components, to other concepts, to the plane on which it is defined, and to the problem it is supposed to resolve; but it is absolute through the condensation it carries out, the site it occupies on the plane, and the conditions it assigns to the problem.

Echoing the view of Deleuze and Guattari, Bal (2006: 17) has considered the intersubjectivity of concepts to represent their value as a learning tool, stating that we gain insight into what concepts can do by 'groping to define what a particular concept may mean'. This groping is seen by Bal to be a collective endeavour and that the value of concepts is 'not because they mean the same thing for everyone, but because they do not'.

Mapping the Teaching Ecosystem

In Chapter 5, we argued that consideration of key ecological concepts such as resilience need to be contextualized so that they are developed by encouraging links with attendant concepts – such as vulnerability, adaptive capacity and transformability (Walker et al. 2004). The map in Figure 8.3 was constructed as part of a conversation with a group of academics to explore how they might link these concepts. Figure 8.3 is offered here, not as an answer, but as a cartographic visualization to open up a dialogue to explore the links as they appear within a particular context and to encourage discussion of the constraints and enablers that are created by the wider university environment. We are working under the assumption here that the act of tracing and articulating this cartography represents a starting point for professional development through promoting enhanced agency. As stated by Charteris et al. (2016: 24):

> The cartographies of academic spaces are tense and precarious, dependent upon hierarchies of power and voice. Yet, recognising and unthreading the perturbations and impasses that we face in the present makes re-threading alternative conditions possible.

The links given in Figure 8.3 are a starting point, gained from an initial discussion with a group of academics. Although this is given in the context of 'university academics', there is no reason why this could not be adapted and to

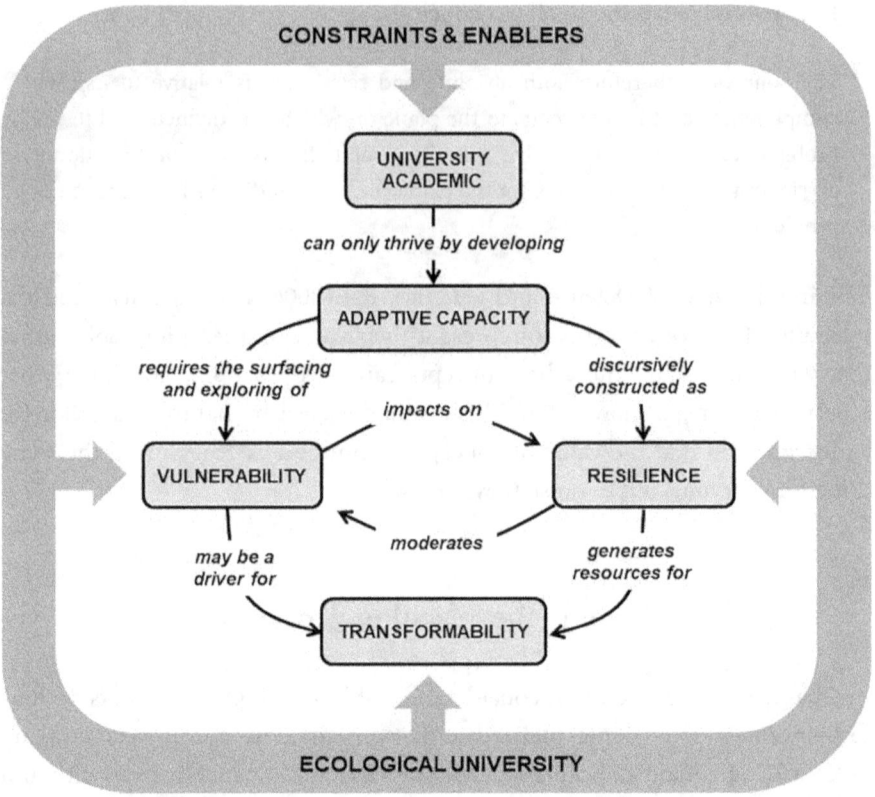

Figure 8.3 Developing links between the key concepts of adaptive capacity, vulnerability, resilience and transformability within the constraints and enablers of the ecological university as a stimulus for further learning.
Source: Author's original.

insert 'student' to replace academics in this figure. A personal reflection on the map was offered to us by one academic:

> First of all, I wondered why adaptive capacity does not also refer to the capacity to influence vulnerability? Vulnerability can be a positive thing too, and so we might want to influence this. Resilience – do we always need to maintain the same identity? Especially with what is going on at the moment and all the changes in education, maybe we need to be flexible and able to change our identity. Changing structures may necessitate a changing identity, and I don't think that changing identity is a bad thing. I find the word 'system' or 'the university' quite scary and intimidating, as I don't think I can change the system or the university in any way at all. I think we can make small steps, change one person in a system, but I would not like responsibility for changing

a whole system. We can influence parts of a system, and sometimes small ripples become bigger waves. So, in the diagram, transformability is about changing a system, and resilience is about changing an identity, but are they so easy to distinguish?

This conceptually rich reflection presents numerous questions inviting more discussion and exploration. It raises questions about academic identity and responsibility for change. In addition, the nature of the links with the wider university needs to be explored to see how they may constrain or enable development, and to consider whether 'resilience' in Figure 8.3 is agreed to represent ecological resilience or engineering resilience (see Chapter 5) and whether the exhibition of a degree of vulnerability is a requirement for such resilience (Mangione and Norton 2020; Wise 2020).

Mapping and Pedagogic Health

Exploration of the teaching ecosystem has resulted in the consideration of pedagogic health as a constellation of related concepts that combine to create a coherent (if unstable) whole – an assemblage. The concept maps that were created to represent teachers' becoming in studies of pedagogic frailty (Kinchin and Winstone 2018), were never intended to 'fix thought' or 'arrest becoming' (*sensu* Mazzei 2017: 676). While historically some maps may have been made with the intention to tame confusion and complexity, the 'situationist cartographies' of pedagogic frailty are intended 'to provoke a view from an unaccustomed angle' and 'expose incoherences and fragmentations' (*sensu* Massey 2005: 109), and to emphasize 'that there are always connections yet to be made' (107). The maps are intended to 'open up' learning and not to 'close it down' (*sensu* Wexler 2001), and acknowledge that such personal narrations are never complete – being part of an ongoing process of reconstruction (Sermijn et al. 2008). Exploratory mapping activities may, therefore, help to deterritorialize dominant narratives, to challenge 'what we all know', and 'what goes without saying'; to destabilize and explore contradictions in dominant plot patterns that organize arguments and saturate scholarly stories (Tomlinson 2013; Ilmonen 2020); and to unsettle what has become sedimented (Murphy 2015). Kinchin and Winstone (2018) used concept maps to help academics identify what was important to them and to start to see how these issues were linked as a precursor to further professional development.

As a starting point, it is important to appreciate the way in which academics perceive the uniqueness of the cultural landscape of their discipline as teaching is never context-free. For example, Behnejad (2018) is keen to offer a distinction between science and engineering by quoting Godfrey and Parker (2010: 9):

> The biggest single thing about engineering is that we are interested in things that work. So in science, you can be interested in science for the theoretical basis of it and whether it works is largely irrelevant, but as far as engineering is concerned, if it doesn't work, if it has no function, has no utility then it is of but academic interest and engineers aren't interested in things for only academic interest.

The engineers' emphasis on 'does it work?' resonates with Deleuze and Guattari's focus on what a concept does (Deleuze and Guattari 1994), and also colours many academics' views on educational research, where intellectual interest is insufficient to encourage many teachers to engage with teaching scholarship unless there is a practical pay-back – that is, 'what does it do for me?' The idea of a broader picture into which learning has to slot is taken up by Ogden (2018: 57), whose teaching approach 'is one where lectures provides students not with detailed content, but with broader conceptual "maps" such that students see the bigger picture related to what they might be learning'. This resonates with views of Winch (2013) that teachers need to be working with a clear conceptual map related to appropriate ways of learning the relevant subject matter. Not only that, but teachers need to provide their students with access to this map.

Conclusion

While concept mapping studies that employ scoring protocols are popular when it comes to conducting systematic reviews, Novak and Gowin (1984: 97) were not convinced of the value of scoring concept maps stating that 'scoring was in many respects irrelevant, for we were looking for qualitative changes in the structure of children's concept maps'. Stuart (1985: 80) commented that 'to rely on numerical scores is to risk missing diagnostic data used to help the pupil', while White and Gunstone (1992: 38) not only doubt the value of such scores but also caution against the damaging effects of scoring, stating, 'Giving any form of grade to a map can alter students' attitudes to them and so threaten their potential to promote learning.' The generation of a final score also reveals little about the nature of the differences between individual maps, reflecting the comment by Caine and Caine

(1994: 166) that 'it is impossible to communicate the scope and depth of a student's abilities by means of a letter or numerical grade'. A focus on a score also increases the focus on the map as a product rather than on mapping as a process – 'being' rather than 'becoming'. It also encourages the construction of larger maps rather than better maps. However, there continues to be a section of the literature that concentrates on the scoring of maps, particularly where maps are being applied to STEM disciplines that traditionally tend to favour quantitative research methods (Watson et al. 2016; Won et al. 2017). This emphasis on scores creates a distraction from Novak's view of the main purpose of concept mapping – supporting the quality of learning and the student's process of becoming.

However, the great potential of concept mapping lies in its versatility and its potential to combine with (and illustrate) a variety of other educational theories. For example, concept mapping can reveal the punctuated nature of learning (Kinchin 2016). Serial mapping of students' learning shows that there may be extended periods of time when students do not learn. By this we mean that the students are unable to elaborate or refine their concept maps. Then there are brief moments of rapid change where ideas seem to fall into place. And yet, the documentation that typically outlines a curriculum is routinely designed with the tacit assumption that knowledge is acquired gradually and evenly over the academic year. While there is an extensive literature that documents the brief moments of change, there is little in the literature to explain what is going on during the longer periods of stasis, or whether these periods are shared across the student population, or if they are wholly personal.

This punctuated pattern of learning has significant implications for teaching and for assessment. Mintzes and Quinn (2007: 303) have speculated on the appearance of an education system that embraced punctuated learning and how it would differ from the traditional institution. They conclude that 'it would be founded on the principle that significant strides in learning are highly individualistic, idiosyncratic and only loosely tied to standard measures of ability. Further, it would acknowledge significant differences among students and in the structure of their prior knowledge'. Importantly, they also suggest that it would not include 'evaluation of students' performance at pre-determined times for the purposes of accountability'. That is, it would reject the neoliberal imperative for testing for the convenience of administration. It would recognize students as fully formed people rather than future workers. The punctuated entanglements between student and learning alluded to by Mintzes and Quinn have been summarized neatly by Charney (2017: 12), which can help to explain how the rhizomatic curriculum may be seen as an active entity rather than an inert track to follow:

> A person enters into the rhizome from a distinct point. It is not possible to re-enter from the same position, or for different people to approach the rhizome from the same position. Each person enters situations and creative processes bringing to bear their own, unique experiences and point of view. Each situation is different, so even a person's point of view changes each situation based on others' contributing perspectives and experiences. Each interaction can change some or all of the other interactions; the sum of the interactions is viewed as a map of the rhizomatic system; therefore every new interaction changes the system's cartography.

Although such a personalized perspective on engagement with the curriculum may be seen by the management as an unfeasible utopia, there are aspects of this perspective that can be adopted, even in a heavily structured, traditional curriculum track. Paradoxically, this is particularly true when we have a clear picture of the structure of knowledge and the ways in which it can be manipulated to support learning (Kinchin 2016), and where knowledge is structured to maximize the recipience of future learning (Kinchin, Winstone and Medland 2020). Therefore, one can benefit from the adoption of multiple perspectives on the challenge of teaching, where traditional, evidence-based approaches can be augmented by less traditional person-centred approaches. As claimed by Hoffman (1980: 418), 'both poetry and science can be means of validating what we apprehend'. Concept mapping (of being and becoming) may help in developing bridges between different conceptions of knowing so that we may put concepts to work, as suggested by Deleuze and Guattari, in ways that may enhance the development of teaching and encourage the becoming teacher.

9

After Method

Introduction

In this book we have experimented with new methods for thinking and researching about higher education including concept mapping and dialogic approaches. However, we have also become increasingly interested in thinking about irruptions within the boundaries of qualitative research itself. This is largely due to the theoretical underpinnings of the book. As Eliabeth Adams St. Pierre explains in an interview with Guttorm, Hohti and Paakkari (2015: 15): 'One of the things that happens when you begin to read poststructural theories and especially when you begin to study ontology ... is that the old words don't work anymore.' We have certainly found this to be true. As our changing thinking fosters a dissatisfaction with normative practices and ways of describing the world, we have found that wider perspectives impact upon the way we think more broadly about research and about methodology itself. The old words no longer work in the same way. However, we have also come to see the dominant view of current scholarship 'which assumes that knowledge can, and indeed should, be presented efficiently: in concise, simplified, methodized forms' (Doll 2006: 86) as a way of excluding revolutionary thoughts that might take teaching in new directions.

Challenges to accepted methodological practices have been posed by authors for some time (Feyerabend 2010). Schulte (2018: 195) goes even further in his critique of our established 'habits' of research methodologies that offer a sense of security and a form of approval that allow us to 'abdicate our ethical and intellectual responsibilities to thinking and doing those aspects of enquiry that are unfamiliar'. Likewise, this critique has been described by Rorty (1999) as 'methodolotry'. Doll (2006) calls for educators to be inventive and creative when considering methods: 'Goals, purposes, and values are neither pre-set nor universal, but actually emerge from the interactional practices in situ; and in this emergence lies the fermentation of creativity' (88). The reductionist outcome of many methodological protocols produces an inappropriate attempt to impose simplicity. This has been explored by

Law (2004: 2) who has argued that when social science attempts to describe things that are complex, diffuse and messy, it makes a mess of it because clear descriptions do not work when what we are describing is itself not very coherent: 'The very attempt to be clear simply increases the mess.' For Law (2004: 2), 'one thing is sure: if we want to think about the messes of reality at all when we're going to have to teach ourselves to think, to practise, to relate, and to know in new ways.'

Similarly, in her innovative book *Reconceptualising Qualitative Research: Methodologies without Methodology*, Koro-Ljungberg (2015) explores the possibilities that methodologies without strict boundaries or normative structures might create, encouraging us to question rigid methodological traditions and neopositivist tenets in qualitative research practice. For Koro-Ljungberg, even traditional labels such as data, qualitative, subjectivity and data analysis warrant problematization (2015: 2). The 'old words' no longer work. Likewise, whether or not a research approach can be understood as 'scientific' (and indeed if and why that matters), has been explored by postqualitative scholars including St. Pierre (2019: 9) who argues for an 'unambiguous incitement' to escape from the dogma of prescribed method. St. Pierre explains that such dogmatic approaches are typical of the natural sciences that aim to validate and territorialize the assemblage. Instead, St. Pierre advocates moving towards research that is at the cutting edge of deterritorialization:

> Social science researchers don't study onto-epistemology (philosophy) because methodology (science) has been foregrounded to try to make the social scientific. But this is an example of social science's logical positivism/logical empiricism at work, which tries to mimic the exact sciences and claims to produce objective, scientific knowledge that is theory-free and value-free.

For scholars like St. Pierre, the ontological focus that problematizes representation, objectivity, binary conceptions and notions of voice mean that the research process and its underpinning certainties must be radically rethought. Claims that social science researchers are able to produce objective, scientific knowledge that is theory-free and value-free are no longer appropriate.

A Dialogue

In exploring the potential for postqualitative enquiry, in the next section, we offer a dialogic exploration of some of the ideas offered by Elizabeth Adams St. Pierre in a recent article (2021). In doing so, we seek to surface some of the key openings for educators offered by a more messy, qualitative research process as well as to share our own challenges with regards to moving beyond qualitative research practices, beliefs, narratives and methodological frameworks. In the following section, extracts from St. Pierre's (2021) article are included and followed by intersections of our own dialogue, responding to the provocations offered within Elizabeth Adams St. Pierre's (ESP) work.

> ESP: Those of us in education had, for several years, been battling the scientifically based, evidence-based police who determined that qualitative research could not be 'scientific' because it was only descriptive and used narratives (see, for example, Shavelson, Phillips, Towne, & Feuer, 2003). If you remember, in 2000, the U.S. No Child Left Behind Act mandated in federal law that randomized controlled trials are the gold standard of educational research, although an article in the current issue of the American Educational Research Association journal, Educational Researcher, reported, almost 20 years later, that rigorous large-scale educational randomized controlled trials are often uninformative (Lortie-Forgues & Inglis, 2019). I wonder if we're surprised? So we desperately needed to come together and decide how to defend qualitative inquiry from neopositivism.

> IK: Arguments about whether 'educational research' should be 'scientific' have followed me throughout my career. Coming from a STEM background, I was naturally drawn to the idea of being scientific. However, the more time that I spent in the classroom, the more I became convinced that the scientific approach to studying teaching was inappropriate. Conversations with teachers in the arts and humanities tended to reinforce this view, while conversations with physicists and engineers tended to be more adversarial. Certainly, randomized controlled trials seemed totally inappropriate to analyse what I was observing. But for many of the 'observed', it was the only tool in their research toolbox.

> KG: I think that qualitative and postqualitative researchers need to feel brave enough to discard both the labels of science, and of quantification, if these frames do not suit their research and their way of seeing the world. In my view, there is absolutely nothing wrong with research being described as unscientific. But I think for many qualitative researchers, declaring this openly requires a bravery as well as an engagement with new definitions of key terms that have become

engrained in the researcher's lexicon: for example, rigour, reliability, impact, data. Linked to this is the question of sample size. There have been too many times when peer reviewers have asked qualitative researchers to defend a small sample size, acknowledging this as a weakness. Or researchers have been asked: how did you achieve reliability in your coding? Again, this adopts a defensive positioning for qualitative research, as it attempts, unsatisfactorily, to fit qualitative research into a mould designed for positivist scientific questions that conceptualize the world entirely differently and seek to represent a measurable reality. Monrouxe and Rees (2019) present an interesting article about this and about the way that qualitative research tries to hide itself behind the markers of positivist frameworks. However, of course it may be easier for me to say this as a result of writers like St. Pierre, Lather, Koro-Ljungberg doing such important work, and what I really like about St. Pierre is how she surfaces the history of qualitative research in order to show just how much how we think about research has already changed. In particular, she writes that:

I would say that research is whatever we say it is; that is, if enough people say a particular set of thoughts and practices counts as research, then it does. This is much about power, of course. We know that, historically, what counts as research has changed. Just think about qualitative research itself, which is now quite legitimate in many areas of social science but at the beginning was not and is still considered illegitimate by those who favor positivist social science approaches. (Guttorm, Hohti, and Paakkari 2015: 19)

But Koro-Ljungberg also talks about loss in terms of moving away from certainty. Is there a sense of loss for you in moving away from your scientific background?

IK: I think that framing this as 'moving away' from my scientific background invites a sense of loss. I have previously referred to my background in biology as 'disciplinary baggage' (Kinchin 2019a), but this suggests that it creates an impediment along a linear pathway of professional development (from structuralist to poststructuralist). I now see this rather differently with my background as an asset in my own rhizomatic becoming (*sensu* Gravett 2021). Borrowing from Youdell and Lindley (2019), I have revised the relationship between past and present in terms of 'social and biological entanglements of learning', where I am able to revisit my biological background using a poststructuralist lens (Chapter 8). Given that a healthy ecosystem exhibits rich biodiversity, then we should expect a healthy ecological university to exhibit a rich diversity of views so that our thinking remains dynamic.

KG: Yes I really like that idea about our thinking being dynamic and I think that we are evolving all the time.

ESP: Qualitative inquiry ... was, indeed, invented in journal articles, book chapters, handbooks, textbooks, in university methodology courses, and in conference papers. Perhaps it's good to remind ourselves that we did, indeed, invent qualitative methodology, we made it up, and we've repeated it again and again so it seems normal, natural, and real. The onto-epistemological arrangement of what I've called conventional humanist qualitative methodology has been able to accommodate interpretive, emancipatory or critical, and even postpositivist inquiry that rely on a particular description of human being. In this way, qualitative methodology has been a big tent, supple enough to serve as a methodology for different kinds of research that begins with the humanist subject.

IK: The idea of 'inventing' a methodology seems outrageous to some of my colleagues. But inventions do not come from nothing. I have spent years teaching and observing teaching. Reading about and writing about teaching. And talking and listening with colleagues about teaching. It would seem, in hindsight, that if no original ideas had emerged during all this activity, then perhaps I wasn't doing it right.

KG: I think here St. Pierre's comments that repetition has led to naturalization are important. We forget that practices are not natural, not given and therefore are open to question. For me this is exciting, and generative, and once you start questioning one area of practice or research you realize just how many other areas can be thought about differently. I also think what's really significant is the move away from a humanist ontology. If you think quite differently about relationality, then concepts like representation, voice, objectivity, data collection become very problematic. I think we have experienced this in terms of the idea of student voice in our work for some time.

IK: The key here, for me, is that we need to think about these things, and not just take things as a given. For example, 'student voice' has become a bit of a sacred cow. But if colleagues stop thinking about voice and what it represents, then inclusion of student voice quickly becomes one of those rituals that can be ticked off the list, and voices become white noise that can be easily blocked out.

ESP: Why are the human sciences and their methodologies problematic in poststructuralism? There're several reasons, but I'll mention two today. The first and most obvious, I think, is that they are inevitably human-centered. Second, poststructuralism refuses pre-existing method and methodology. Foucault (1997/2003), for example, wrote:

> I do not have a methodology that I apply in the same way to different domains. On the contrary, I would say that I try to isolate a single field of objects, a domain of objects, by using the instruments I can find or that I forge as I am actually doing my research, but without privileging the problem of methodology in any way (287–8).

So Foucault wrote that he used no pre-existing methodology, which he then applied in his research. Instead, he made it up as he went.

IK: The issue of 'human-centredness' being problematic is itself perhaps one of the most problematic leaps to be made when peering into the posthuman tent. Teaching seems appropriate to call 'human-centred', though I am interested in the counter-arguments.

KG: The label posthuman can definitely be daunting. In this book we have explored how posthuman theories can enable us to think in new ways about a breadth of learning and teaching questions. Posthumanism is about decentring the human. It is not saying that teaching does not involve humans or that humans don't matter. Rather it reminds us to expand our lens more widely to permit the inclusion of other nonhuman actors as important within teaching and within the world. This is an ethical practice too, as once the human is not the centre of the world then other forces become equally as important and must be considered: spaces, objects, bodies, materialities. All these things matter, but posthuman theorists contend that they have for too long been neglected within a limited, humanist, gaze.

IK: Perhaps it is the 'post' prefix that causes problems for me? The transition from pre to post conjures up an image of a linear trajectory from one to the other, and that is probably not helpful. Also, in my mind it is difficult to think of something becoming 'post' (e.g. poststructuralist) without first having been structuralist. The way in which these challenging concepts are also bound up in language whose meaning has changed, provides a considerable conceptual challenge. How do we get academics to engage in this challenge and disturb a system in which those colleagues with agency have already done well?

KG: I guess all labels can be limiting if they are not used carefully and are not problematized, but I think the 'post' prefix suggests an important break. I suppose we just need to continue to engage colleagues in debates and pose questions that encourage them to reflect upon concepts. Perhaps we have to encourage others to realize that without thoughtfulness and criticality we cannot be effective teachers and researchers. Challenging our own thinking is also pleasurable too, I think.

ESP: Deleuze and Guattari's philosophical concepts, such as the rhizome, are deliberately anti-method, and Deleuze argued that 'thought does not need a method', that method will, in fact, shut down thought, capture it, and consign it to the strata, to the normal, to what everyone knows, to the dogmatic image of thought that prohibits experimentation and creation. Furthermore, as they explained, Deleuze and Guattari's and St. Pierre's philosophical concepts are composed of specific components which change when the concept is taken from its specificity on the plane on which appears, so those concepts don't travel. That is, they cannot be taken from Deleuze's plane of immanence which is pre-personal, pre-individual, pre-subjective, and pre-conceptual and then be sprinkled throughout a conventional humanist qualitative study that's grounded in an onto-epistemology and an empiricism that is not Deleuzian. Deleuze and Guattari also made it clear that their philosophical concepts cannot be applied to organize, contain, and describe human experience as do concepts in the applied social or human sciences, like the concept's role in sociology and culture in anthropology. Deleuzo-Guattarian concepts are philosophical, not intended for application to lived human experience but for re-orienting thought.

IK: I guess the apparent separation of thought from application is the difficult leap here for me. And while I do get the idea that 'concepts don't travel' at a philosophical level, that does create a barrier when I am talking to STEM colleagues for whom their disciplinary currency is concepts that *do* travel. It is difficult to merge these two worlds in a way that allows me to function in both. And yet, by keeping them separate I feel that I am somehow missing out on something – like hearing a joke in a foreign language, where you understand the words, but don't appreciate the subtle cultural references that are left unsaid, but nonetheless carry the humour.

KG: This really encapsulates one of the main problems with binary concepts for me. Binaries unhelpfully juxtapose concepts as artificially separate. Thinking can be understood as doing; theory and practice as intertwined. Theoretical concepts can re-orientate thought. This is much more than a simple concept of applying theory. This is something that we explore in greater depth in Chapter 2. I am interested in why it is difficult for you to make this leap given that you are so committed to disrupting binaries in other contexts? Do you not consider thinking to be research, reading to be research?

IK: I consider thinking and reading to be essential, but these are often down-played in the research discourses and are not given due consideration in much of the literature. As St. Pierre suggests, everyone rushes to method. Unless you want to claim to be a philosopher (not something I can really do), thinking seems to play no part in the publication game. Editors and reviewers require that you run a focus group or conduct an interview with a random participant in order to provide a spurious data set that confirms your thoughts. It seems to carry more weight to have a small sample (and to cite this as a weakness in the study) than to think deeply about an issue. In my more cynical moments, I might even suggest that some research papers indicate a lack of thought, but compensate with a rigorous methodology.

KG: If you think that can be the case, where even the most limited kind of methodology is sometimes prized over deep thought or engagement with the literature/ideas, then blurring the boundaries can only help with the kinds of issues you describe.

ESP: From the beginning of my doctoral research, my methodology training in qualitative research trumped my theoretical training in poststructuralism, which I confined to the literature review chapter of my dissertation, and I automatically leaped to methodology and implemented the qualitative research process. In other words, I began with methodology and not poststructuralism. It didn't occur to me that methodology might not be thinkable in poststructuralism. It didn't occur to me there might be a way to inquire without using a pre-existing social science research methodology. But my choices seemed to be either qualitative or quantitative methodology.

IK: At what point does an academic have sufficient agency to break the mould and challenge orthodoxy? For St. Pierre, this seems to have occurred after she gained her doctorate – after she was inducted into her academic tribe. But she works in a field where challenging the orthodoxy is seen as the norm (Kneebone 2002).

KG: Yes and doesn't it still require considerable bravery to challenge research norms in the ways that St. Pierre and other 'post' scholars have done? I would argue that an academic should be always evolving and critiquing our own and others' work. I particularly like what Patti Lather writes about the concept of 'rigorous confusion' (2001: 207), that we have explored elsewhere in this book. Lather advises that our ongoing reading and learning might very well upend everything we believe and she suggests that this is mark of rigorous scholarship. For me, this offers a radical and exciting reinterpretation of the notion of rigor, which I find often problematic and limiting as a concept via its normative definitions. Here, Lather is openly suggesting that we actively turn towards confusion, and that we can be comfortable in admitting that our thinking may be muddled and evolving over time. I think that these are powerful ideas for researchers and academics to play with.

But I also think that we are indebted to the bravery of scholars who have challenged norms before us. I really like what St. Pierre writes about how for her she feels like she is always collaborating with authors living and dead when she writes, meaning that all her work then becomes a collaboration (St. Pierre 2014). I really like this idea of collaboration as intertextuality. It suggests that we are always entangled in an assemblage with other ideas and writers and destabilizes the idea of the author as a single individual. What do you think about that? It's very indebted to Barthes's ideas (1986) about the death of author. Unlike, St. Pierre, however, I love to collaborate with living authors too!

IK: I agree that collaborating with others is not only helpful in the research process, but also exciting. However, I think most of the collaborations that we witness in the literature are not between colleagues who might challenge each other. It is a bit like the arguments about social media – you only read the things that you already agree with. We tend not to seek out contrary points of view or counter-arguments. There is a danger that such dynamic collaborations may not be able to produce a neat answer to the problem that fits with the journal style.

KG: It can certainly be challenging to collaborate with others who think very differently from you or have a different epistemological or ontological perspective. I guess we have also had some differences, although, as we explore in Chapter 1, we have tried not to compromise too much and more often to reach agreement and greater awareness through discussion. I think what can be more useful is to critique published research when it is out there in a constructive way and engage in debate with other authors. I love it when I read something that completely upturns my thinking.

ESP: It's important to remember that, following Derrida, deconstruction does not reject what it deconstructs. Rather, it overturns and displaces a structure to make room for something different. So postqualitative inquiry is not a rejection of qualitative inquiry or any other pre-existing social science research methodology. It's something different altogether and cannot be recognized and understood in the same grid of intelligibility as those methodologies.

KG: I think the term rejection here suggests a simplicity – a new binary – that is not especially helpful. I really like what Koro-Ljungberg (2015: 2) writes when she suggests that she uses and problematizes labels simultaneously. So what I would hope that we can do in our work is critique, and then create openings for new ideas, that build and work with what is already there but offer entirely new perspectives. I also really like St. Pierre and Pillow's (2000) idea of working within 'the ruins'. For example, they write:

We are always speaking within the language of humanism, our mother tongue, a discourse that spawns structure after structure – binaries, categories, hierarchies ... poststructural feminists are interested in different discourses in which different statements and different material and political conditions might be possible .... such spaces, gaps, and interstices are seductive. (2000: 4.)

IK: The language is still problematic for me, and I think for many in the STEM world. As soon as we invoke terms such as 'poststructural feminists', many colleagues feel they are actively being excluded from the conversation. I realize that a shift in language complements the shift in thinking, and that new concepts require new terms, but some of these terms appear to raise a barrier to inclusion for some colleagues. If we want colleagues to think differently about their teaching, we need to ease them into the discourse. Finding areas of overlap is important. For me, it was the concept of the rhizome that connected to my STEM background and allowed me to start to engage with dangerous ideas. We need to help other colleagues to find their own entry points to this discourse, so they can see possibilities for their own development.

KG: Yes entry points are important, but I think it's also important to acknowledge that just because something is uncomfortable doesn't mean that we shouldn't engage with it. Theories such as feminism, postcolonialism, antiracism will of course be uncomfortable. Perhaps when something is uncomfortable that's when we need to engage with it even more!

ESP: Post qualitative inquiry doesn't have pre-existing methods of data analysis like coding data or thematic analysis in which themes somehow miraculously emerge from the data. It refuses representationalist logic that relies on a two-world ontology, which assumes there is the real out there and then a representation of the real in a different ontological order. The robust critique of representation in poststructuralism is crucial in post qualitative inquiry because so much effort in pre-existing social science research methodologies focuses on how to represent the real, authentic lived experiences of human beings. Representation is not the goal of post qualitative inquiry. Its goal is, instead, experimentation and the creation of the new, which is very difficult. Finally, and importantly, post qualitative inquiry is aligned with the humanities, with philosophy, history, the arts, the sciences, and literature, and not with the social sciences.

IK: Re: thematic analysis.

I might be called by some as a 'representationalist', given my earlier work with concept mapping (Kinchin 2016). But I guess the real issue is what is being represented, and for what purpose. The 'creation of the new' is something that I would align myself with. But I need to know if what has been created is 'new' – not just for me, but for others around me. How can I do that if I don't represent it somehow in a manner that can promote scrutiny by others? Perhaps the key term here is 'real'?

KG: I think it's really interesting how far you have departed from your origins within science education! As we have seen, the concept of representation is totally problematic if you don't believe that there is an objective reality out there that can be viewed, researched and measured by the researcher, and if you don't believe that meaning is single and stable. Instead, poststructural, posthumanist and postqualitative researchers often believe that researchers do not exist independently of the world and cannot objectively represent any reality. Objectivity, reality and representation are deeply problematic concepts. This is why the notion of emerging themes is so problematic in qualitative research as it implies that themes somehow emerge from data in a process that is entirely divorced from the researcher's input! Postqualitative research deconstructs and muddles all these ideas, de-centring the humanist all-knowing researcher, and challenging the normative ordering of research processes. I think you could perhaps still use the term representation with the caveat that your 'representation' is only one of many interpretations, open to a multiple of readings and meanings and is no way indicative of a pre-existing reality?

I think this is what St. Pierre is talking about in her interview with Guttorm and Hohti, and Paakkari (2015: 15) when she talks about how when you begin to study ontology the old words don't work anymore because so many are grounded in the subject of humanism. She continues to argue:

In science, so many are grounded in epistemology with hardly a nod to ontology. Those humanist words embed you in a particular discursive and material structure. Derrida wrote that when you use a concept you bring with it the entire structure in which it is thinkable. So, if you use the word 'individual,' you situate yourself in a human-centered structure. If you think the 'researcher begins a study', then you think the researcher exists before the study, ahead of language and materiality, that the researcher is not always already in the middle of everything.

Do you not see yourself, the researcher, as entangled within a wider set of relations that you can't step outside?

IK: When I am researching classroom practice, I totally see myself as part of ecosystem that I am looking at. But the historic requirement of detaching yourself from the research environment is a difficult habit to break. When I used to teach science in school, we spent hours training the pupils to write up their experiments in the third person. And this is the way that science needs to proceed. So, to then switch to a different perspective (where I might matter) is against all my training. However, I do feel tensions within educational research that contradict my training. For example, the obsession with thematic analysis is something that seems like method gone mad. Why should there be a nice neat number of themes to emerge from a study? Why can we not be satisfied with complexity? But if I represent that visually, so I can hold ideas in my head and share them with others, that is not to deny complexity, but to help me explore it.

KG: I am delighted that you are going against all your training and switching to a new perspective!

ESP: The goal of post qualitative inquiry is not to systematically repeat a pre-existing research process to produce a recognizable result but to experiment and create something new and different that might not be recognizable in existing structures of intelligibility.

IK: Repetition of pre-existing processes is not interesting. But the demand for 'recognizable results' is a pressure that we all face in the neoliberal university. And if our colleagues need to use existing structures to make this work intelligible, then we have an impasse that constrains unbridled creativity. We need to be intelligible – it provides the basis for teaching.

KG: I agree we need to take people with us in our work and at times use the words and concepts that others understand and are familiar with. As we have seen, Koro-Ljungberg (2015) explores this challenge and explains how we may need to use words that are sometimes problematic to us in order to have meaningful discussions with others and to engage with methodological conversations and discourses. I think we have tried to take colleagues with us on this journey too? What else can we do?

IK: We need to keep talking and sharing ideas without necessarily needing to 'win' the argument. I think dialogue is the key. And we need to recognize that not everyone will accept all the ideas that are on offer. I have started this part of my academic journey from the standpoint of a biology graduate. You started as an English literature graduate. We started at different points. Who says we need to 'end' at the same point?

KG: Yes – who says we need to or can end anywhere at all?

Moving Beyond Method: Challenges for Qualitative and Postqualitative Researchers

We have seen how making our work intelligible is important if we are to communicate effectively with our colleagues and within and beyond our field. In the next section, we explore further some of the barriers we have experienced in our work, as we attempt to experiment with more messy qualitative approaches, and to create new openings for new ways of thinking and doing in the sector. One of the most visceral, and perhaps problematic, of these challenges is the process of peer review, where we have both experienced the need to work with peer reviewers who may be resistant to new ways of writing and researching but who when anonymous may be very difficult to engage in dialogue. We consider what solutions and ways forward might exist for writers who want to innovate.

Peer Review and Its Constraints

Peer review of published research is widely perceived to represent 'the gold standard' when it comes to academic rigour. And yet, peer review can pose a barrier to the creation of new ideas. Colleagues deliberately target prestige research journals that demonstrate clearly defined processes of peer review so that readers can have some assurance about the quality of the work they are reading. However, this is a system not without its critics. The debilitating impact of peer review feedback has been highlighted frequently in recent literature (Hyland 2012; Horn 2016; Day and Porter 2018; Bozalek, Zembylas and Shefer 2019). Hyland (2012: 7) writes that following negative reviews writers may be 'so disheartened by criticism that they give up', and Mercer (2013) and Hartley and Dobele (2009) explore the particular impact of publication rejection upon female and early career researchers. Bozalek, Zembylas and Shefer (2019: 351) highlight that peer reviewers' critical comments can 'unnerve' even experienced authors.

Gernert (2008) lays out the basic pros and cons of peer review. The pros include the exclusion of poor-quality research; safeguarding of standards; the correction of minor flaws, and preventing a flood of useless material. However, the longer list of objections to peer review include the time it takes and the way it slows down publication; the lack of guarantees about the validity of the process; the bias nature of acceptance and rejection; the suppression of innovation; the gatekeeping role of a small number of 'elites', and the unfair advantage obtained by reviewers about up-and-coming publications. Smith (2006) sees, 'peer review as a flawed process', and describes how it may proceed in some instances:

> There may even be some journals using the following classic system. The editor looks at the title of the paper and sends it to two friends whom the editor thinks know something about the subject. If both advise publication the editor sends it to the printers. If both advise against publication the editor rejects the paper. If the reviewers disagree the editor sends it to a third reviewer and does whatever he or she advises. This pastiche – which is not far from systems I have seen used – is little better than tossing a coin, because the level of agreement between reviewers on whether a paper should be published is little better than you'd expect by chance. (Smith 2006: 178)

We have both experienced a number of challenging peer review-related incidents in the past few years. In recalling one incident, we decided to send a paper to a leading journal in the field that had a very rigorous review system – sending the manuscript to four referees. However, in hindsight, it seems that more is not necessarily better. If you ask more and more people about anything, you will eventually find someone that disagrees and in the eyes of many editors, one negative review is more important than three positive reviews. In this example Reviewer #1 commented on the high quality of the writing and how enjoyable the paper was. Reviewer #2 said how the paper would be of interest to the journal readership, and Reviewer #3 was very keen to express how the paper would resonate with the teaching reality for many colleagues. However, the fourth reviewer had a very different perspective on the paper, and on his/her role as a reviewer, and adopted a more negative tone describing how they were not interested in reading the views of selected individuals. Inevitably, the editor's decision was to reject – influenced largely by the voice of Reviewer #4, who was concerned about having a series of papers in the same style – we had only submitted one. Perhaps this reviewer was reluctant to embrace new perspectives or novel methodologies that might challenge the status quo and disrupt a field of enquiry? Of course, as most reviews are still anonymous, we have no idea who Reviewer #4 was. He or she may be the most eminent researcher in the field. Or s/he may not. Reviewer #4 above demonstrates the bias in the peer review process, and the homophily that has been discussed by Brezis and Birukou (2020), in which reviewers are more likely to appreciate innovations that are similar to their own research tendency. Notably, this reviewer refers to 'we as an academic community'. And yet who is this community, who is this 'we' whose views have already been decided upon? As such, the peer review process can lead to to conformity and selects less controversial papers for publication.

Interestingly, biographies of the celebrated biologist Lynn Margulis often refer to the fact that her seminal paper on cellular evolution was rejected by fifteen journals before it was finally accepted for publication (Knoll 2012; Schaechter 2012). While such stories provide us all with hope when we have just received a rejection letter from an editor, one wonders how many other significant papers might now be sitting on a shelf somewhere, if their authors had not had the same tenacity as Margulis to resubmit their work for publication. Furthermore, our experiences prompt wider questions regarding how disciplinary communities are created and constrained and how we are to effectively exist and thrive within the spaces, gaps and interstices of such constraints. How can new knowledge be created within such boundaries?

One potentially positive solution may lie in seeking opportunities for dialogue. In this much more positive experience, we received a final response from an anonymous peer reviewer after three rounds of review, during which we attempted to be open and explicit about the rationale for our method and approach. The reviewer thanked us for our responses to their feedback and commented that 'although we are not exactly on the same page when it comes to reporting qualitative research, I feel that you have sufficiently described the process in the revision letter and manuscript.'

This outcome was positive, but was made more difficult due to the anonymous peer review process. Potentially a move towards more open reviewing processes, as already being adopted by some academic journals, may pose one solution, offering a positive direction for change. Additionally, Bozalek, Zembylas, and Shefer (2019: 349) call for a more transformative practice of 'response-able reviewing' whereby reviewers and authors openly and collaboratively negotiate changes to be made. Interestingly, Bozalek and colleagues also advocate 'making reviews "count" in publishing, hiring, tenure and promotion' (2019: 355). They contend that it would be then possible to reward 'careful attentiveness and quality in reviewing' (2019: 355) as well as opening the way for more dialogic opportunities.

Conclusions

In this chapter we have been inspired by St. Pierre and other postqualitative scholars to discuss the potential for thinking about method and qualitative research in new and different ways. Real challenges do exist to thinking differently. Peer review processes can be exclusionary, and pressures remain for researchers to 'dress up' subjectivity as objectivity, and to quantify the unquantifiable. However, we believe that working in new ways remains possible, and that scholars within the higher education field are doing so. We are keen to continue to experiment in our work, to collaborate and learn from one another, and we hope that other educators too will take up the baton from some of the thinkers we have discussed here. As St. Pierre and Pillow explain: 'poststructural feminists have indeed shown that discourses are not closed systems and that shifts in historical thought and material conditions are possible' (2000: 4). What might such shifts in thought be able to achieve?

10

Towards a Relational Pedagogy

Where Are We Now?

It is clear that 'common sense' is not sufficient for the systematic enhancement of university teaching and the adoption of approaches that have been demonstrated to promote meaningful learning. This is because rational, linear, logical and common-sense narratives are too narrow to attend to the complexity of human and social phenomena (Strom and Martin 2017b). This has been summarized nicely by Snir (2018: 302) who identifies that the problem lies

> in the imperialism of common sense, in the way it takes over thought and action, casting them in conformist patterns ... even when trying to be critical, common sense thought in fact reaffirms and reproduces the prevailing political order and the meanings it assigns to subjects and objects.

So, as we enter the third decade of the twenty-first century, we find that after following 'rational' trajectories of development that have been dominated by market forces, universities are portrayed in the research literature as largely unhappy places – operating in an education system that has been described as 'frail' (Kinchin and Winstone 2017), or 'toxic' (Smyth 2017), creating 'theatres of cruelty' (Giroux 2010b: 2) that enact violence upon their employees (Liu and Pechenkina 2019). Far from being centres of social justice and care, they are accused of creating an 'un-liveable life' (Taylor 2020: 2), promoting 'carelessness' (Lynch 2010; Blackmore 2020). While these characteristics of the neoliberal university were once seen as a problem of Western universities, it seems that they have now travelled to the Global South (Bianchini 2002; Kazemi and Safari 2020). In part, we see this as a result of reductionist policies that support measurement and control at the expense of professional values. As a result, we observe teachers engaged in what are often called 'traditional' teaching styles, for example, lecturing without any interaction to large, passive audiences. Unsurprisingly, this is viewed as an unfulfilling activity by many of our colleagues who become trapped in this cycle of non-learning (Kinchin, Lygo-Baker and Hay 2008), as they feel that any deviation from this norm would be seen as unorthodox and risky.

In this volume, we have argued against simplistic views of teaching and learning, and through an interplay of structuralist, poststructuralist and posthuman lenses, we argue not just for the acceptance of complexity in higher education, but the need for active engagement with complexity to support a scholarly, antifragile advancement of teaching and learning. Thoughtfulness matters. Using the ecological analogies offered by Orr (1992: 87), this would see the university teacher acting as a field naturalist: a participant observer, 'deeply impressed by the overwhelming intricacy of phenomena and revelling in their very complexity'. A by-product of the reductionist, simplification of teaching discourse is the relegation of the scholarship of teaching to a peripheral activity that only concerns staff members who are not actively engaged in disciplinary research. As a result, the Scholarship of Teaching and Learning (SoTL) is seen by some (rightly or wrongly) as little more than watered-down educational research (Canning and Masika 2020).

By bringing together structuralist, poststructuralist and posthuman perspectives in this book, we have introduced unsettling ideas and unfamiliar connections to the higher education literature. In turn, this generates potential 'lines of flight' to the disciplinary assemblage that will doubtless cause discomfort to some observers as we 'tamper' with the accepted wisdom and approved discourses of the field, for example, by challenging central dogmas such as student-centredness and employability. In a similar vein, Roy (2003: 31) encourages teachers not to be passively affected by conditions and instead urges them to breach or rupture old boundaries, and contends that in the process of deterritorializing

> we make small ruptures in our everyday habits of thought and start minor dissident flows and not grand 'signifying breaks,' for grand gestures start their own totalizing movement, and are easily captured. Instead, small ruptures are often imperceptible, and allow flows that are not easily detected or captured by majoritarian discourses.

This is analogous to the subterranean, academic 'potholing' described by Bengtsen and Barnett (2017), or the 'life within the cracks' of the neoliberal university that is described by Manathunga and Bottrell (2019), which can lead to subversive, 'guerrilla teaching' (Lee 2008). However, Lee cautions us about employing such guerrilla tactics as it can lead to a 'bleak existence' where you are forever seen as an 'outlier'. This would seem to be a trajectory likely to lead to a state of pedagogic frailty (Kinchin and Winstone 2017). Similarly, in his book, *The Skillful Teacher* (2015: 254), Stephen Brookfield warns that although 'working on the margins can sometimes be exhilaratingly edgy and creative. In times of economic austerity or in situations of professional isolation, it can also become debilitating and demoralizing'. Brookfield advises new colleagues to choose their battles carefully and to attend to their emotional survival.

Towards a Complex Turn

We recall an exchange with a new university teacher several years ago. He really did not want to engage on a teacher development course that he was attending, and stated, 'It's only teaching. It's not rocket science!'. To which he received the reply, 'No, it's much more complicated than that.' While that might have been a slightly facetious response to close down an awkward conversation, there is some truth regarding the complex nature of teaching, and in the way it compares with rocket science, as summarized by Glouberman and Zimmerman (2002: 1) in their summary of complex and simple problems:

> Simple problems like following a recipe may encompass some basic issues of technique and terminology, but once these are mastered, following the recipe carries with it a very high assurance of success. Complicated problems contain subsets of simple problems but are not merely reducible to them. Their complicated nature is often related not only to the scale of a problem like sending a rocket to the moon, but also to issues of coordination or specialized expertise. Complicated problems, though generalizable, are not simply an assembly of simple components. Complex problems can encompass both complicated and simple subsidiary problems, but are not reducible to either since they too have special requirements, including an understanding of unique local conditions, interdependency with the added attribute of non-linearity, and a capacity to adapt as conditions change. Unavoidably, complex systems carry with them large elements of ambiguity and uncertainty that are in many ways similar to the problems associated with raising a child.

This is summarized in Table 10.1. If teaching was as simple as following a recipe then the life of the university teacher would be easy. However, within the classroom the 'ingredients' are constantly changing. Students are not homogeneous or standardized, and there is no guarantee of easily replicable outcomes every time

Table 10.1 Comparing simple and complex problems

Following a recipe	Sending a rocket to the moon	Raising a child
The recipe is essential	Formulae are critical and necessary	Formulae have a limited application
Recipes are tested to assure easy replication	Sending one rocket increases assurance that the next will be OK	Raising one child provides experience, but no assurance of success with the next
No particular expertise is required, but cooking expertise increases success rate	High levels of expertise in a variety of fields are necessary for success	Expertise can contribute, but is neither necessary or sufficient to ensure success
Recipes produce standardized products	Rockets are similar in critical ways	Every child is unique and must be understood as an individual
The best recipes give good results every time	There is a high degree of certainty of outcome	Uncertainty of outcome remains
Optimistic approach to problem possible	Optimistic approach to problem possible	Optimistic approach to problem possible

Source: After Glouberman and Zimmerman (2002).

a module is taught. There is no recipe for excellent teaching. Teaching is much more like raising a child (Table 10.1). Experience and expertise are both helpful, but not sufficient to guarantee success. Every teaching episode is unique and there is always some uncertainty about the outcome. Very few of the variables that impact upon a student's learning are under the control of the teacher.

In their rejection of reductionist conceptions of teaching that can strip professional practice down to a recipe or a set of competencies, Strom and Viesca (2020: 14) move towards the 'complex turn' to 'create meaningful lines of flight that can disrupt our inequitable educational status quo'. Building on the seven strands of the complex framework proposed by Strom and Viesca (2020), we offer our own interpretations of the non-linear shifts in perspective that are required to move teaching forward.

1. From Dualism to Ecosystem

We have seen in Chapter 2 how binary thinking can constrain practice. However, new entrants to academia are bombarded with simplistic binaries during their induction to the profession. The question of whether they should focus on research activities or teaching practice is often given prominence by senior colleagues charged with mentoring responsibilities. For many new teachers, emphasis within the teaching-research binary is dictated by their contracts ('research-active' or 'teaching-only'). For those who focus on teaching (by choice or contractual obligation), a range of more subtle binaries gradually come into view, leading to a number of questions to be addressed: should my teaching focus on efficiency (i.e. economy of effort) or on innovation? Should I view teaching as an administrative duty or as a scholarly endeavour? Each decision has the result of aligning with or potentially alienating other members of the department.

After arrival at the university, most novice teachers may find some refuge with teaching specialists offering formal support on an accredited programme of professional development. But even here the binaries may persist. One of the most widely presented binaries to those who are starting to reflect on the complexity of teaching is the notion of deep and surface learning (Marton and Säljö 1976). The simplicity of the 'deep-surface' idea often resonates with new academics' perceptions of teaching. However, Tormey (2014: 8) has warned that 'a framework that is simple enough to be a powerful metaphor may be too simple to adequately account for learning in different contexts', and that its blind acceptance by new entrants to the profession has 'imposed blinkers that make useful alternative conceptualisations invisible'. Likewise, Brookfield (2015: 269) writes that

> teaching and learning are such complex processes, and teachers and learners are such complex beings, that no curricular model or instructional approach will ever apply to all people in all settings. Not surprising, peddlers of such things would have us believe otherwise. Their pitch is that if we just adopt their model or approach we will rid our teaching of ambiguities, problems, and contradictions. It ain't necessarily so.

Being wary of standardized approaches may then be very wise. Moreover, once accepted, the deep-surface binary can lead logically into other associated binaries, such as passive and active learning. The conscientious teacher who tries to put these ideas together to make a logical framework to support their practice will see that by opting towards efficiency of teaching, this can be optimized by encouraging passivity among the students and satisfaction with rote learning. Those elements all fall into place so long as the assessment regime rewards the students for their compliance to facilitate the university as a centre of non-learning (Kinchin, Lygo-Baker and Hay 2008). The alternative pathway through the set of binaries sees the teacher engaged in innovative practices to encourage active participation and meaningful learning. This can be more taxing (or rewarding) for the teacher and the student, but becomes untangled if the assessment regime fails to recognize quality of learning over quantity. Without support, or suitable role models, new teachers may fall into line and revert to the efficiency of practice as a guiding principle for their teaching, even when they see that it falls short of their aspirations. An institution that is split by the efficiency-innovation binary is likely to experience the symptoms of pedagogic frailty (Kinchin and Winstone 2017).

However, where new teachers do have role models who are advocates of different kinds of approaches to education, we have seen entrants to the profession blossom into teachers who are eager to engage with their students and who see the intellectual challenge inherent in teaching. Teachers who want to be in the classroom. Invariably, these are teachers who question orthodoxy and recognize the complexity of the classroom as something more than a series of binary choices. These are teachers who see themselves as part of the evolving ecology of the classroom, and who have a personal investment in their professional practice as a teacher. In such an environment, traditional binaries such as student-centred versus teacher-centred become redundant and inhibitory.

2. From Individuals to Multiplicity

Within the neoliberal university, there is a relentless focus on the performance of the individual teacher. The successful individual is lauded as the 'hero teacher' when things are going well (Madriaga and Morley 2016) but is blamed when things are not so smooth. The evaluation of teaching quality in the UK is partly determined by student responses to the National Student Survey (NSS). The NSS focusses on individual teacher actions with questions like 'do your teachers explain things well', but never attend to the wider ecology of teaching. This suggests a rather low level of expectation regarding the ability of students to engage with sophisticated discussions about teaching – something that does not align with our experiences of working with students and their often insightful commentary on their observations (Gravett, Yakovchuk and Kinchin 2020). This style of questioning in the NSS focuses the blame for poor student satisfaction on individual teachers who may score badly within the survey. However, it is the same survey irrespective of the expertise of the teacher or the popularity of the module. The NSS relies on evaluating teaching based on historical norms and fails to look forward to emerging innovations or creativity of practice. In short, it does not support a philosophy of becoming.

Rather, what we need is an approach in which 'the quality of a teacher's activity is determined by both how it fits with, and how it shapes, the educational ecology' (Fawns, Aitken and Jones 2021: 74). So how would the focus change if the unit of analysis was not the individual teacher, but broadened the lens to attend to the wider teaching assemblage? What if the NSS included questions such as the following?

> Q. Does the university offer sufficient support and incentive to the teaching staff that allows them to enact their professional values?

Such a question presupposes a more scholarly dialogue about teaching with the students, some of whom are aware that teachers are sometimes absent from their classes to go on training courses, but are never a part of that dialogue (Kinchin and Kinchin 2019). This perspective would have to assume that agency was more distributed throughout the teaching assemblage, and would shift the discourse from simplistic notions of 'satisfaction' towards an understanding of learning and teaching as a complex process in which a multiple of actors are actively entangled and engaged. In summary, 'evaluation should consider not just what teachers do but also the relationship between teachers and students' (Fawns, Aitken, and Jones 2021: 71).

3. From Isolated to Collective

A centralized command-and-control style of leadership can often fail to generate a shared sense of purpose between different groups within the university (Erickson, Hanna and Walker 2020). Wright and Greenwood (2017: 47) comment:

> A core pathology of current higher education institutions is that the legitimate participants (students, faculty, staff and administration) are not held together by shared interests and understandings. They compete with each other rather than being required to harmonise their different interests and operate in solidary ways.

This would be typical of the arborescent university in which tree-like structures are evident in the branching management charts that are often produced to convey the arrangement to the workforce. This is the antithesis of the rhizomatic university in which every part of the rhizome communicates with every other part. It also seems that within universities, there is a quiet form of alternative leadership that may be operating, which is unseen and 'eludes reductively diminutive branding via quantifiable metrics in the academy of knowledge, slipping silently away from any easy observation and definition' (Jameson 2018: 379). This has been described by Jameson as 'unrecorded conversations exchanged amongst the mutually wounded'. These exchanges of survival mechanisms are recognized anecdotally as instrumental in academic success. A combination of poorly appreciated rhizomatic structures and underground alternative leadership may help to explain why lines of communication within universities are often so fragile.

In contrast, what would happen if we conceptualize universities as assemblages of interrelated people and things who have a responsibility to one another? Indeed, Taylor and Fairchild describe how we might understand institutions as assemblages in which 'collections of heterogeneous bodies – human and nonhuman, social, material, abstract and physical – which emerge and come into relations around particular events' (Taylor and Fairchild 2020: 520). Attending to institutions as collective ecologies, or assemblages, creates new questions about relationality, relational pedagogies, and about our intra-actions and responsibilities. This has been described by Bozalek et al. (2018a) as leading us towards a 'pedagogy of response-ability' where we become accountable, responsible and entangled, leading us to think differently about how we relate to one another within a collective context.

4. From Human-Centred to Posthuman

The ideas explored above, of disrupting binaries and of understanding institutions as complex ecologies and assemblages, are all prevalent themes within a posthuman perspective. A posthuman perspective can offer openings for us to think entirely differently about learning and teaching, leading to an enriched understanding of higher education and relational pedagogies. Crucially, it enables us to problematize notions of learning and teaching as a performative, measurable experience with an agentic, autonomous individual at the centre. Instead, posthumanism offers an affirmative, values-based, ethical approach to understanding learning, teaching and our relationship to the world. Posthuman theories do this, first, by depicting experiences as messy, fluid, evolving and complex. Second, posthuman theorists contend that individuals can be more helpfully be understood as entangled with their environment and with one another (Barad 2007). As a result, posthuman perspectives offer a way to rethink our relationships with students, with our colleagues and with our environments, drawing new attention to how we intra-act. Such a wider conception of the relational encourages us to ask new questions about concepts such as agency, engagement, voice, as well as how we intra-act ethically with one another and with our contexts. Such a change in direction requires teachers to recognize that each meeting matters, to develop their own personal philosophy of teaching, while attending to the wider impact of such a philosophy within a collaborative, relational and ethical approach that recognizes the role of the teacher as part of a wider whole.

5. From Neutral and Universal to Political and Situated

The move from a monoculture of acceptable knowledge to a recognition of a rich ecology of knowledges is a difficult one to make for many academics. As Morrice (2019: 26) confirms, 'the exclusionary monopoly operated by Western conceptions of learning and what constitutes relevant or valid knowledge has the effect of negating the knowledges, experiences and practices of whatever does not fit within the dominant epistemological canon' and describes this as an example of the 'sociology of absences' that unveils social conditions that have been successfully suppressed by the dominant culture (*sensu* Santos 2001). However, there are instances within the research literature where authors are now giving voice to their awareness of other ways of thinking. For example, Wooten (2018: 212) gives a personal account of how she had considered her study in the sciences as a neutral practice as her research used so many bias-eliminating procedures, but then adopts a different gaze and comments, 'My cartographic inquiry connects to philosophic inquiring that regards research as political in terms of how research methods' effects extend beyond their intentions including for whom their productions come to matter.' There are certainly those in the higher education community who act as gatekeepers, maintaining the status quo and deterring deviations from the norm. This will be experienced by anyone who submits a research paper for review that does not conform tightly to the established pattern (see our discussion of peer review in Chapter 9). Gatekeepers have contributed to the structured formalizing and normalizing of method in such a way that some observers complain that now, 'most studies look the same' and that being forced into a narrow repertoire of methodologies can 'almost prevent us from doing something different' (Guttorm and Hohti 2015: 16–17). Recognition of the political environment in which we are working, and the inhibitions this imposes on creativity, is a first step to wanting to think and practice differently.

6. From Being to Becoming

As teachers we can be understood as always evolving, always in process (see our discussion of becoming in Chapter 6). This is a notion that has been employed by Braidotti (2019: 34) who contends that posthumanism offers a frame in which 'to understand the ongoing processes of becoming-subjects in our fast-changing times'. Within this perspective, teachers are always learning, always in transition, always 'becoming-subjects'. These ideas resonate with Deleuze and Guattari's notion of the rhizome which they describe as 'always in the middle … interbeing, intermezzo' (1987: 26). If we understand teaching as rhizomatic and as about continuous becoming, it can be incredibly helpful in disrupting normative notions of teaching expertise and reminding ourselves that we too are always learning, always 'intermezzo'. As Strom and Viesca (2020) contend, 'teacher development is a non-linear activity that happens not in a stable trajectory but as a series of "becomings" – temporal realisations of teacher-self, instances of learning, and/or practice events that occur as "thresholds" within a larger ongoing process of "becoming different" – all of which emerge out of the collective activity of a particular assemblage' (Strom and Viesca 2020: 12)

7. From Sameness and Homogeneity to Difference and Diversity

Examination of the contemporary research literature will give the reader a flavour of how academia likes to constrain and constrict difference. Many studies that look at the richness of student experience or teaching practice will turn on their rich data sets and seek to fit them to a handful of categories or themes. This simplifies the representation of data and offers a control mechanism for practitioners and managers – to fit their participants to the definitions of their categories. Famously, this was done with the observations of student learning styles. As a result of this research, teachers were encouraged 'to VAK' their teaching plans and highlight where the needs of different categories of students would be catered for – by stressing the visual, auditory or kinaesthetic components of the lesson. Work on student learning styles has now fallen out of favour (Franklin 2006; Dembo and Howard 2007), as the focus on the categories became more important than the teachers' relationships with the students being categorized. However, the categorization of teachers and students continues in educational research, in studies where the richness and messiness of the data fails to serve the reporting needs of the researcher.

The emphasis on themes and categories promotes an emphasis on 'sameness' and 'conformity' through a philosophy of being. Where individuals do not align to our themes and categories, individuals or groups are seen to be different – outliers. This difference is then taken as an indicator of something that has not been achieved – a deficit:

> We need to recognize deficit thinking when we see it. This can be difficult because such ideas are all around us and we are accustomed to them. It requires critically reflecting on how we are socialized into perpetuating these myths and how our identities are socially constructed and change over time. It is key to understanding that differences – especially differences from us and how we learn, speak or listen – are not deficits. (Tewell 2020: 155)

Throughout this book, we have emphasized the potential of becoming. This promotes a conceptualization of teaching as always evolving, and of a move towards 'becoming different'. We acknowledge this may be in tension with the need for new academics to assimilate within their departmental or disciplinary culture and to gain recognition among a closed community of peers. This is especially true of academics who migrate from one national context to another and already feel labelled as 'different', where different can also imply 'less' (Hosein et al. 2018). Addressing this subtext is a major hurdle for higher education. To achieve a state where different simply means different. And where 'sameness' only contributes to an unhealthy monoculture, and 'difference' is seen to contribute to a healthy state of diversity.

From Binary Logic to Care-full Assemblage

Few would argue against the idea that academics should care about their students, and the idea of care as an ethical imperative within higher education has a long history within the research literature and particularly within feminist research (Noddings 1986; 2012; Gilligan 1982; Tronto 1993). In recent years, the concept of care and relationships has been explored in ever more detail (Anderson et al. 2020; Bozalek, Zembylas and Tronto 2020; Gravett and Winstone 2020). This is partly in response to the recognition that the neoliberal university appears to place increasing emphasis on market forces, and this seems to be in tension with the labour-intensive practices of caring for students – so that university life appears to be placing the mental health of our students at risk (Broglia, Millings and Barkham 2017). It is also a response to concerns for more socially just pedagogies and more nuanced understandings of relationships and connections in higher education.

How we might understand care and begin to think about its role within higher education is complex. The isolation and description of the concept of care may be analogous to the chemist extracting a rare mineral from the ore in which it occurs. Once isolated, the mineral is structurally and functionally distinct from the ore in which it is naturally found. It is no longer bound to the other components of the ore. This idea resonates with the managerial tendency to latch on to a definition, reduce it to a series of simplified terms that can be quantified and turn it into a metric for the evaluation of practice. Once care is defined, then the deficit condition (care-less) can also be defined (Lynch 2010), and we can set up a binary logic. Again, this seems to be for the purposes of *rigorous* reporting rather than to actually support teachers and teaching practice.

An initial step towards the recognition of closely allied elements within the assemblage in which care may operate has been described by Kinchin (2019) as a triple point – a point where the components function without barriers or borders and become indistinguishable from each other. These close elements, of pedagogic health and wellbeing (salutogenesis), can be visualized as a heuristic (Figure 10.1) to help in the description of the potential messiness and complexity of the situation. Such a visualization is necessarily a simplification and does not represent a comprehensive description of the larger context. However, it provides an entry point for wider appreciation of the dynamic and complex nature of the care-pedagogy-wellness assemblage; a point for dialogue and exploration.

We must also recognize that even if we understand care as contextualized, and recognize the complex environment in which it may operate, the use of the term 'care' brings with it accompanying expectations and inequalities. For example, the gendered nature of caring practices within society and education (Mariskind 2014) result in uneven caring practices across campuses, with the result that the burden of care often falls on part-time, female, teaching-focused staff – leaving those more 'successful' academics free from the responsibility of caring and able to offload care (Clegg and Rowland 2010: 721). As summarized by the Puāwai Collective (2019: 34):

> The gendering of workloads generally, and the gendered constructions of women as fulfilling a caring role for staff and students within academic departments means women are likely to bear the brunt of the emotional, psychological and physical effects arising from increased workloads and changes in university cultures. Outside of the university environment, caring responsibilities are also most likely to affect women and, subsequently, women's ability to perform according to the expectations imposed by research quality and productivity

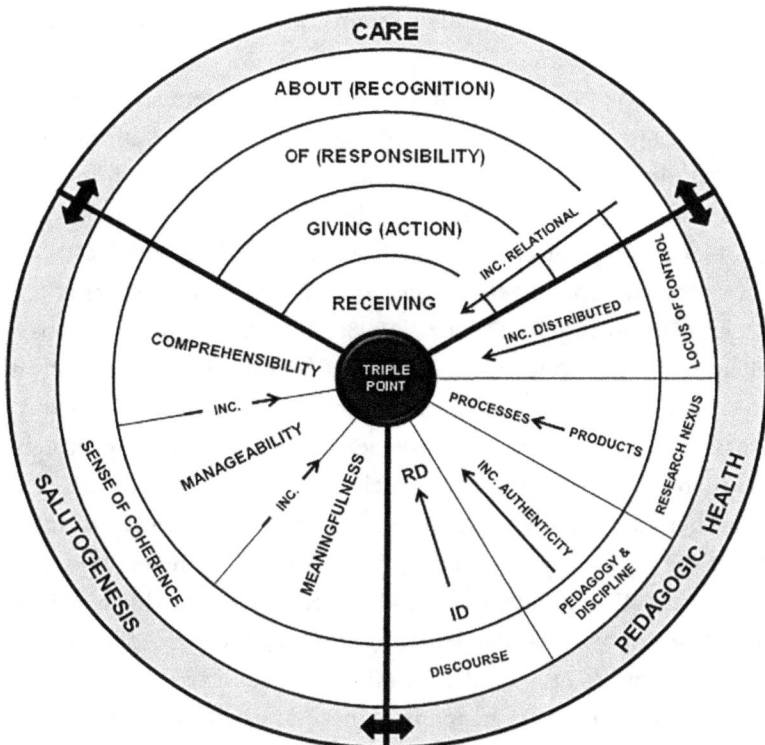

Figure 10.1 Three lines in the care-pedagogy-salutogenesis assemblage suggesting a tendency towards a triple point.
ID = Instructional Discourse; RD = Regulative Discourse; INC = Increasing[ly].
Source: After Kinchin (2020).

metrics. The seeming impossibility of reconciling career and home/family responsibilities can therefore give rise to feelings of selfishness and guilt and compound stress and anxiety.

Such entrenched systemic inequalities can break down the reciprocal nature of caring – where staff no longer feel cared for. In such instances, they are not in a position to care for others. A paradoxical situation then evolves where a managerial imperative to care can result in a reduction in being cared for across the campus. It is, therefore, essential that we are sensitive to the language that is used when trying to improve the environment for learning, and that we avoid the seductive tendency towards reductionism and binary thinking that can emerge through the obsessive search for complete definitions of difficult concepts. The complexity inherent in the thoughtful university is something that should be shared and explored, rather than being simplified and measured.

This exaptation of the triple point concept (from chemistry to educational research) is a move away from the reductionist tendencies of the dominant science paradigm, in line with Deleuze's bio-philosophical perspectives (Marks 2006). In particular, this highlights Deleuze's distinction between a map of *extensions* (of external relations, space, time and matter), and a map of *intensities* (of affective constellations composed of relations and *becomings*) (Deleuze 1998). Deleuze (1998: 64) situates intensive maps within the felt transitions of becoming (including becoming teacher – Strom and Martin 2017a), as part of 'the cartographic activity of the unconscious'. Those academics who have achieved their triple point (even fleetingly) will have probably done so without conscious reflection on the process. The model is therefore a tool to help in the exploration of a map of intensities and raises the possibility of achieving a triple point to the conscious level of deliberative practice. Academics who have engaged with this heuristic have found it to be empowering, particularly within a philosophy of becoming that removes the tyranny of a fixed endpoint to be achieved, stating: 'Reaching my triple point sometimes happens – these are transient moments which are easily destabilised – sadly the triple point is not sustainable at all times, but understanding this and what I need to do to move back towards it is enormously helpful' (Kinchin et al. 2021: 104).

Stein (2019: 144) contends that 'if we simply re-imagine higher education from where we currently stand, we will likely continue to imagine and create more of the same', and suggests that we might 'denaturize the epistemological and ontological categories and assemblages that enable higher education as we know it to exist and persist'. Stein is critical of the research within the higher education community and how it fails to encourage any form of denaturization, categorizing it as descriptive or prescriptive, with the former simply providing data that represents existing reality and the latter offering solutions to identified problems that clearly delineate ideal means to a predetermined end. In either case, there are few opportunities taken to question the epistemological or ontological frameworks that orientate our work or shape the questions we ask. Therefore, we end up presuming that 'all worthwhile knowledge production should be immediately instrumentalizable'. According to Stein, this fits with the dominant higher education 'field-imaginary' – the collective norms, working assumptions and self-understandings that characterize a particular field and allow the field's practitioners to make sense of shared objects, theories and methods of study. Stein explains that the currently dominant field-imaginary in higher education was sedimented in the period after the Second World War and that while the political, social and economic contexts have shifted dramatically, the higher education field-imaginary has remained relatively static. The result of this is that higher education is constructed to serve a context that is detached from the sociomaterial conditions of the present. This situation leads us to make minor adjustments so that when the system appears to fail students who are not representative of the post-war context, we have to talk about 'attainment gaps' among groups that we can recognize as 'other'. While marginalized 'others' (notably women and racial minorities) are actively encouraged to enter higher education in the name of diversity and representation, they too are compelled to behave in accordance with the rules set by the dominant group, thereby reproducing privilege rather than challenging it. Being allowed into the space comes at the cost of suppressing those aspects of their identity that are considered incongruent to the context (Dawson 2020). Based on these observations Shilliam (2015: 32) comments that while 'the doors to higher education have been opened ... the architecture of the building has hardly changed'. This longstanding situation in UK higher education has been described by Ross et al. (2018: 111) as a 'significant moral and economic failure'. Stein (2019: 147) concludes:

> Within a sedimented field-imaginary, knowledge is produced through a set of taken for granted epistemological norms and conceptual-ideological assemblages. ... As a result, we do not often think to ask whether the questions that orient our field-imaginary are still the questions that need asking, and whether the terms of our scholarly conversations are adequate to the task of responding to contemporary ethical-political challenges.

This may be a result of the sidelining of academic imaginaries in favour of short-term economically driven policies. Morley (2012: 354) talks about the mythological binary between the university of the past (associated with elitism, exclusion and inequality) and the university of today that is represented as diversified, globalized, borderless, marketized and neoliberalized. Morley summarizes this confused cartography as a 'binary of hyper-modernism and archaism'. We have attempted to nudge the reader to ask fundamental questions about the field-imaginary of higher education, and to consider adopting polyvalent lines of enquiry (Chapter 2), investigating the 'other' side of the epistemological abyss (Chapter 6), and by questioning the boundaries of method (Chapter 9).

Continuing Thoughts

In weaving together our discussions of the discourses that dominate the confused cartography of higher education, and drawing upon a rich assemblage of theoretical paradigms to theorize resistance to dominant conceptions, we identify the dangers inherent in linear thinking, binary oppositions and taken-for-granted assumptions. We have suggested that too often such discourses offer an artificially narrow perspective that fails to consider the messy, day-to-day and situated experiences of staff and students. We have suggested that this reduces university teaching to a series of approved habits (masquerading as 'best practice' that shelters behind a sanitized instructional discourse), rather than a scholarship of teaching (with all the messiness and unpredictability that entails) as the sector claims. The creation of an ecological university requires the maintenance of (bio)diversity rather than a monoculture of regulation and standardization. This is essential to create a healthy and sustainable university ecosystem that can thrive in a changing environment.

We suggest that moving towards a perspective that considers a teaching and learning ecosystem as relational may be generative in offering new openings to engage more thoughtfully. Enacting a relational pedagogy in which we understand bodies, matter and our environment as an interwoven web of relations, and where we attend to connections and intra-actions as opposed to oppositions, may enable us to see past neoliberal dominant discourses that offer only homogenized depictions of learning in higher education. In their discussion of relational pedagogies, Bingham and Sidorkin (2004) summarized their perspective in the following points:

1. A relationship is more real than the things it brings together and defines our reality.
2. The self is a knot in a web of relations. Outside the web, the self cannot be defined.
3. Authority and knowledge are subordinate to relations and require others for their enactment.
4. Human relations exist in and through shared practices.
5. Relations are complex and can only be described as a multi-voiced text.
6. Actions are subordinate to relations. Actions only acquire meaning in context.
7. Teaching is the building of educational relations.
8. Educational relations exist to include the student in a wider web of relations - beyond the limits of education.
9. Relations are not necessarily 'good'. Relationality is not an ethical value.

These points offer enormous scope for continuing research into pedagogy and offer a framework in which to embed scholarly reflection on teaching. Such perspectives prioritize attention to the material as well as to the human, enabling the blurring of all binaries and boundaries in a radical way. Crucially, such a perspective also invites a focus on the situated, localized and granular context of the individual within higher education and speaks back to universalist conceptions of experience. This focus can support the reader in their own process of becoming.

References

Adam, B. (1998), *Timescapes of Modernity: Environment and Invisible Hazards*, London: Routledge.

Adams, E. (2021), 'Being before: Three Deleuzian becomings in teacher education', *Professional Development in Education*, 1–14. doi.org/10.1080/19415257.2021.1891954.

Adcroft, A. (2018), 'Business', in I. M. Kinchin and N. E. Winstone (eds), *Exploring Pedagogic Frailty and Resilience: Case Studies of Academic Narrative*, 77–90, Leiden: Brill.

Ahmed, S. (2017), *Living a Feminist Life*, Durham, NC: Duke University Press.

Ahn, M. Y., and Davis, H. H. (2020), 'Four domains of students' sense of belonging to university', *Studies in Higher Education*. doi.org/10.1080/03075079.2018.1564902.

Ainsworth, S., and Oldfield, J. (2019), 'Quantifying teacher resilience: Context matters', *Teaching and Teacher Education*, 82: 117–28.

Ali, X., Tatam, J., Gravett, K., and Kinchin, I. (2021), 'Partnership values: An evaluation of student-staff research projects at a UK higher education institution', *International Journal for Students at Partners*, 5(1): 12–25.

Althusser, L. (1971), 'Ideology and ideological state apparatuses (notes towards an investigation)', in L. Althusser (ed.), *Lenin and Philosophy and Other Essays*, 127–86, New York: Monthly Review Press.

Anderson, V., Rabello, R., Wass, R., Golding, C., Rangi, A., Eteuati, E., Bristowe, Z., and Waller, A. (2020), 'Good teaching as care in higher education', *Higher Education*, 79(1): 1–19.

Andreotti, V. de O., Ahenakew, C., and Cooper, G. (2011), 'Epistemological pluralism: Ethical and pedagogical challenges in higher education', *AlterNative*, 7(1): 40–50.

Andreotti, V. de O., Stein, S., Pashby, K., and Nicolson, M. (2016), 'Social cartographies as performative devices in research in higher education', *Higher Education Research & Development*, 35(1): 84–99.

Arao, B., and Clemens, K. (2013), 'From safe spaces to brave spaces: A new way to frame dialogue around diversity and social justice', in L. M. Landremann (ed.), *The Art of Effective Facilitation: Reflections from Social Justice Educators*, 135–50, Sterling, VA: Stylus Publishing.

Ashwin P., Boud, D., Coate, K., Hallett, F., Keane, E., Krause, K. L., Leibowitz, B., MacLaren, I., McArthur, J., McCune, V., and Tooher, M. (eds) (2015), *Reflective Teaching in Higher Education*, London: Bloomsbury.

Bacevic, J. (2019), 'With or without U? Assemblage theory and (de)territorialising the university', *Globalisation, Societies and Education*, 17(1): 78–91.

Baker, S., and Irwin, E. (2019), 'Disrupting the dominance of 'linear pathways': How institutional assumptions create "stuck places" for refugee students' transitions into higher education', *Research Papers in Education*. doi.org/10.1080/02671522.2019.1633561.

Bal, M. (2002), *Travelling Concepts in the Humanities: A Rough Guide (Green College Lecture Series)*, Toronto: University of Toronto Press.

Bal, M. (2006), 'Working with concepts', *European Journal of English Studies*, 13(1): 13–23.

Ball, S. (1997), 'Policy sociology and critical social research: A personal review of recent education policy and policy research', *British Educational Research Journal*, 23(1): 257–74.

Ball, S. J., and Olmedo, A. (2013), 'Care of the self, resistance and subjectivity under neoliberal governmentalities', *Critical Studies in Education*, 54(1): 85–96.

Barad, K. (2007), *Meeting the Universe Halfway*, Durham, NC: Duke University Press.

Barnett, R. (2017), *The Ecological University: A Feasible Utopia*, London: Routledge.

Barthes, R. (1986), 'The death of the author', in R. Barthes (ed.), R. Howard (trans.), *The Rustle of Language*, 49–55, Berkeley, CA: University of California Press.

Behnejad, S. A. (2018), 'Engineering', in I. M. Kinchin and N. E. Winstone (eds), *Exploring Pedagogic Frailty and Resilience: Case Studies of Academic Narrative*, 33–45. Leiden: Brill.

Bell, A. (1980), 'The vascular pattern of a rhizomatous ginger (*Alpinia speciosa* L. Zingiberaceae). 2. The rhizome', *Annals of Botany*, 46: 213–20.

Bengtsen, S., and Barnett, R. (2017), 'Confronting the dark side of higher education', *Journal of Philosophy of Education*, 51(1): 114–31.

Benner, P. (1984), *From Novice to Expert: Excellence and Power in Clinical Nursing Practice*, Menlo Park, CA: Addison-Wesley.

Bennett, A., and Burke, P. J. (2018), 'Re/conceptualising time and temporality: An exploration of time in higher education', *Discourse: Studies in the Cultural Politics of Education*, 39(6): 913–25.

Bernstein, B. (2000), *Pedagogy, Symbolic Control and Identity*, Oxford: Rowman & Littlefield.

Bhabha, H. K. (1994), *The Location of Culture*, London: Routledge.

Bianchini, P. (2002), 'Education as a market. Travelling concepts and discourses: views from Africa', *Education and Social Justice*, 4(3): 32–40.

Biesta, G. (2013), *The Beautiful Risk of Education*, London: Routledge.

Biesta, G. (2015), 'Freeing teaching from learning: Opening up existential possibilities in educational relationships', *Studies in Philosophy and Education*, 34(3): 229–43.

Biesta, G. J. J., and van Braak, M. (2020), 'Beyond the medical model: Thinking differently about medical education and medical education research', *Teaching and Learning in Medicine*, 32(4): 449–56.

Bingham, C. W., and Sidorkin, A. M. (2004) (eds), *No Education without Relations*, New York: Peter Lang.

Blackmore, J. (2020), 'The carelessness of entrepreneurial universities in a world risk society: A feminist reflection on the impact of Covid-19 in Australia', *Higher Education Research & Development*. doi.org/10.1080/07294360.2020.1825348.

Blackmore, P. (2015), *Prestige in Academic Life: Excellence and Exclusion*, London: Routledge.

Bleazby, J. (2015), 'Why some school subjects have a higher status than others: The epistemology of the traditional curriculum hierarchy', *Oxford Review of Education*, 41(5): 671–89.

Bottrell, D., and Manathunga, C. (eds) (2019), *Resisting Neoliberalism in Higher Education: Volume 1: Seeing Through the Cracks*, Cham: Palgrave Macmillan.

Bozalek, V., Bayat, A., Gachago, D., Motala, S., and Mitchell, V. (2018a), 'A pedagogy of response-ability', in V. Bozalek, R. Braidotti, T. Shefer and M. Zembylas (eds), *Socially Just Pedagogies: Posthumanist, Feminist and Materialist Perspectives in Higher Education*, 82–97, London: Bloomsbury.

Bozalek, V., Braidotti, R., Shefer, T., and Zembylas, M. (eds) (2018b), *Socially Just Pedagogies: Posthumanist, Feminist and Materialist Perspectives in Higher Education*, London: Bloomsbury.

Bozalek, V., Shefer, T., and Zembylas, M. (2018), 'Introduction', in V. Bozalek, R. Braidotti, T. Shefer and M. Zembylas (eds), *Socially Just Pedagogies: Posthumanist, Feminist and Materialist Perspectives in Higher Education*, 1–11, London: Bloomsbury.

Bozalek, V., Zembylas, M., and Shefer, T. (2019), 'Response-able (peer) reviewing matters in higher education: A manifesto', in C. Taylor and A. Bayley (eds), *Posthumanism and Higher Education*, 349–57, Cham: Palgrave Macmillan.

Bozalek, V., Zembylas, M., and Tronto, J. C. (2020), *Posthuman and Political Care Ethics for Reconfiguring Higher Education Pedagogies*, London: Routledge.

Braidotti, R. (2006), 'Posthuman, all too human: Towards a new process ontology', *Theory, Culture & Society*, 23(7–8): 197–208.

Braidotti, R. (2018), 'Foreword', in V. Bozalek, R. Braidotti, T. Shefer and M. Zembylas (eds), *Socially Just Pedagogies: Posthumanist, Feminist and Materialist Perspectives in Higher Education*, xiii–xxvii, London: Bloomsbury.

Braidotti, R. (2019), 'A theoretical framework for the critical posthumanities', *Theory, Culture & Society*, 36(6): 31–61.

Braidotti, R., and Bignall, S. (eds) (2019), *Posthuman Ecologies: Complexity and Process After Deleuze*, London: Rowman and Littlefield.

Brand, F. S., and Jax, K. (2007), 'Focusing the meaning(s) of resilience: Resilience as a descriptive concept and a boundary object', *Ecology and Society*, 12: 23.

Brewer, M. L., van Kessel, G., Sanderson, B., Naumann, F., Lane, M., Reubenson, A., and Carter, A. (2019), 'Resilience in higher education students: A scoping review', *Higher Education Research & Development*, 38(6): 1105–20.

Brezis, E.S. and Birukou, A. (2020), 'Arbitrariness in the peer review process', *Scientometrics*, 123: 393–411.

Brink, C. (2018), *The Soul of a University: Why Excellence Is not Enough*, Bristol: Bristol University Press.

Broglia, E., Millings, A., and Barkham, M. (2017), 'Challenges to addressing student mental health in embedded counselling services: A survey of UK higher and further education institutions', *British Journal of Guidance and Counselling*, 46: 441–55.

Brookfield, S. (1986), *Understanding and Facilitating Adult Learning*, Milton Keynes: Open University Press.

Brookfield, S. D. (2015), *The Skillful Teacher: On Technique, Trust, and Responsiveness in the Classroom*, San Francisco, CA: Jossey-Bass.

Brooks, M. A. (2009), 'Medical education and the tyranny of competency', *Perspectives in Biology and Medicine*, 52(1): 90–102.

Brooks, R. (2018), 'The construction of higher education students in English policy documents', *British Journal of Sociology of Education*, 39(6): 745–61.

Brooks, R. (2021), 'The construction of higher education students within national policy: A cross-European comparison', *Compare: A Journal of Comparative and International Education*, 51(2): 161–80

Broughan, C., and Prinsloo, P. (2020), '(Re)centring students in learning analytics: in conversation with Paulo Freire', *Assessment & Evaluation in Higher Education*, 45(4): 617–28.

Browne, J. (2010), *Securing a Sustainable Future for Higher Education: An Independent Review of Higher Education Funding and Student Finance* (Report BIS/10/1208), London: Department for Business, Innovation and Skills

Buckley, A. (2021), 'The tyranny of "teaching and learning"', *Studies in the Philosophy of Education*, 40, 415–27.

Bunce, L., King, N., Saran, S., and Talib, N. (2021), 'Experiences of black and minority ethnic (BME) students in higher education: Applying self-determination theory to understand the BME attainment gap', *Studies in Higher Education*, 46(3): 534–47.

Caine, R. N., and Caine, G. (1994), *Making Connections: Teaching and the Human Brain*. Menlo Park, CA: Addison-Wesley.

Canning, J., and Masika, R. (2020), 'The scholarship of teaching and learning (SoTL): The thorn in the flesh of educational research', *Studies in Higher Education*. doi.org/10.1080/03075079.2020.1836485.

Capra, F. (2005), 'Speaking nature's language: Principles for sustainability', in M. K. Stone and Z. Barlow (eds), *Ecological Literacy: Educating our Children for a Sustainable World*, 18–29, San Francisco: Sierra Book Club Books.

Capra, F., and Luisi, L. (2014), *The Systems View of Life: A Unifying Vision*, Cambridge: Cambridge University Press.

Caputo, J. D. (1997), *Deconstruction in a Nutshell: A Conversation with Jacques Derrida*, New York: Fordham University Press.

Carpenter, S. R., Folke, C., Scheffer, M., and Westley, F. (2009), 'Resilience: Accounting for the noncomputable', *Ecology and Society*, 14(1): 13.

Cassiano, A. D. N., Menezes, R. M. P. D., Medeiros, S. M. D., Silva, C. J. D. A., and Lima, M. C. R. A. D. A. D. (2021), 'Performance of nurse-midwives from the perspective of Epistemologies of the South', *Escola Anna Nery*, 25(1): e20200057.

Chambers, D. W. (2003), 'The mumpsimus', *The Journal of the American College of Dentists*, 70(1): 31–5.

Charney, R. (2017), 'Rhizomatic learning and adapting: A case study exploring an interprofessional team's lived experiences', PhD Thesis, Antioch University. Available online at http://aura.antioch.edu/etds/382.

Charteris, J. (2014), 'Epistemological shudders as productive aporia: A heuristic for transformative teacher learning', *International Journal of Qualitative Methods*, 13(1): 104–121.

Charteris, J., Gannon, S., Mayes, E., Nye, A., and Stephenson, L. (2016), 'The emotional knots of academicity: A collective biography of academic subjectivities and spaces', *Higher Education Research & Development*, 35(1): 31–44.

Charteris, J., Jones, M., Nye, A., and Reyes, V. (2017), 'A heterotopology of the academy: Mapping assemblages as possibilised heterotopias', *International Journal of Qualitative Studies in Education*, 30(4): 340–53.

Clarke, D. A. G., and Mcphie, J. (2016), 'From places to paths: Learning for sustainability, teacher education and a philosophy of becoming', *Environmental Education Research*, 22(7): 1002–24.

Clark/Keefe, K. (2014), 'Becoming artist, becoming educated, becoming undone: toward a nomadic perspective of college student identity development', *International Journal of Qualitative Studies in Education*, 27(1): 110–34.

Clegg, S. (2005), 'Evidence-based practice in educational research: A critical realist critique of systematic review', *British Journal of Sociology of Education*, 26(3): 415–28.

Clegg, S. (2007), 'The demotic turn – excellence by fiat', in A. Skelton (ed.), *International Perspectives on Teaching Excellence in Higher Education: Improving Knowledge and Practice*, 91–102, London: Routledge.

Clegg, S., and Rowland, S. (2010), 'Kindness in pedagogical practice and academic life,' *British Journal of Sociology of Education*, 31(6): 719–35.

Cook-Sather, A., Bovill, C., and Felten, P. (2014), *Engaging Students as Partners in Learning and Teaching: A Guide for Faculty*, San Francisco, CA: Jossey-Bass.

Cotton, D. R. E., Joyner, M., George, R., and Cotton, P. A. (2016), 'Understanding the gender and ethnicity attainment gap in UK higher education', *Innovations in Education and Teaching International*, 53(5): 475–86.

Cribb, A., and Gewirtz, S. (2013), 'The hollowed-out university? A critical analysis of changing institutional and academic norms in UK higher education', *Discourse: Studies in the Cultural Politics of Education*, 34(3): 338–50.

Cristancho, S., and Fenwick, T. (2015), 'Mapping a surgeon's becoming with Deleuze', *Medical Humanities*, 41(2): 128–135.

Dawson, M. C. (2020), 'Rehumanising the university for an alternative future: Decolonisation, alternative epistemologies and cognitive justice', *Identities*, 27(1): 71–90.

Day, N., and Porter, T. (2018), 'Lacerations of the soul: Rejection-sensitive business school faculty and perceived publication performance', *Journal of Leadership and Organizational Studies*, 25(1): 101–15.

De Arment, S. T., Reed, E., and Wetzel, A. P. (2013), 'Promoting adaptive expertise: A conceptual framework for special educator preparation', *Teacher Education and Special Education*, 36(3): 217–30.

Deleuze, G. (1989), *Cinema II: The Time Image*, London: Bloomsbury.

Deleuze, G. (1998), *Essays Critical and Clinical*. Trans. D. W. Smith and M. A. Greco, London: Verso.

Deleuze, G. and Foucault, M. (1977), 'Intellectuals and power', in D. F. Bouchard (ed.), *Language, Counter-memory, Practice: Selected Essays and Interviews*, 205–17, Ithaca: Cornell University Press.

Deleuze, G., and Guattari, F. (1987), *A Thousand Plateaus*. Trans. B. Massumi, London: Bloomsbury.

Deleuze, G., and Guattari, F. (1994), *What Is Philosophy?* Trans. H. Tomlinson and G. Burchell, London: Verso.

Dembo, M. H., and Howard, K. (2007), 'Advice about the use of learning styles: A major myth in education', *Journal of College Reading and Learning*, 37(2): 101–9.

Derrida, J. (1967), *Of Grammatology*, Baltimore: Johns Hopkins University Press.

Derrida, J. (1972), *Positions*, London: Continuum.

Derrida, J. (1973), *Speech and Phenomena and Other Essays on Husserl's Theory of Signs*, Evanston, IL: Northwestern University Press.

Dewey, J. (1910), *How We think*, New York: Heath.

Dobzhansky, T. (1973), 'Nothing in biology makes sense except in the light of evolution', *American Biology Teacher*, 35(3): 125–9.

Doll, W. (2006), 'Method and its culture: An historical approach', *Complicity: An International Journal of Complexity in Education*, 3(1): 85–9.

Dollinger, M., and Lodge, J. (2019), 'What learning analytics can learn from student as partners', *Educational Media International*, 56(3): 218–32.

Donald, J. G. (2002), *Learning to Think: Disciplinary Perspectives*, San Francisco, CA: Jossey-Bass.

Donelan, M. (2020), 'Universities minister calls for true social mobility', Speech delivered on 1 July 2020, https://www.gov.uk/government/speeches/universities-minister-calls-for-true-social-mobility (accessed 8 August 2021).

Drach-Zahavy, A., Broyer, C., and Dagan, E. (2017), 'Similarity and accuracy of mental models formed during nursing handovers: A concept mapping approach', *International Journal of Nursing Studies*, 74: 24–33.

Dreyfus, H. L., and Dreyfus, S. E. (1986), *Mind over Machine: The Power of Human Intuition and Expertise in the Era of the Computer*, New York: Free Press.

Duong, H. (2020), 'How bad were Ofqual's grades?' Available at https://www.hepi.ac.uk/2020/08/18/how-bad-were-ofquals-grades-by-huy-duong/ (accessed 8 August 2021).

Edwards, R. (2006), 'A sticky business? Exploring the "and" in teaching and learning', *Discourse: Studies in the Cultural Politics of Education*, 27(1): 121–33.

Ellsworth, E. (1989), 'Why doesn't this feel empowering? Working through the repressive myths of critical pedagogy', *Harvard Educational Review*, 59(3): 297–324.

Elvira, Q., Imants, J., Dankbaar, B., and Segers, M. (2017), 'Designing education for professional expertise development', *Scandinavian Journal of Educational Research*, 61(2): 187–204.

Eppler, M. J. (2006), 'A comparison between concept maps, mind maps, diagrams, and visual metaphors as complementary tools for knowledge construction and sharing', *Information Visualization*, 5(3): 202–210.

Erikson, M. G., and Erikson, M. (2019), 'Learning outcomes and critical thinking – good intentions in conflict', *Studies in Higher Education*, 44(12): 2293–303.

Erickson, M., Hanna, P., and Walker, C. (2020), 'The UK higher education senior management survey: A statactivist response to managerialist governance', *Studies in Higher Education*. doi.org/10.1080/03075079.2020.1712693.

Evans, B., and Reid, J. (2013), 'Dangerously exposed: The life and death of the resilient subject', *Resilience*, 1(2): 83–98.

Fath, B. D., Dean, C. A., and Katzmair, H. (2015), 'Navigating the adaptive cycle: an approach to managing the resilience of social systems', *Ecology and Society*, 20(2): 24.

Fawns, T., Aitken, G., and Jones, D. (2021), 'Ecological teaching evaluation vs the datafication of quality: Understanding education with, and around, data'. *Postdigital Science and Education*, 3: 65–82.

Fenwick, T., and Landri, P. (2012), 'Materialities, textures and pedagogies: Socio-material assemblages in education'. *Pedagogy, Culture & Society*, 20(1): 1–7.

Fernandez, A. A., and Shaw, G. P. (2020), 'Academic leadership in a time of crisis: The coronavirus and Covid-19', *Journal of Leadership Studies*, 14(1): 39–45.

Feyerabend, P. (2010), *Against Method*. (4th edn), London: Verso.

Folke, C. (2006), 'Resilience: The emergence of a perspective for social-ecological systems analysis', *Global Environmental Change*, 16: 253–67.

Folke, C., Carpenter, S. R., Walker, B., Scheffer, M, Chapin, T., and Rockström, J. (2010), 'Resilience thinking: Integrating resilience, adaptability and transformability', *Ecology & Society*, 15(4): 20.

Fortunato, M. W. P. (2017), 'Advancing educational diversity: Antifragility, standardization, democracy, and a multitude of education options', *Cultural Studies of Science Education*, 12: 177–87.

Foucault, M. (1969), 'What is an author', in M. Foucault, D. F. Bouchard and S. Simon (eds), *Language, Counter-memory, Practice: Selected Essays and Interviews*, 113–38, London: Blackwell.

Foucault, M. (1970), *The Order of Things*, Harmondsworth: Penguin.

Foucault, M. (1997), 'Friendship as a Way of Life', in Foucault, M., *Ethics: Subjectivity and Truth* (P. Rabinow, ed.), 135–49, New York: New Press.

Franklin, S. (2006), 'VAKing out learning styles – why the notion of 'learning styles' is unhelpful to teachers', *Education 3–13*, 34(1): 81–7.

Freire, P. (1970), *Pedagogy of the Oppressed*, Harmondsworth: Penguin.

Gale, K. (2007), 'Teacher education in the university: Working with policy, practice and Deleuze', *Teaching in Higher Education*, 12(4): 471–83.

Gale, T., and Hodge, S. (2014), 'Just imaginary: Delimiting social inclusion in higher education', *British Journal of Sociology of Education*, 35(5): 688–709,

Gallopín, G. C. (2006), 'Linkages between vulnerability, resilience, and adaptive capacity', *Global Environmental Change*, 16: 293–303.

Geertsema, J. (2016), 'Academic development, SoTL and educational research', *International Journal for Academic Development*, 21(2): 122–34.

Gernert, D. (2008), 'How to reject any scientific manuscript', *Journal of Scientific Exploration*, 22(2): 233–43.

Gilligan, C. (1982), *In a Different Voice: Psychological Theory and Women's Development*, Cambridge, MA: Harvard University Press.

Giroux, H. A. (2010a), 'Bare pedagogy and the scourge of neoliberalism: Rethinking higher education as a democratic public sphere', *Educational Forum*, 74(3): 184–96.

Giroux, H. A. (2010b), *Neoliberalism's War on Higher Education*, Chicago: Haymarket Books.

Giroux, H. A. (2014), *Neoliberalism's War on Higher Education*, Chicago: Haymarket Books.

Giroux, H., and Proasi, L. (2020), 'La pandemia de Covid-19 está exponiendo la plaga del Neoliberalismo', *Praxis Educativa*, 24(2): 1–13.

Glouberman, S., and Zimmerman, B. (2002), 'Complicated and complex systems: What would successful reform of medicare look like?', Commission on the Future of Healthcare in Canada: Discussion Paper No. 8. https://www.researchgate.net/profile/Sholom-Glouberman/publication/265240426_Complicated_and_Complex_Systems_What_Would_Successful_Reform_of_Medicare_Look_Like/links/548604670cf268d28f044afd/Complicated-and-Complex-Systems-What-Would-Successful-Reform-of-Medicare-Look-Like.pdf (accessed 8 August 2021).

Godfrey, E., and Parker, L. (2010), 'Mapping the cultural landscape in engineering education', *Journal of Engineering Education*, 99(1): 5–22.

Gorski, P. (2016), 'Poverty and the ideological imperative: A call to unhook from deficit and grit ideology and to strive for structural ideology in teacher education', *Journal of Education for Teaching*, 42(4): 378–86.

Gould, S. J. (1991), 'Exaptation: A crucial tool for an evolutionary psychology', *Journal of Social Issues*, 47(3): 43–65.

Gourlay, L. (2015), '"Student engagement" and the tyranny of participation', *Teaching in Higher Education*, 20(4): 402–11.

Gourlay, L. (2017), 'Student engagement, "Learnification" and the sociomaterial: critical perspectives on higher education policy', *Higher Education Policy*, 30(1): 23–34.

Gourlay, L. (2021), *Posthumanism and the Digital University: Texts, Bodies and Materialities*, London: Bloomsbury.

Gourlay, L. and Oliver, M. (2018), *Student Engagement in the Digital University: Sociomaterial Assemblages*, London: Routledge.

Grant, M. J., and Booth, A. (2009), 'A typology of reviews: An analysis of 14 review types and associated methodologies', *Health Information and Libraries Journal*, 26: 91–108.

Gravett, K. (2020), 'Feedback literacies as sociomaterial practice', *Critical Studies in Education*. doi.org/10.1080/17508487.2020.1747099.

Gravett, K. (2021), 'Troubling transitions and celebrating becomings: from pathway to rhizome', *Studies in Higher Education*, 46(8): 1506–17.

Gravett, K., and Ajjawi, R. (2021), 'Belonging as situated practice', *Studies in Higher Education*. doi.org/10.1080/03075079.2021.1894118.

Gravett, K., and Kinchin, I. M. (2020), 'Revisiting "A 'Teaching Excellence' for the times we live in": Posthuman possibilities', *Teaching in Higher Education*. 25(8): 1028–34.

Gravett, K., Kinchin, I. M., and Winstone, N. E. (2020a), 'Frailty in transition: Troubling the norms, boundaries and limitations of transition theory and practice', *Higher Education Research and Development*, 39(6): 1169–85.

Gravett, K., Kinchin, I. M., and Winstone, N. E. (2020b), 'More than customers': Conceptions of students as partners held by students, staff, and institutional leaders, *Studies in Higher Education*, 45(12): 2574–87.

Gravett, K., Kinchin, I. M., Winstone, N. E., Balloo, K., Heron, M., Hosein, A., Lygo-Baker, S., and Medland, E. (2020), 'The development of academics' feedback literacy: Experiences of learning from critical feedback via scholarly peer review', *Assessment and Evaluation in Higher Education*, 45(5): 651–65.

Gravett, K., and Winstone, N. E. (2020), 'Making connections: Authenticity and alienation within students' relationships in higher education', *Higher Education Research and Development*. doi.org/10.1080/07294360.2020.1842335.

Gravett, K., and Winstone, N. E. (2021), 'Storying students' becomings into and through higher education', *Studies in Higher Education*, 46(8): 1576–89.

Gravett, K., Yakovchuk, N., and Kinchin, I. M. (eds) (2020), *Enhancing Student-Centred Teaching in Higher Education: The Landscape of Student-Staff Partnerships*, Cham: Palgrave Macmillan.

Guattari, F. (2014), *The Three Ecologies*. Trans. I. Pindar and P. Sutton, London: Bloomsbury.

Guerin, C. (2013), 'Rhizomatic research cultures, writing groups and academic research identities', *International Journal of Doctoral Studies*, 8: 137–50.

Guttorm, H., Hohti, R., and Paakkari, A. (2015), 'Do the next thing: An interview with Elizabeth Adams St. Pierre on post-qualitative methodology', *Reconceptualizing Educational Research Methodology*, 6(1).

Guyotte, K. W., Flint, M. A., and Latopolski, K. S. (2019), 'Cartographies of belonging: Mapping nomadic narratives of first-year students', *Critical Studies in Education*. doi.org/10.1080/17508487.2019.1657160.

Guzmán-Valenzuela, C., and Barnett, R. (2013), 'Marketing time: Evolving timescapes in academia', *Studies in Higher Education*, 38(8): 1120–34

Hamshire, C., Forsyth, R., Bell, A., Benton, M., Kelly-Laubscher, R., Paxton, M., and Wolfgramm-Foliaki, E. (2017), 'The potential of student narratives to enhance quality in higher education', *Quality in Higher Education*, 23(1): 50–64.

Hanley, P., Chambers, B., and Haslam, J. (2016), 'Reassessing RCTs as the "gold standard": Synergy not separation in evaluation design', *International Journal of Research & Method in Education*, 39(3): 287–98.

Haraway, D. (1988), 'Situated knowledges: The science question in feminism and the privilege of partial perspective', *Feminist Studies*, 14(3): 575–99.

Haraway, D. (2016), *Staying with the Trouble: Making Kin in the Chthulucene*, Durham, NC: Duke University Press.

Harris, D. (2016), 'Rhizomatic education and Deleuzian theory', *Open Learning: The Journal of Open, Distance and e-Learning*, 31(3): 219–32.

Hartley, N., and Dobele, A. (2009), 'Feathers in the nest: Establishing a supportive environment for women researchers', *Australian Educational Researcher*, 36(1): 43–58.

Havnes, A., and Prøitz, T.S. (2016), 'Why use learning outcomes in higher education? Exploring the grounds for academic resistance and reclaiming the value of unexpected learning', *Educational Assessment, Evaluation and Accountability*, 28(3): 205–23.

Healey, M., Flint, A., and Harrington, K. (2014), *Engagement through Partnership: Students as Partners in Learning and Teaching in Higher Education*, New York: Higher Education Academy.

Healy, S. (2003), 'Epistemological pluralism and the "politics of choice"', *Futures*, 35: 689–701.

Heisenberg, W. (2000), *Physics and Philosophy: The Revolution in Modern Science*, London: Penguin Classics.

Heron, M., Kinchin, I. M., and Medland, E. (2018), 'Interview talk and the co-construction of concept maps', *Educational Research*, 60(4): 373–89.

Higher Education Academy (2017), 'What works? Student retention and success change programme'. Available online at https://www.heacademy.ac.uk/individuals/strategic-priorities/retention/what-works (accessed 8 August 2021).

Hine, C. (2013), 'The emergent qualities of digital specimen images in biology', *Information, Communication & Society*, 16(7): 1157–75.

Hirst, P. H. (1974), *Knowledge and the Curriculum*, London: Routledge.

Hodson, D. (1998), *Teaching and Learning Science: Towards a Personalized Approach*, Buckingham: Open University Press.

Hoffman, R. R. (1980), 'Metaphor in science', in R. P. Honeck and R. R. Hoffman (eds), *Cognition and Figurative Language*, 393–423, Hillsdale, NJ: Lawrence Erlbaum Associates.

Holling, C. S. (1996), 'Engineering resilience vs. ecological resilience', in P. C. Schultze (ed.), *Engineering within Ecological Constraints*, 31–43, Washington, DC: National Academy Press.

Holling, C. S. (2001), 'Understanding the complexity of economic, ecological, and social systems', *Ecosystems*, 4: 390–405.

Holling, C. S. and Gunderson, L.H. (2002), 'Resilience and adaptive cycles', in L. H.Gunderson and C. S. Holling (eds), *Panarchy: Understanding Transformation in Human and Natural Systems*, 25–62, Washington, DC: Island Press.

Holmes, A. G. (2019), 'Learning outcomes – a good idea, yet with problems and lost opportunities', *Educational Process International Journal*, 8(3): 159–70

hooks, b. (1989), *Talking Back: Thinking Feminist, Thinking Black*, Boston, MA: South End Press.

Horn, S. (2016), 'The social and psychological costs of peer review: Stress and coping with manuscript rejection', *Journal of Management Inquiry*, 25(1): 11–26.

Hosein, A., Rao, N., Yeh, C. S.-H., and Kinchin, I. M. (2018), *Academics' International Teaching Journeys: Personal Narratives of Transitions in Higher Education*, London: Bloomsbury.

Hroch, P. (2014), 'Deleuze, Guattari, and environmental pedagogy and politics: Ritournelles for a planet-yet-to-come', in M. Carlin and J. Wallin (eds), *Deleuze and Guattari, Politics and Education: For a People-Yet-To-Come*, 49–75, London: Bloomsbury.

Hussey, T., and Smith, P. (2010), *The Trouble with Higher Education: A Critical Examination of Our Universities*, London: Routledge.

Hutchings, C. (2014), 'Referencing and identity, voice and agency: Adult learners' transformations within literacy practices', *Higher Education Research and Development*, 33(2): 312–24.

Hyland, K. (2012), 'Welcome to the machine: Thoughts on writing for scholarly publication', *Journal of Second Language Teaching and Research*, 1(1): 58–68.

Ilmonen, K. (2020), 'Feminist storytelling and narratives of intersectionality', *Signs: Journal of Women in Culture and Society*, 45(2): 347–71.

Jackson, A. Y. (2003), 'Rhizovocality', *Qualitative Studies in Education*, 16(5): 693–710.

Jackson, A. Y., and Mazzei, L. A. (2012), *Thinking with Theory in Qualitative Research: Viewing Data across Multiple Perspectives*, London: Routledge.

Jameson, J. (2018), 'Critical corridor talk: Just gossip or stoic resistance? Unrecognised informal higher education leadership', *Higher Education Quarterly*, 72: 375–89.

Jax, K. (2007), 'Can we define ecosystems? On the confusion between definition and description of ecological concepts', *Acta Biotheoretica*, 55(4): 341–55.

Jensen, K., and Bennett, L. (2016), 'Enhancing teaching and learning through dialogue: A student and staff partnership model', *International Journal for Academic Development*, 21(1): 41–53.

Jin, H., and Wong, K. Y. (2010), 'Training on concept mapping skills in geometry', *Journal of Mathematics Education*, 3(1): 104–19.

Kahu, E. R. (2013), 'Framing student engagement in higher education', *Studies in Higher Education*, 38(5): 758–73.

Kazemi, A. V., and Safari, S. (2020), 'Travelling concepts: The story of the commodification of higher education in Iran', *Critique*, 48(4): 405–28.

Keiny, S. (2003), *Ecological Thinking: A New Approach to Educational Change*, Lanham, MD: University Press of America.

Kemmis, S., Edwards-Groves, C., Wilkinson, J., and Hardy, I. (2012), 'Ecologies of practices', in P. Hager, A. Lee and A. Reich (eds), *Practice, Learning and Change*, 33–49, Dordrecht: Springer.

Kinchin, I. M. (2009), 'A knowledge structures perspective on the scholarship of teaching and learning', *International Journal for the Scholarship of Teaching and Learning*, 3(2): article 5, https://doi.org/10.20429/ijsotl.2009.030205 (accessed 8 August 2021).

Kinchin. I. M. (2011), 'Visualising knowledge structures in biology: Discipline, curriculum and student understanding', *Journal of Biological Education*, 45(4): 183–9.

Kinchin, I. M. (2012), 'Visualizing knowledge structures of university teaching to relate pedagogic theory and academic practice', in J. E. Groccia, M. A. T. Al-Sudairi and W. Buskist (eds), *Handbook of College and University Teaching: A Global Perspective*, 314–32, Thousand Oaks: Sage.

Kinchin, I. M. (2014), 'Concept mapping as a learning tool in higher education: a critical analysis of recent reviews', *Journal of Continuing Higher Education*, 66(1): 39–49.

Kinchin, I. M. (2016), *Visualising Powerful Knowledge to Develop the Expert Student: A Knowledge Structures Perspective on Teaching and Learning at University*, Rotterdam: Sense Publishers.

Kinchin, I. M. (2019a), 'Accessing expert understanding: The value of visualising knowledge structures in professional education', in K. Trimmer, T. Newman, D. Thorpe and F. Padro (eds), *Ensuring Quality in Professional Education Volume 2*, 71–89, Cham: Palgrave MacMillan.

Kinchin, I. M. (2019b), 'Care as a threshold concept for teaching in the salutogenic university', *Teaching in Higher Education*. doi.org/10.1080/13562517.2019.1704726.

Kinchin, I. M. (2020), 'Concept mapping and pedagogic health in higher education (a rhizomatic exploration in eight plateaus)'. DLitt thesis, University of Surrey. Available online at https://openresearch.surrey.ac.uk/esploro/outputs/doctoral/Concept-mapping-and-pedagogic-health-in-higher-education-a-rhizomatic-exploration-in-eight-plateaus/99545423202346 (accessed 8 August 2021).

Kinchin, I. M. (2021), 'Towards a pedagogically healthy university: The essential foundation for excellence in student-staff partnerships', in M. Heron, K. Balloo and L. Barnett (eds), *Exploring Disciplinary Teaching Excellence in Higher Education: Student-Staff Partnerships for Research*, 183–97, Cham: Palgrave Macmillan.

Kinchin, I. M., Alpay, E., Curtis, K., Franklin, J., Rivers, C., and Winstone, N. E. (2016), 'Charting the elements of pedagogic frailty', *Educational Research*, 58(1): 1–23.

Kinchin, I. M., and Cabot, L. B. (2010), 'Reconsidering the dimensions of expertise: from linear stages towards dual processing', *London Review of Education*, 8(2): 153–66.

Kinchin, I. M., Cabot, L. B., and Hay, D., B. (2008), 'Visualising expertise: towards an authentic pedagogy for higher education', *Teaching in Higher Education*, 13(3): 315–26.

Kinchin, I. M., Chadha, D., and Kokotailo, P. (2008), 'Using PowerPoint as a lens to focus on linearity in teaching', *Journal of Further and Higher Education*, 32(4): 333–46.

Kinchin, I. M., Derham, C., Foreman, C., McNamara, A., and Querstret, D. (2021), 'Exploring the salutogenic university: Searching for the triple point for the becoming-caring-teacher through collaborative cartography', *Pedagogika*, 141(1): 94–112.

Kinchin, I. M., and Francis, R. A. (2017), 'Mapping pedagogic frailty in geography education: A framed autoethnographic case study', *Journal of Geography in Higher Education*, 41(1): 56–74.

Kinchin, I. M., and Gravett, K. (2020), 'Concept mapping in the age of deleuze: fresh perspectives and new challenges', *Education Sciences*, 10(3): 82.

Kinchin, I. M., Heron, M., Hosein, A., Lygo-Baker, S., Medland, E., Morley, D., and Winstone, N. E. (2018), 'Researcher-led academic development', *International Journal for Academic Development*, 23(4): 339–54.

Kinchin, I. M., and Kinchin, A. M. (2019), 'Finding an identity in the crowd: A single-case framed narrative of being in the invisible majority', in S. Lygo-Baker, I. M. Kinchin and N. E. Winstone (eds), *Engaging Student Voices in Higher Education: Diverse Perspectives and Expectations in Partnership*, 19–36, Cham: Palgrave Macmillan.

Kinchin, I. M., Kingsbury, M., and Buhmann, S. Y. (2018), 'Research as pedagogy in academic development', in E. Medland, R. Watermeyer, A. Hosein, I. M. Kinchin and S. Lygo-Baker (eds), *Pedagogical Peculiarities at the Edge of University Teaching and Learning*, 49–67, Rotterdam: Brill/Sense.

Kinchin, I. M., Lygo-Baker, S., and Hay, D. B. (2008), 'Universities as centres of non-learning', *Studies in Higher Education*, 33(1): 89–103.

Kinchin, I. M., and Winstone, N. E. (eds) (2017), *Pedagogic frailty and resilience in the university*, Rotterdam: Sense.

Kinchin, I. M., and Winstone, N. E. (eds) (2018), *Exploring Pedagogic Frailty and Resilience: Case Studies of Academic Narrative*, Leiden: Brill.

Kinchin, I. M., Winstone, N. E., and Medland, E. (2020), 'Considering the concept of recipience in student learning from a modified Bernsteinian perspective'. *Studies in Higher Education.* doi.org/10.1080/03075079.2020.1717459.

Kneebone, R. (2002), 'Total internal reflection: An essay on paradigms', *Medical Education*, 36(6): 514–18.

Knoll, A. H. (2012), 'Lynn Margulis, 1938–2011', *PNAS*, 109(4): 1022.

Knysh I. V., and Kochubey, N. V. (2017), 'Etymological discrepancy: rhizoma vs. radix vs. Hyphe', *SWorld Journal*, 12: 377–91.

Koro-Ljungberg, M. (2015), *Reconceptualising Qualitative Research: Methodologies without Methodology*, London: Sage.

Koro-Ljungberg, M., and Löytönen, T. (2017), 'A slow reading [of] notes and some possibilities of liberated, open, becoming universities', *Cultural Studies ↔ Critical Methodologies*, 17(3): 294–303.

Larson, G., Stephens, P. A., Tehrani, J. J., and Layton, R. H. (2013), 'Exapting exaptation', *Trends in Ecology & Evolution*, 28(9): 497–8.

Lather, P. (1996), 'Troubling clarity: The politics of accessible language', *Harvard Educational Review*, 66: 525–45.

Lather, P. (2001), 'Postbook: Working the ruins of feminist ethnography', *Signs*, 27(1): 199–227.

Lather, P., and St. Pierre, E. A. (2013), 'Post-qualitative research', *International Journal of Qualitative Studies in Education*, 26(6): 629–33.

Law, J. (2004), *After Method: Mess in Social Science Research*, London: Routledge

Leber, J., Renkl, A., Nűckles, M., and Wäschle, K. (2018), 'When the type of assessment counteracts teaching for understanding', *Learning: Research and Practice*, 4(2): 161–79.

Lee, Y-J. (2008), 'Thriving in-between the cracks: Deleuze and guerilla science teaching in Singapore', *Cultural Studies of Science Education*, 3: 917–35.

Leijen, Ä., Pedaste, M., and Lepp, L. (2020), 'Teacher agency following the ecological model: How it is achieved and how it could be strengthened by different types of reflection', *British Journal of Educational Studies*, 68(3): 295–310.

Lenz Taguchi, H. (2016), '"The concept as method": Tracing-and-mapping the problem of the neuro(n) in the field of education', *Cultural Studies ↔ Critical Methodologies*, 16(2): 213–23.

Lenz Taguchi, H., and St. Pierre, E. A. (2017), 'Using concept as method in educational and social science inquiry', *Qualitative Inquiry*, 23(9): 643–8.

Liu, H., and Pechenkina, E. (2019), 'Innovation-by-numbers: An autoethnography of innovation as violence', *Culture and Organization*, 25(3): 178–88.

Lortie-Forgues, H., and Inglis, M. (2019), ''Rigorous large-scale educational RCTs are often uninformative: Should we be concerned?', *Educational Researcher*, 48: 158–66.

Loughlin, C., Lygo-Baker, S., and Lindberg-Sand, Å. (2021), 'Reclaiming constructive alignment', *European Journal of Higher Education*, 11(2): 119–36.

Lumb, M., and Burke, P. J. (2019), 'Re/cognising the discursive fr/ames of equity and widening participation in higher education', *International Studies in Sociology of Education*, 28(3–4): 215–36.

Lussi, I. A. O. (2020), 'Social emancipation and occupational therapy: Approaches from epistemologies of the south and the ecology of knowledges', *Cadernos Brasileiros de Terapia Ocupacional*, 28(4): 1335–45.

Lygo-Baker, S., Kinchin, I. M., and Winstone, N. E. (2019), eds. *Engaging Student Voices in Higher Education: Diverse Perspectives and Expectations in Partnership*. Cham: Palgrave.

Lygo-Baker, S., Kingston, E., and Hay, D. B. (2008), 'Uncovering the diversity of teachers' understanding of their role: The importance of individual values', *International Journal of Learning*, 15(5): 245–53.

Lynch, K. (2010), 'Carelessness: A hidden doxa of higher education', *Art & Humanities in Higher Education*, 9(1): 54–67.

Macfarlane, B. (2015), 'Dualisms in higher education: A critique of their influence and effect', *Higher Education Quarterly*, 69(1): 101–18.

Macfarlane, B. (2020), 'Myths about students in higher education: Separating fact from folklore', *Oxford Review of Education*, 46(5): 534–48.

Macfarlane, B. (2021), 'The neoliberal academic: Illustrating shifting academic norms in an age of hyper-performativity', *Educational Philosophy and Theory*, 53(5): 459–68.

Macfarlane, B., and Tomlinson, M. (2017), 'Critiques of student engagement', *Higher Education Policy*, 30(1): 6–21.

Machado, C. T., and Carvalho, A. A. (2020), 'Concept mapping: Benefits and challenges in higher education', *Journal of Continuing Higher Education*, 68(1): 38–53.

Maclure, M. (2010), 'The offence of theory', *Journal of Education Policy*, 25(2): 277–86.

MacRury, I. (2007), 'Institutional creativity and pathologies of potential space: The modern university', *Psychodynamic Practice*, 13(2): 119–40.

Madriaga, M., and Morley, K. (2016), 'Awarding teaching excellence: 'What is it supposed to achieve?' Teacher perceptions of student-led awards', *Teaching in Higher Education*, 21(2): 166–74.

Mahon, K., Heikkinen, H. L., and Huttunen, R. (2019), 'Critical educational praxis in university ecosystems: Enablers and constraints', *Pedagogy, Culture & Society*, 27(3): 463–80.

Malcolm, J., and Zukas, M. (2003), 'Dirty language: Reclaiming pedagogy', in I. Davidson, D. Murphy and B. Piette (eds), *Speaking in Tongues: Languages of Lifelong Learning*, 145–9, Bangor: University of Wales/Standing Conference on University Teaching and Research in the Education of Adults. Available online at https://drive.google.com/file/d/1EAsGFznbVILNQa1svJJYRKl3sOklC16R/view (accessed 8 August 2021).

Manathunga, C. (2011), 'The field of educational development: Histories and critical questions', *Studies in Continuing Education*, 33(3): 347–62.

Manathunga, C., and Bottrell, D. (eds) (2019), *Resisting Neoliberalism in Higher Education: Volume 2: Prising Open the Cracks*, Cham: Palgrave Macmillan.

Manathunga, C., Selkrig, M., Sadler, K., and Keamy, K. (2017), 'Rendering the paradoxes and pleasures of academic life: Using images, poetry and drama to speak back to the measured university', *Higher Education Research & Development*, 36: 526–40.

Mangione, D., and Norton, L. (2020), 'Problematising the notion of "the excellent teacher": Daring to be vulnerable in higher education'. *Teaching in Higher Education*. doi.org/10.1080/13562517.2020.1812565.

Mann, S. J. (2005), 'Alienation in the learning environment: A failure of community?', *Studies in Higher Education*, 30(1): 43–55.

Mariskind, C. (2014), 'Teachers' care in higher education: Contesting gendered construction', *Gender and Education*, 26(3): 306–20.

Marks, J. (2006), 'Molecular biology in the work of Deleuze and Guattari', *Paragraph*, 29(2): 81–97.

Marton, F., and Säljö, R. (1976), 'On qualitative differences in learning: 1 – Outcome and process', *British Journal of Educational Psychology*, 46(1): 4–11.

Massey, D. (2005), *For Space*. London: Sage.

Maton, K. (2014), 'Building powerful knowledge: The significance of semantic waves', in E. Rata and B. Barrett (eds), *Knowledge and the Future of the Curriculum*, 181–97, London: Palgrave Macmillan.

Matthews, K. E., Cook-Sather, A., Acai, A., Dvorakova, S. L., Felten, P., Marquis, E., and Mercer-Mapstone, L. (2019), 'Toward theories of partnership praxis: An analysis of interpretive framing in literature on students as partners in teaching and learning', *Higher Education Research and Development*, 38(2): 280–93.

Matthews, K. E., Cook-Sather, A., and Healey, M. (2018), 'Connecting learning, teaching, and research through student-staff partnerships: Toward universities as egalitarian learning communities', in V. Tong, A. Standen and M. Sotiriou (eds), *Research Equals Teaching: Inspiring Research-Based Education Through Student-Staff Partnerships*, 23–9, London: University College of London.

Matthews, K. E., Dwyer, A., Russell, S., and Enright, E. (2019), 'It is a complicated thing: Leaders' conceptions of students as partners in the neoliberal university', *Studies in Higher Education*, 44(12): 2196–207.

May, T. (2003), 'When is a Deleuzian becoming?', *Continental Philosophical Review*, 36: 139–53.

Mazzei, L. A. (2016), 'Voice without a subject', *Cultural Studies ↔ Critical Methodologies*, 16(2): 151–61.

Mazzei, L. A. (2017), 'Following the contour of concepts towards a minor inquiry', *Qualitative Inquiry*, 23(9): 675–85.

Mazzei, L. A., and Jackson, A. Y. (2017), 'Voice in the agentic assemblage', *Educational Philosophy and Theory*, 49(11): 1090–98.

McNaughton, S., Barrow, M., Bagg, W., and Frielick, S. (2016), 'Capturing the integration of practice-based learning with beliefs, values and attitudes using modified concept mapping', *Journal of Medical Education and Curricular Development*, 3: 17–24.

Meehan, C., and Howells, K. (2019), 'In search of the feeling of "belonging" in higher education: Undergraduate students transition into higher education', *Journal of Further and Higher Education*, 43(10): 1376–90.

Mercer, J. (2013), 'Responses to rejection: The experiences of six women early career researchers in the education department of an English university', *Women's Studies International Forum*, 38(38): 125–34.

Mercer-Mapstone, L., and Bovill, C. (2020), 'Equity and diversity in institutional approaches to student–staff partnership schemes in higher education', *Studies in Higher Education*, 45(12): 2541–57.

Meyerhoff, E. (2019), *Beyond Education: Radical Studying for another World*, Minneapolis: University of Minnesota Press.

Mignolo, W. (2000), *Local Histories/Global Designs: Coloniality, Subaltern Knowledges and Border Thinking*, Princeton: Princeton University Press.

Miller, T. R., Baird, T. D., Littlefield, C. M., Kofinas, G., Chapin, F., and Redman, C. L. (2008), 'Epistemological pluralism: Reorganizing interdisciplinary research', *Ecology and Society*, 13(2): 46.

Mintzes, J. J., Cañas, A., Coffey, J., Gorman, J., Gurley, L., Hoffman, R., McGuire, S. Y., Miller, N., Moon, B., Trifone, J., and Wandersee, J. H. (2011), 'Comment on "retrieval practice produces more learning than elaborative studying with concept mapping"', *Science*, 334(6055): 453.

Mintzes, J., and Quinn, H. J. (2007), 'Knowledge restructuring in biology: Testing a punctuated model of conceptual change', *International Journal of Science and Mathematics Education*, 5: 281–306.

Molina-Motos, D. (2019), 'Ecophilosophical principles for an ecocentric environmental education', *Education Sciences*, 9(1): 37

Monrouxe, L. V., and Rees, C. E. (2019), 'When I say … quantification in qualitative research'. *Medical Education*, 54(3): 186–7.

Moon, J. (1999), *Guidance for Writing and Using Learning Outcomes*, Exeter: University of Exeter.

Mooney Simmie, G., Moles, J., and O'Grady, E. (2019), 'Good teaching as a messy narrative of change within a policy ensemble of networks, superstructures and flows', *Critical Studies in Education*, 60(1): 55–72.

Morcke, A. M., and Eika, B. (2009), 'Medical faculty and curriculum design – "No, no, it's like this: You give your lectures …"' *Medical Teacher*, 31: 642–8.

Morley, L. (2012), 'Researching absences and silences in higher education: Data for democratisation', *Higher Education Research & Development*, 31(3): 353–68.

Morley, L. (2016), 'Troubling intra-actions: Gender, Neo-liberalism and research in the global academy', *Journal of Education Policy*, 31(1): 28–45.

Morrice, L. (2019), 'Abyssal lines and cartographies of exclusion in migration and education: Towards a reimagining', *International Journal of Lifelong Education*, 38(1): 20–33.

Mowat, J. G. (2018), 'Closing the attainment gap – a realistic proposition or an elusive pipe-dream?', *Journal of Education Policy*, 33(2): 299–321.

Muller, J. (2009), 'Forms of knowledge and curriculum coherence', *Journal of Education and Work*, 22(3): 205–26.

Murphy, M. (2015), 'Unsettling care: Troubling transnational itineraries of care in feminist health practices', *Social Studies of Science*, 45: 717–37.

Nicoara, S. M., Szamoskozi, S. E., Mitrea, D. A., and Leucuta, D. C. (2020), 'Concept mapping, an effective tool for long-term memorization of anatomy – a quasi-experimental research carried out among 1st year general medicine students', *European Journal of Investigation in Health, Psychology and Education*, 10(1): 530–43.

Nicol, D. (2010), 'From monologue to dialogue: Improving written feedback processes in mass higher education', *Assessment and Evaluation in Higher Education*, 35(5): 501–17.

Nixon, J. (2007), 'Excellence and the good society', in A. Skelton (ed.), *International Perspectives on Teaching Excellence in Higher Education: Improving Knowledge and Practice*, 15–31, London: Routledge.

Noddings, N. (1986), 'Fidelity in teaching, teacher education, and research for teaching', *Harvard Educational Review*, 56(4): 496–511.

Noddings, N. (2012), 'The caring relation in teaching', *Oxford Review of Education*, 38(6): 771–81.

Novak, J. D., and Cañas, A. J. (2006), 'The origins of concept maps and the continuing evolution of the tool', *Information Visualization Journal*, 5(3): 175–84.

Novak, J. D., and Cañas, A. J. (2007), 'Theoretical origins of concept maps, how to construct them, and uses in education', *Reflecting Education*, 3(1): 29–42.

Novak, J. D., and Gowin, D. B. (1984), *Learning How to Learn*, Cambridge: Cambridge University Press.

Ogden, J. (2018), 'Psychology', in I. M. Kinchin and N. E. Winstone (eds), *Exploring Pedagogic Frailty and Resilience: Case Studies of Academic Narrative*, 47–59, Leiden: Brill.

O'Leary, S. (2017), 'Graduates' experiences of, and attitudes towards, the inclusion of employability-related support in undergraduate degree programmes; trends and variations by subject discipline and gender', *Journal of Education and Work*, 30(1): 84–105.

Oliver, B., and Jorre de St Jorre, T. (2018), 'Graduate attributes for 2020 and beyond: Recommendations for Australian higher education providers', *Higher Education Research & Development*, 37(4): 821–36.

Opdal, P. A. (2020), 'Inside the black box: On the concepts "teaching" and "learning" and the connections between them', *Scandinavian Journal of Educational Research*, 64(3): 457–70.

Orr, D. W. (1992), *Ecological Literacy: Education and the Transition to a Postmodern World*, Albany, NY: SUNY Press.

Osborne, E., Anderson, V., and Robson, B. (2021), 'Students as epistemological agents: Claiming life experience as real knowledge in health professional education', *Higher Education*, 81: 741–56.

O'Shea, S., Lysaght, P., Roberts, J., and Harwood, V. (2016), 'Shifting the blame in higher education – social inclusion and deficit discourses', *Higher Education Research & Development*, 35(2): 322–36.

Park, S., Pelletier, C., and Klingenberg, M. (2014), 'The missing self: Competence, the person and Foucault', *Medical Education*, 48: 740–7.

Pijl-Zieber, E. M., Barton, S., Konkin, J., Awosoga, O., and Caine, V. (2014), 'Competence and competency-based nursing education: finding our way through the issues', *Nurse Education Today*, 34: 676–8.

Pinar, W. F. (2019), *What Is Curriculum Theory?* (3rd edn), Oxford: Routledge.

Pines, A. L. (1985), 'Toward a taxonomy of conceptual relation', in T. West and A. L. Pines (eds), *Cognition Structure and Conceptual Change*, 101–16, Orlando, FL: Academic Press.

Polowy, B. (2016), 'Teaching and learning from an anti-fragile perspective', *Taboo: The Journal of Culture and Education*, 15(1): ar.10.

Postma, D. (2016), 'The ethics of becoming in a pedagogy for social justice: A posthuman perspective', *South African Journal of Higher Education*, 30(3): 310–28.

Priestley, M., Biesta, G., and Robinson, S. (2015), *Teacher Agency: An Ecological Approach*, London: Bloomsbury.

Puāwai Collective (2019), 'Assembling disruptive practice in the neoliberal university: An ethics of care', *Geografiska Annaler: Series B, Human Geography*, 101(1): 33–43.

Quinn, J. (2010), 'Rethinking "failed transitions" to higher education', in K. Ecclestone, G. Biesta and M. Hughes (eds), *Transitions and Learning through the Lifecourse*, 118–29. London: Routledge.

Rajchman, J. (2001), *The Deleuze Connections*, Cambridge: MIT Press.

Reay, D. (2020), 'Sociology of education: A personal reflection on politics, power and pragmatism', *British Journal of Sociology of Education*, 41(6): 817–29.

Reay, D., Crozier, G., and Clayton, J. (2010) ' "Fitting in" or "standing out": Working-class students in UK higher education', *British Educational Research Journal*, 36(1): 107–24.

Reimann, N., and Sadler, I. (2017), 'Personal understanding of assessment and the link to assessment practice: The perspectives of higher education staff', *Assessment & Evaluation in Higher Education*, 42(5): 724–36.

Robinson, C., and Taylor, C. (2013), 'Student voice as a contested practice: Power and participation in two student voice projects', *Improving Schools*, 16(1): 32–46.

Roberts, R. (2016), 'Understanding the validity of data: A knowledge-based network underlying research expertise in scientific disciplines', *Higher Education*, 72: 651–68.

Roberts, R., and Johnson, P. (2015), 'Understanding the quality of data: A concept map for 'the thinking behind the doing' in scientific practice', *Curriculum Journal*, 26(3): 345–69.

Rorty (1999), *Philosophy and Social Hope*, London: Penguin.

Ross, F. M., Tatam, J. C., Hughes, A. L., Beacock, O. P., and McDuff, N. (2018), '"The great unspoken shame of UK higher education": Addressing inequalities of attainment', *African Journal of Business Ethics*, 12(1): 104–15.

Roy, K. (2003), *Teachers in Nomadic Spaces: Deleuze and Curriculum*, New York: Peter Lang.

Ruitenberg, C. W. (2007), 'Here be dragons: Exploring cartography in educational theory and research', *Complicity: An International Journal of Complexity and Education*, 4: 7–24.

Sabri, D. (2010), 'Absence of the academic from higher education policy', *Journal of Education Policy*, 25(2): 191–205.

Salmon, D., and Kelly, M. (2015), *Using Concept Mapping to Foster Adaptive Expertise: Enhancing Teacher Metacognitive Learning to Improve Student Academic Performance*. New York: Peter Lang.

Santos, B. de Sousa (2001), 'Nuestra America: Reinventing a subaltern paradigm of recognition and redistribution', *Theory, Culture & Society*, 19(2–3): 185–217.

Santos, B. de Sousa (2007), 'Beyond abyssal thinking: From global lines to ecologies of knowledges', *Review (Fernand Braudel Center)*, 30(1): 45–89.

Santos, B. de Sousa. (2014), *Epistemologies of the South: Justice against epistemicide*, London: Routledge.

Saunders, D. B., and Ramírez, G. B. (2017), 'Against 'teaching excellence': Ideology, commodification, and enabling the neoliberalization of postsecondary education', *Teaching in Higher Education*, 22(4): 396–407.

Schaechter, M. (2012), 'Lynn Margulis (1938–2011), *Science*, no. 335: 302.

Schön, D. A. (1971), *Beyond the Stable State*, New York: W.W. Norton.

Schulte, C. M. (2018), 'Deleuze, concept formation, and the habit of shorthand inquiry', *Qualitative Inquiry*, 24(3): 194–202.

Schwendimann, B. A. (2019), 'Concepts maps as versatile learning, teaching, and assessment tools', in M. Spector, B. Lockee and M. Childress (eds), *Learning, Design, and Technology*, 1–64, Cham: Springer.

Scriven, M. (2008), 'A summative evaluation of RCT methodology: An alternative approach to causal research', *Journal of Multidisciplinary Evaluation*, 5(9): 11–24.

Sellar, S. (2015), 'A feel for numbers: Affect, data and education policy', *Critical Studies in Education*, 56(1): 131–46.

Selwyn, N. (2019), 'What's the problem with learning analytics?', *Journal of Learning Analytics*, 6(3): 11–19.

Sermijn, J., Devlieger, P., and Loots, G. (2008), 'The narrative construction of the self: Selfhood as a rhizomatic story', *Qualitative Inquiry*, 14(4): 632–50.

Shavelson, R. J., Phillips, D. C., Towne, L., and Feuer, M. J. (2003), 'On the science of education design studies', *Educational Researcher*, 32: 25–8.

Shavelson, R. J., Ruiz-Primo, M. A., and Wiley, E. W. (2005), 'Windows into the mind', *Higher Education*, 49(4): 413–30.

Shilliam, R. (2015), 'Black academia: The doors have been opened but the architecture remains the same', in C. Alexander and J. Arday (eds), *Aiming Higher: Race, Inequality and Diversity in the Academy*, 32-4. London: Runnymede Trust.

Skelton, A. M. (2009), 'A "teaching excellence" for the times we live in?', *Teaching in Higher Education*, 14(1): 107–12.

Smagorinsky, P., Augustine, S. M. and Gallas, K. (2006), 'Rethinking rhizomes in writing about research', *Teacher Educator*, 42(2): 87–105.

Smith, R. (2006), 'Peer review: A flawed process at the heart of science and journals', *Journal of the Royal Society of Medicine*, 99(4): 178–82.

Smyth, J. (2017), *The Toxic University: Zombie Leadership, Academic Rock Stars and Neoliberal Ideology*, London: Palgrave Macmillan.

Smyth, J. (2020), 'The neoliberal toxic university: Beyond no is not enough and daring to dream a socially just alternative into existence', *Educational Philosophy and Theory*, 52(7): 716–25.

Snir, I. (2018), 'Making sense in education: Deleuze on thinking against common sense', *Educational Philosophy and Theory*, 50(3): 299–311.

Stein, S. (2019), 'Beyond higher education as we know it: Gesturing towards decolonial horizons of possibility', *Studies in Philosophy and Education*, 38: 143–61.

Stewart, A. (2015), 'Rhizocurrere: A Deleuzo-Guattarian approach to curriculum autobiography', *International Journal of Qualitative Studies in Education*, 28(10): 1169–85.

St. Pierre, E. A. (1997), 'Circling the text: Nomadic writing practices', *Qualitative Inquiry*, 3(4): 403–17.

St. Pierre, E. A. (2000), 'Poststructural feminism in education: An overview', *International Journal of Qualitative Studies in Education*, 13(5): 477–515.

St. Pierre, E. A. (2014), 'An always already absent collaboration', *Cultural Studies-Critical Methodologies*, 14(4): 374–9.

St. Pierre, E. A. (2016), 'The empirical and the new empiricisms', *Cultural Studies ↔ Critical Methodologies*, 16(2): 111–24.

St. Pierre, E. A. (2019), 'Post qualitative inquiry in an ontology of immanence', *Qualitative Inquiry*, 25(1): 3–16.

St. Pierre. E. A. (2021), 'Post qualitative inquiry, the refusal of method, and the risk of the new', *Qualitative Inquiry*, 27(1): 3–9.

St. Pierre, E. A., and Pillow, W. S. (2000), *Working the Ruins: Feminist Poststructural Theory and Methods in Education*, London: Routledge.

Stratford, R., and Wals, A. E. (2020), 'In search of healthy policy ecologies for education in relation to sustainability: Beyond evidence-based policy and post-truth politics', *Policy Futures in Education*. doi.org/10.1177/1478210320906656.

Strom, K. J. (2018), 'That's not very Deleuzian: Thoughts on interrupting the exclusionary nature of "high theory"', *Educational Philosophy and Theory*, 50(1): 104–13.

Strom, K. J., and Martin, A. D. (2017a), *Becoming-Teacher: A Rhizomatic Look at First-Year Teaching*, Rotterdam: Sense.

Strom, K. J., and Martin, A. D. (2017b), 'Thinking with theory in an era of Trump', *Issues in Teacher Education*, Fall: 3–22.

Strom, K. J., and Viesca, K. M. (2020), 'Towards a complex framework of teacher learning-practice', *Professional Development in Education*, 47(2–3): 209–24.

Stronach, I., and Maclure, M. (1997), *Educational Research Undone: The Postmodern Embrace*, Buckingham: Open University Press.

Stuart, H. (1985), 'Should concept maps be scored numerically?', *European Journal of Science Education*, 7(1): 73–81.

Sundstrom, S. M., and Allen, C. R. (2019), 'The adaptive cycle: More than a metaphor', *Ecological Complexity*, 39: 100767.

Suri, H. (2013), 'Epistemological pluralism in research synthesis methods', *International Journal of Qualitative Studies in Education*, 26(7): 889–911.

Svenkerud, S. W., Madsen, J., Ballangrud, B. B., Strande, A. L., and Stenshorne, E. (2020), 'Sustainable use of ecological concepts in educational science', *Discourse and Communication for Sustainable Education*, 11(1): 153–62.

Talbot, M. (2004), 'Monkey see, monkey do: A critique of the competency model in graduate medical education', *Medical Education*, 38(6): 587–592.

Taleb, N. N. (2012), *Antifragile: Things That Gain from Disorder*, London: Penguin.

Taylor, C. A. (2018a), 'Each intra-action matters: Towards a posthuman ethics for enlarging response-ability in higher education pedagogic practice-ings', in V. Bozalek, R. Braidotti, T. Shefer and M. Zembylas (eds), *Socially Just Pedagogies: Posthumanist, Feminist and Materialist Perspectives in Higher Education*, 81–97, London: Bloomsbury.

Taylor, C. A. (2018b), 'Edu-crafting posthumanist adventures in/for higher education: A speculative musing', *Parallax*, 24(3): 371–81.

Taylor, C. A. (2020), 'Slow singularities for collective mattering: New material feminist praxis in the accelerated academy', *Irish Educational Studies*, 39(2): 255–72.

Taylor, C. A., and Bayley, A. (2019), *Posthumanism and Higher Education: Reimagining Pedagogy, Practice and Research*, Cham: Palgrave Macmillan.

Taylor, C. A., and Fairchild, N. (2020), 'Towards a posthumanist institutional ethnography: Viscous matterings and gendered bodies', *Ethnography and Education*, 15(4): 509–27.

Taylor, C. A., and Harris-Evans, J. (2018), 'Reconceptualising transition to higher education with Deleuze and Guattari', *Studies in Higher Education*, 43(7): 1254–67.

Teelken, C. (2012), 'Compliance or pragmatism: How do academics deal with managerialism in higher education? A comparative study in three countries', *Studies in Higher Education*, 3(3): 271–90.

Teodorescu, T. (2006), 'Competence versus competency: What is the difference?', *Performance Improvement*, 45(10): 27–30.

Tewell, E. (2020), 'The problem with grit: Dismantling deficit thinking in library instruction', *Portal: Libraries and the Academy*, 20(1): 137–59.

Tight, M. (2004), 'Research into higher education: An a-theoretical community of practice?', *Higher Education Research and Development*, 23(4): 395–411.

Tight, M. (2014), 'Discipline and theory in higher education research', *Research Papers in Education*, 29(1): 93–110.

Tight, M. (2020), 'Student retention and engagement in higher education', *Journal of Further and Higher Education*, 44(5): 689–704.

Tomlinson, B. (2013), 'To tell the truth and not get trapped: Desire, distance and intersectionality at the scene of argument', *Signs: Journal of Women in Culture and Society*, 38(4): 993–1017.

Tomlinson, M., Enders, J., and Naidoo, R. (2020), 'The teaching excellence framework: Symbolic violence and the measured market in higher education', *Critical Studies in Education*, 61(5): 627–42.

Tormey, R. (2014), 'The centre cannot hold: Untangling two different trajectories of the 'approaches to teaching' framework', *Teaching in Higher Education*, 19(1): 1–12.

Toulmin, S. (1972), *Human Understanding. Volume 1, General Introduction and Part 1*, Clarendon Press: Oxford.

Trifone, J. D. (2019), *From Being to Becoming: Living an Authentic and Meaningful Life*. James Trifone Books.

Tronto, J. (1993), *Moral Boundaries: A Political Argument for an Ethic of Care*, London: Routledge.

Trowler, V. (2010), *Student Engagement: A Literature Review*, York: Higher Education Academy.

Ungar, M. (2008), 'Resilience across cultures', *British Journal of Social Work*, 38: 218–35.

Ungar, M. (2011), 'The social ecology of resilience: Addressing contextual and cultural ambiguity of a nascent construct', *American Journal of Orthopsychiatry*, 81(1): 1–17.

van den Bogaart, A. C., Schaap, H., Hummel, H. G., and Kirschner, P. A. (2017), 'Combining concept maps and interviews to produce representations of personal professional theories in higher vocational education: effects of order and vocational domain', *Instructional Science*, 45(3): 359–76.

Varey, W. (2011), 'Viability of psychological panarchy: Thought as an ecology', *Systems Research and Behavioral Science*, 28: 509–25.

Wald, N., and Harland, T. (2019), 'Graduate attributes frameworks or powerful knowledge?', *Journal of Higher Education Policy and Management*, 41(4): 361–74.

Walker, B., Holling, C. S., Carpenter, S. R., and Kinzig, A. (2004), 'Resilience, adaptability and transformability in social-ecological systems', *Ecology & Society*, 9(2): 5.

Walker, C., Gleaves, A., and Grey, J. (2006), 'Can students within higher education learn to be resilient and, educationally speaking, does it matter?', *Educational Studies*, 32(3): 251–64.

Walker, S. (2014), 'Tree exhaustion', *Studies in Art Education*, 56(1): 355–8.

Walk-Shannon, E., Batzli, J., Pultorak, J., and Boehmer, H. (2019), 'Biological variation as a threshold concept: Can we measure threshold crossing?', *CBE – Life Sciences Education*, 18: ar36, 1–15.

Waller, M. A. (2001), 'Resilience in ecosystemic context: Evolution of the concept', *American Journal of Orthopsychiatry*, 71(3): 290–7.

Wallin, J. (2010), *A Deleuzian Approach to Curriculum: Essays on a Pedagogical Life*, New York: Palgrave MacMillan.

Wang, C. L. (2015), 'Mapping or tracing? Rethinking curriculum mapping in higher education', *Studies in Higher Education*, 40(9): 1550–9.

Watermeyer, R., Crick, T., Knight, C., and Goodall, J. (2021), 'Covid-19 and digital disruption in UK universities: Afflictions and affordances of emergency online migration'. *Higher Education*, 81: 623–41.

Watson, M. K., Pelkey, J., Noyes, C. R., and Rodgers, M. O. (2016), 'Assessing conceptual knowledge using three concept map scoring methods', *Journal of Engineering Education*, 105(1): 118–46.

Watson, R. (2002), 'Clinical competence: Starship Enterprise or straitjacket?', *Nurse Education Today*, 22: 476–80.

Webster, D., and Rivers, N. (2019), 'Resisting resilience: Disrupting discourses of self-efficacy', *Pedagogy, Culture and Society*, 27(4): 523–35.

Wexler, M. N. (2001), 'The who, what and why of knowledge mapping', *Journal of Knowledge Management*, 5: 249–63.

Wheelahan, L. (2007), 'How competency-based training locks the working class out of powerful knowledge: A modified Bernsteinian analysis', *British Journal of Sociology of Education*, 28(5): 637–51.

Wheelahan, L. (2010), *Why Knowledge Matters in Curriculum: A Social Realist Argument*, Oxford: Routledge.

White, R., and Gunstone, R. (1992), *Probing Understanding*, London: Falmer Press.

Wignell, P. (2007), 'Vertical and horizontal discourses and the social sciences', in F. Christie and J. R. Martin (eds), *Language, Knowledge and Pedagogy: Functional Linguistic and Sociological Perspectives*, 184–204, London: Continuum.

Wilkins, A., and Burke, P. J. (2015), 'Widening participation in higher education: The role of professional and social class identities and commitments', *British Journal of Sociology of Education*, 36(3): 434–52.

Wilkinson, C., Silverio, S. A., and Wilkinson, S. (2021), 'The neoliberal university and the neurotic academic: A textual analysis of ITV drama, *Cheat*', *Journal of Further and Higher Education*, 45(2): 257–69.

Wilson, E. O. (1998) *Consilience: The Unity of Knowledge*. London: Abacus.

Wilson, J., Mandich, A., and Magalhães, L. (2016), 'Concept mapping: A dynamic, individualized and qualitative method for eliciting meaning', *Qualitative Health Research*, 26(8): 1151–61.

Winch, C. (2013), 'Curriculum design and epistemic ascent', *Journal of Philosophy of Education*, 47(1): 128–46.
Winstone, N., Balloo, K., Gravett, K. Jacobs, D., and Keen, H. (2020), 'Who stands to benefit? Wellbeing, belonging and challenges to equity in engagement in extra-curricular activities at university', *Active Learning in Higher Education*. doi.org/10.1177/1469787420908209.
Wise, K. A. (2020), 'Educational mindfulness: Embracing vulnerability', *Transformative Dialogues: Teaching and Learning Journal*, 13(1): 105–12.
Wooten, M. M. (2018), 'A cartographic approach toward the study of academics' of science teaching and learning research practices and values', *Canadian Journal of Science, Mathematics and Technology Education*, 18(3): 210–21.
Won, M., Krabbe, H., Ley, S. L., Treagust, D. F., and Fischer, H. E. (2017), 'Science teachers' use of a concept map marking guide as a formative assessment tool for the concept of energy', *Educational Assessment*, 22(2): 95–110.
Woolf, V. (1938), *Three Guineas*, London: Hogarth Press.
Wright, S., and Greenwood, D. J. (2017), 'Universities run for, by, and with the faculty, students and staff: Alternatives to the neoliberal destruction of higher education', *Learning and Teaching*, 10(1): 42–65.
Wyse, D., Brown, C., Oliver, S., and Poblete, X. (2020), 'Education research and educational practice: The qualities of a close relationship', *British Educational Research Journal*. doi.org/10.1002/berj.3626.
Youdell, D., and Lindley, M. R. (2019), *Biosocial Education: The Social and Biological Entanglements of Learning*. London: Routledge.
Young, M., and Muller, J. (2013), 'On the powers of powerful knowledge', *Review of Education*, 1(3): 229–50.
Young, P. (2006), 'Out of balance: Lecturers' perceptions of differential status and rewards in relation to teaching and research', *Teaching in Higher Education*, 11(2): 191–202.
Yue, M., Zhang, M., Zhang, C., and Jin, C. (2017), 'The effectiveness of concept mapping on development of critical thinking in nursing education: A systematic review and meta-analysis', *Nurse Education Today*, 52: 87–94.
Zdebik, J. (2019), *Deleuze and the Map-Image: Aesthetics, Information, Code and Digital Art*, London: Bloomsbury.
Zembylas, M. (2020), 'Against the psychologization of *resilience*: Towards an onto-political theorization of the concept and its implications for higher education', *Studies in Higher Education*. doi.org/10.1080/03075079.2019.1711048.

Index

abyssal thinking 86, 87
adaptive
   capacity 127, 128
   cycle 74, 75
affirmative ethics 27
antifragility 79
aspirational poverty 52

bare pedagogy 64
becoming 23, 26, 74, 90–2, 95, 116, 120,
      121, 136, 160, 161
   parallel states of 43, 90, 92
   teacher 66, 74, 80
belonging 43
binaries 7, 19, 140, 154

care 161, 162
cartography 9, 26
centredness 15
complex problems 153, 154
concept mapping 27, 115, 118–21
concepts 125, 127, 140
   travelling 11
consilience 3, 76
consumerism 51
currere 67, 68

deconstruction 17, 142
deficit discourse 54, 161, 162
dialogue 40, 99, 146
dualisms 7

ecological
   analogies 72, 152
   literacy 73
   perspective 126
   thinking 8, 73
ecologies 57
ecology 72
   of knowledges 85, 87, 159
   of practices 85

ecosystem 73, 74, 137, 145, 154
employability 81, 92
engagement 35, 104–8
entangled matterings 17
epistemological
   agents 88
   cartography 81, 86–8
   flexibility 81, 88
   frameworks 86
   pluralism 76, 88
   shudders 4
evidence-based policy 77
exaptation 11, 72, 164
expert student 82, 87, 90

fetishization 58
field imaginary 165

graduate attributes 81
grit 55, 56

hero teacher 156
humanist ethics 52

inclusion 49
individualism 55
inequality 50, 51, 163
intra-action 53

learnification 35, 65
learning 65, 116
   analytics 93, 94
   outcomes 68–70, 81
   punctuated 131
   styles 160
   and teaching 63, 66
linearity 7

methodological conservatism 116, 133,
      134, 159

mumpsimus 82
myths (about students) 34

neoliberalism 12, 28, 49, 151
nomadism 25, 26, 45
non-learning 121, 152, 155

pathologized practices 35
pathology of the university 15, 157
pedagogic
    frailty 129, 153, 156
    health 129, 162
pedagogy 66
peer review 21, 136, 143, 146–9
plurality (pluralism) 17, 42
polyvalent lines of enquiry 17, 28
postqualitative research 23, 143
posthumanism 11, 138, 152, 158
poststructuralism 11, 23, 24, 25, 138, 150
powerful knowledge 89, 93, 121
prestige 7
process-ontology 45, 74

randomized control trials 116, 135
recipience 82, 132
redundancy of expertise 78
relational pedagogies 60, 158, 166
representationism 143
resilience 55, 56, 77, 78, 80, 127
    ecological 79
    engineering 79
response-ability 52, 60
    pedagogy of 53, 158
rhizomatic
    researchers 15, 90

    thinking 123
rhizomatics 74, 117, 121
rhizovocality 42

salutogenic university 121, 162, 163
semantic
    plane 84
    weaving 90
situated knowledges 46
social justice 49, 50
social mobility 50
sociology of absences 13, 159
SoTL 21, 152
standardized excellence 13
St. Pierre, Elizabeth 10, 14, 18, 47, 133, 134, 135–45
structure
    of expertise 83, 84
    of knowledge 83, 122
student
    experience 36
    satisfaction 102
    voice 38, 138
student-staff partnership 42

teaching excellence 53, 100–3
theory and practice 17, 85
timescapes 57

virility culture 55
vulnerability 56, 127, 128

widening participation 49

www.ingramcontent.com/pod-product-compliance
Lightning Source LLC
Chambersburg PA
CBHW061830300426
44115CB00013B/2320